NO
FREE
PARKING

THE CURIOUS HISTORY OF LONDON'S MONOPOLY STREETS

NO FREE PARKING

NICHOLAS BOYS SMITH

BLINK
bringing you closer

First published in the UK by Blink Publishing
an imprint of Bonnier Books UK
Fourth Floor, Victoria House, Bloomsbury Square,
London WC1B 4DA

Owned by Bonnier Books
Sveavägen 56, Stockholm, Sweden

www.facebook.com/blinkpublishing
twitter.com/blinkpublishing

First published in hardback in 2022

Hardback: 978-1-78946 538 9
eBook: 978-1-78946 539 6
Audio: 978-1-78946 540 2

British Library Cataloguing-in-Publication Data:

A catalogue record for this book is available from the British Library.

Design by www.envydesign.co.uk

Printed and bound in Great Britain by Clays Ltd, Elcograf S.p.A.

1 3 5 7 9 10 8 6 4 2

Blink Publishing is an imprint of Bonnier Books UK
www.bonnierbooks.co.uk

For my parents
'La reconnaissance est une dette que les enfants n'acceptent
pas toujours à l'inventaire.'

CONTENTS

'The poetry of history lies in the quasi-miraculous fact that once, on this earth, once, on this familiar spot of ground, walked other men and women, as actual as we are to-day, thinking their own thoughts, swayed by their own passions, but now all gone, one generation vanishing after another, gone as utterly as we shall shortly be gone as ghosts at cock-crow.'

G.M Trevelyan

'What have you in common with the child of five whose photograph your mother keeps on the mantelpiece? Nothing, except that you happen to be the same person.'

George Orwell

INTRODUCTION

Streets of woe
and gold

I wander thro' each charter'd street,
Near where the charter'd Thames does flow.
And mark in every face I meet
Marks of weakness, marks of woe.
William Blake, *London*

Monopoly was a game designed to criticise capitalism that became a worldwide capitalist success; a product of the New World that is normally associated with the old; and a game which has defined for millions globally their knowledge of London's streets, but whose actual selection of twenty-two streets was cobbled together by the elderly boss of a printing firm and his secretary on a day trip down from Leeds.

One street is misnamed: it is *Great* Marlborough Street, not Marlborough Street. And two of them are not even streets. You will search in vain for an Angel Street in Islington. (It was a coaching inn, a hotel and then a Lyons tea shop, miraculously saved from 1960s destruction for 'road widening', which now serves as a Co-op bank.) Nor does London have any street called Mayfair; though there are at least 121 streets within the neighbourhood of that name, nearly all of them sheening with that perennial London favourite – ready money.

There is little evidence of precisely where Victor Watson and Marjory Phillips went on their 1935 day trip to London. But it seems probable that they did not head south or east. Only one street, Old Kent Road, is south of the Thames. And only one, Whitechapel Road, is east of the City of London. (And both, colour-coded brown, have suffered now from the *Monopoly* ignominy of being the cheapest streets on the board for nearly a century.) Even the City of London, where the Thames was first bridged and Dick Whittington was Lord Mayor, gets short shrift. Only one street on the board even touches the ancient city walls: Fleet Street, formerly Fleet Bridge Street, which since 1769 has merely bridged the drain channelling the largest of London's now subterranean rivers into the Thames.

Many other *Monopoly* streets are within the London that grew around the ancient Cities of Westminster and London in the seventeenth to nineteenth centuries. Some were what we now call greenfield development: streets and squares carved from Middlesex fields and named after developing landowners (Leicester Square), passing fashion (Piccadilly), or sporting pastime (Pall Mall). Others were brownfield development: Trafalgar Square replaced the former royal stables.

Some streets were ancient routes whose purpose and character altered as the capital grew around them. The Angel may be a pub not a street, but it stands on a still busy crossroads whose location predates the Romans. Oxford Street is now a place to shop, not the high road west or the final route along which the condemned passed before their execution at the village of Tyburn (pretty much precisely where Marble Arch now stands). But it follows the same route.

Still other streets have turned full circle. Whitehall evolved from being a public road through a royal palace to a maze of sublet homes, offices and shops to being, again, a place of governance with the building of the great Victorian public palaces of Treasury and Foreign Office. But, as a 2016 study showed, there is remarkable consistency in the relative values of London's *Monopoly* streets from 1936 to the twenty-first century. Streets can change completely and yet stay the same.

London's *Monopoly* streets do not only illuminate the city's history. They also open up an entirely new way of thinking about London's past. Probably no other city is as richly written about as London. Its neighbourhoods, bridges, sewers, politicians, clubs, suburbs, railways, people and ages have been explored in almost endless detail. Yet, curiously, there has never been a history of London focused on the city's most obvious, important and timeless piece of infrastructure – her streets. And none have made use of what we now understand about how streets do (or don't) work for humans.

How were streets built and who owned them? Where did people walk and where could they *not* walk? How did people move about the city? Why were some streets prosperous and others not? Where were rich and poor separated and where were they together? Who controlled what streets were built, what went in them, and how Londoners could use them? Understand this and you understand much about London.

When you approach the history of London street-first, when you are street-focused, then the history of London takes on a rather different shape. It is a cliché, for example, that London is a city of villages. But this is far truer than most people realise. The best way to understand where Londoners live today and why they make the daily journeys they do from home to work and back again is to understand not Roman Londinium but the network of Celtic, Roman and Anglo-Saxon roads, villas and villages that surround it. These are the true origins of most of modern London. *Lundenwic. Lambehita. Hemstede. Fulan Hamme.* This is why the Old Kent Road or Whitechapel Road matter even if you can buy them (in *Monopoly*) for only £60.

London's chaotic, unplanned development is often contrasted with the more organised development of great continental cities. There is some truth in this, but not much. Medieval streets were places of control as much as of licence. The building, growth and development of London has been far more regulated for hundreds of years than most people have realised. It is true that central London never experienced widespread rebuilding in the nineteenth century in the way that Paris, Vienna and Barcelona did. But it did experience something pretty similar, though far less beautiful, in the twentieth century.

Running through all these points, like the flavours of a good pudding, is one theme. And the theme is that the nature, ownership, design, management, sanitation, use and regulation of our streets and squares has a hitherto underappreciated role in London's history. The English may or may not be a nation of shopkeepers whose homes are our castles.[1] But our shops and our homes, our work and our lives have been, at least in part, defined by our streets. They are London's most perennial infrastructure.

From medieval London to today, to add the word 'street' to a word or phrase is to talk the language of revolt or danger, dirt or poverty. The mob takes to the street. The lady of the night walks them. A riot is a street protest. An abandoned child is a street Arab. Even the components of the street can provide a verbal admixture of moral or physical degradation: gutter press, night on the tiles. Streets are verbally dangerous places from which the masses break the windows of their masters safely ensconced away from the street in club, mansion or palace. The Duke of Wellington was known as the 'Iron Duke' not because of his military prowess, but because of the iron bars with which he shuttered his Piccadilly mansion against the depredations of the mob.

And yet London streets could be paved with gold, not just marked with woe. They were not normally places of riot or poverty. The Dick Whittington of folklore came to London to make his fortune as the 'streets were paved with gold'. The Dick Whittington of historical reality made his actual fourteenth-century fortune in that most English of trades as a mercer or cloth merchant. He then used his time as Mayor of London to improve the lighting, drainage and drinking fountains of the city's streets.

Streets could be fashionable; dandies walked on streets. Streets were beautified; shops looked out on streets with growing expanses of glass. 'Never was such painting and guilding, such sashings and looking-glasses among the shopkeepers as there is now,' wondered Daniel Defoe in 1726. And a series of statutes over hundreds of years (medieval city regulations such as Whittington's, the Westminster Paving Act, the London Lighting Act) and landowners' leasehold stipulations ensured that streets were paved, lit and controlled long before there were policemen to patrol them.

Streets could be safe. In 1788 the French diplomat, Henri Decremps, told how a father carried out an experiment to see if his five-year-old could safely return to Temple Bar from Charing Cross: 'He arrived at his father's house, safe and sound, eating the sweets that had been given him on the way.'

London's streets were certainly paved with gold for Victor Watson, the head of the Leeds-based printing business, John Waddington Limited. Persuaded by his son, Norman, after a weekend playing a new American game called *Monopoly*, Watson made the first trunk call of his life to America in spring 1935 and swiftly bought the exclusive rights to the game for most of the world beyond North America. The deal was done on the phone and an exchange of letters followed. It was an excellent decision. London streets were rapidly substituted for the Atlantic City originals after Watson's day trip to London, the printing presses rolled, and the London version of *Monopoly* was soon on sale first in the United Kingdom and then around the world.

Although localised editions were later produced in much of Europe (a Dutch version pirated by Nazi invaders was widely rejected in favour of the English language original), it was the London version that outsold them all. It was exported to much of Europe, Australia, New Zealand, South Africa, and most of the Empire and Commonwealth. Sales were sensational. By the time war came, the game was so ubiquitous that the British Secret Intelligence Service hid clandestine escape maps in Red Cross *Monopoly* games sent to British prisoners of war in occupied Europe.

The game whose near global rights Waddingtons had so swiftly and astutely bought was marketed not just as the 'rage of America', but also as the very latest thing. It was not. While *Monopoly* had first been sold widely in 1935 by the Massachusetts-based game manufacturer, Parker Brothers, the game itself was already a generation old. Like *Magna Carta*, the board game *Monopoly* was 'born with a grey beard'.[2] It had initially been designed in 1902 by the American inventor, game designer, writer and actress, Elizabeth Magie. She had called it *The Landlord's Game*.

It was intended to help popularise the teachings of the American economist Henry George, who argued that a single land tax should be used to prevent any income derived from land

and indeed to reduce the value of land to almost zero. 'It is a practical demonstration of the present system of land-grabbing with all its usual outcomes and consequences,' she said. But it did not catch on. There has never been much of a leisure market for learning about economics.

Nevertheless, the game survived as a niche interest. It was played, adapted, copied and pirated by economics teachers, Quakers, followers of Henry George, and university students in Ivy League universities and in Midwest and East Coast cities for over thirty years. Different variants became less didactic and more about simply winning (or losing). Only in 1934, however, did a failed domestic-heater salesman, Charles Darrow, manage to make something of it. Having lost his job and then learnt the game at a dinner party, he improved the design, patented it as *Monopoly*, and started selling it successfully in Philadelphia and New York.

Within a year he had sold the rights to Parker Brothers, who were able to manufacture 20,000 copies a year. *Monopoly* was the best-selling game in the United States in 1935. And Charles Darrow was the first millionaire game designer in history. Elizabeth Magie got nothing. Didactic anti-capitalist games don't pay. But games that are fun do.

At the same time that Parker Brothers and Waddingtons were cashing in on streets of gold, houses and hotels, the street itself was falling sharply out of fashion with architects and town planners. You can hardly blame them. All around were smoke-begrimed cities, 'seared with trade' as the Victorian poet Gerard Manley Hopkins put it, and smeared with the filth of the age of coal. Smogs hid the sun. Children coughed up the filth of sitting-room fires or city-centre coal power stations. The nineteenth-century city had grown beyond its ability to provide a clean or decent life to its inhabitants.

In fact, sanitation and improved public health had largely solved the 'urban penalty' of Victorian cities by the 1920s. However, you could be forgiven for not noticing. The Spanish flu pandemic from 1918–20 disproportionately killed the young and fit, and thousands were ill-housed after the deprivations of the First World War.

'The street,' wrote the Swiss architect Le Corbusier in 1929, 'wears us out; it is altogether disgusting. Why, then, does it still exist?' Modernist architects were encouraged in their beliefs by two seismic technological changes. Firstly, it became possible to build large towers and sheds, comparatively cheaply, in a way that had simply not been technically possible before.

Humanity also invented the motor car and then, hypnotised by the joy of driving on empty 1930s roads, became fundamentally confused about the role that cars should play in towns and inner cities. Too much traffic, with its consequent pollution, noise, speed and general risk of killing pedestrians, has the consistent consequence of making town centres less prosperous, attractive or valuable.

The gospel of 'traffic modernism' sought to replace urban streets and squares essentially designed for walking or riding with flyovers and city-centre motorways segregated from pedestrian walkways and underpasses. In Paris, Le Corbusier's *Plan Voisin* dreamed of sweeping away the blocks and boulevards of Paris and replacing them with sixty-storey concrete towers and fast roads in open parkland. In London, 1930s architects such as Charles Glover and the Corporation of London evolved lunatic plans to run city airports down the Thames or in a cartwheel of elevated runways above King's Cross.

The *Monopoly* streets of London were a threatened commodity eighty years ago: dirty, out of fashion and then bombed in the Second World War. The eighteenth bomb to hit London on the first full night of the Blitz (7 September 1940) hit 503 Old Kent Road damaging, according to London Fire Brigade records, the back room on the first floor. In total, eleven bombs hit *Monopoly* roads on that night and thousands more destroyed or damaged 1.7 million buildings across London throughout the war.

It got worse afterwards. In the twenty years after 1955, landowners and councils demolished 1.5 million homes and countless streets, many of them in London. Even more insidiously, two generations of highways engineers insisted on turning even the surviving city streets into monocultures for cars.

A successful street is a place where people wish to come to meet, to converse, to buy, to sell, and to be amused in the process. Highways engineers were having none of it. The Old Kent Road, once a haven of pubs and costermongers, was turned into a dual carriageway and was dehumanised by a flyover in 1968. Whatever happened to city life, the car had to get through.

However, London's streets, or rather their residents, fought back. Dozens of community groups were formed to argue for the rehabilitation of their streets rather than their wholesale demolition. A life of towers and overpasses did not appeal. At one protest meeting, one question summed up the mood of London's residents perfectly: 'You claim you're bettering us but you're not. You're nicking space off us – you are going to give us less than we started with. It's a bloody farce.'

Almost immediately, much of the new multi-storey housing which swept away London's streets became 'hard-to-let' – to use the contemporary officialese. Families and households simply refused to move in. And in a London whose population was still shrinking, they could afford not to. One east London estate, completed in 1968, was only 40 per cent full by 1974. In north London, 55 per cent of housing applicants would not move to one new estate within five years of its completion.

By the late 1970s, the destruction of London's streets had largely stopped. *Monopoly* is *not* a game of merely historic interest. Its streets survive. Indeed, they are thriving. Over the last thirty years, London's economic vitality has been transformed. This was made possible by cleaner air thanks to the 1956 Clean Air Act. And it was driven by the growth in service and financial industries, by deregulation, and by London's ability to function as a high-growth, high-employment, English-speaking, European time-zone magnet for rich, talented or hard-working immigrants from all over the world.

London is certainly an anomaly within the UK, often cited as the world's most influential city. It is no longer really an English city but a gloriously international one. Thirty-seven per cent of the current population were born abroad. This seems fitting for the capital of a nation with such a complex trading history. Although many pockets of poverty remain, London's overall economy has effectively been booming for thirty years. In early 2015, London's population finally surpassed that of August 1939, when frightened parents had started evacuating their children from a bomb-threatened city.

Funded by local tax income of which other cities can only dream, London's boroughs have also started to correct the disastrous errors of their predecessors, with street trees re-planted and cars tamed. Many of London's *Monopoly* streets are being rehumanised. Most notably Trafalgar Square has been transformed from a roost for pigeons and fleeting tourists into a teeming and attractive square worthy of its status as the geospatial heart of London, mile zero for all the road signs signalling the distance to the capital from Somerset to the Isle of Skye.

You may think you know the history of London. You don't. Or at least not entirely. This is the history of the capital as you have never, quite, read it before.

Chapter 1

OLD KENT ROAD

Ancient route to the Thames

See you our pastures wide and lone,
Where the red oxen browse
O there was a City thronged and known,
Ere London boasted a house.
And see you, after rain, the trace
Of mound and ditch and wall?
O that was a Legion's camping-place,
When Caesar sailed from Gaul.
Rudyard Kipling, 'Puck's Song'

The most ancient surviving image of London is a gold medallion of 10 aurei struck for the Roman emperor Constantius Chlorus, father of Constantine the Great, in AD 297. On the medal's reverse, London is symbolised by the city's towered walls beside the Thames. That symbolism of London as city walls and river dominated the iconography of London for a thousand years from the marginalia sketches of the thirteenth-century chronicler Matthew Paris to the first extant painting of London in a fifteenth-century French illuminated manuscript.

But cities rarely start with towered city walls. They start where roads meet to trade food, reach the sea, pass through hills or, as in the case of London, to bridge rivers. The walls on Constantius's medal were only a hundred years old when the medal was struck. But London, and the roads that led to her and through her, were already unimaginably older.

In the high summer of AD 43 the British chieftain Caratacus, fleeing the invading Roman legions led by Aulus Plautius, retreated from his defeat on the Medway to the Thames, which he crossed pursued by Roman legions, most of whom probably made use of an existing network of British fords, bridges and causeways. (Though some Batavian troops apparently swam across.)

We cannot be certain what route Caratacus took or where he crossed the Thames. However, it is probable that he took the ancient trackway that ran from the Medway to Thorney Island (now Westminster) with another branch running north to the two hills we know as Cornhill and Ludgate Hill where the Thames could readily be crossed. It is possible that the Celts had already built defended enclosures on London's twin hills as they did on so many other prominences beside their trackways and ridgeways. But we cannot know for sure.

What we do know is that many hundreds of prehistoric finds have emerged underneath the Roman city and just south of the Thames where the ancient trackway met the bridge, ford or ferry that crossed the river: bowls, pots, tools, fragments of weapons, evidence of metal-working. We do know that the very word London is almost certainly of Celtic and prehistoric origin. *Lundonjon* means the settlement by the Thames where it becomes too wide to ford – and, Latinised to Londinium, was being referred to in surviving Roman letters within twenty short years of their invasion.

We also know that the Roman road from Dover through Canterbury and Chatham to London has pre-Roman origins, like so many Roman roads, and follows that Celtic trackway along which Caratacus probably retreated. This road has been known by many names during its more than 2,000-year history: *Casingc Stræt*, Key Street, Watling Street, the Pilgrims' Way. Most of it is now the A2. As it approaches the Thames, and passes the Cheers Cash and Carry and Deptford Ambulance Station, it becomes known, and has been since the late eighteenth century, as the Old Kent Road.

It is changed beyond recognition and yet it is still performing the same function that it did for invading legions or Chaucer's pilgrims, who spent their first night at roughly 320 Old Kent Road: helping people journey to and from London in the direction of Kent's pre-Roman settlement of *Durouernon* (now known as Canterbury) and the Roman port of *Portus Dubris* (better known to us as Dover).

Old Kent Road may be the cheapest street on the *Monopoly* board, but it is well named for it is certainly the oldest. The antiquity of its route, linking the river Thames and the county of Kent, almost sings to you etymologically. For Kent is England's oldest recorded place name and the Thames is probably the second oldest.

Uniquely among English county names, the word 'Kent' is very close to what linguistic scholars call proto-Indo European. Three hundred generations ago, about 6000 BC in the late Stone Age, there existed a tribe somewhere in the Russian steppes, the Danube valley or Asia Minor. Their (unwritten) language, of which we can only guess, contained words whose echoes, astonishingly, we can still hear ringing through our spoken languages today. *Oynos, dwoh, treyes, ketwores, penke, sweks, septm, okto, hnewn, dekm* is roughly how they counted to ten.

Sometime during the Bronze Age, probably between 3500 to 2500 BC, they began to fan out across Europe and Asia. The different tribes carried with them basic grammar (*hei, wei, tuh, yuh*), words for cold weather (for snow and cold), tree names (for oak, willow and birch), animal names (for sheep, goat, pig and dog) and much besides, whose distant descendants can still be heard in languages as remote as Urdu and English or Persian and Portuguese.

One of this tribe's words was probably *kanthos*. As those tribespeople wandered west into what became Gaul and Britain, we know not via what route, *kanthos* evolved into the Celtic work *cant* meaning 'coastal district', 'corner land', 'land on the rim' and, possibly also, 'land of the armies'. Similar words survive in Welsh or Breton. *Cant* means 'bordering a circle' in Welsh and 'circle' in Breton. Cantabria in Spain (a Celtic-speaking coastal region before the arrival of the Romans) probably has the same origin. The Celts seem to have called the south-east of Britain *Cantio*, as it was literally in the corner of the island.

At any rate this is the place name that the ancient Greek geographer Strabo used to refer to the 'eastern extremity of Britain' and which the Roman general Julius Caesar Latinised as *Cantium* when he wrote about his raids into Britain in 55 and 54 BC. All other English county names are infants in comparison, a mere 1,500 years old. They recognise Anglo-Saxon local government (shire is the Old English for a 'district under a governor'), Anglo-Saxon kingdoms (Essex is the kingdom of the East Saxons), or the tribes who lived there in the Dark Ages (the Nor folk or the tribe of the Dumonii in Devon). Kent is unimaginably older.

The name 'Thames' is similarly ancient. There are also rivers Tamar, Teme and Taff in Britain, a Temes in Hungary, a Tamese in Italy and even a tributary of the Ganges known in Sanskrit as the Tamasa. The common Indo-European origin, something like *teme*, might have meant darkness or holy. *Tywyll* means darkness in Welsh. Thames itself is based on two words: the Celtic *tam*, which probably meant smooth or wide-spreading, and the word *isa* meant running water.

The Thames is thus the wide-spreading running ooze or water, possibly with an overtone of mysterious darkness: highly appropriate for a sacred, life-giving river that was twice as wide as it is now, before it was steadily embanked by generations of Londoners, and spread broadly to the south as low lying marshes and swampy islands. (Bermondsey means the 'island' or 'dry piece of land in a fen' belonging to Beornmund.)

If you had visited *Brettanike* or *Albion* (the two oldest surviving names for Britain) from the Continent in, say, 60 BC, a little before Julius Caesar, and travelled inland to the Thames, you would have journeyed along the road to and then on the Old Kent Road itself. What would it have been like? And what would you have found when you arrived at the two hills that the Celts probably called *Lundonjon*, where a mixture of islands and low tides on the Thames made is so easy to ford the river? It would have been a journey, much slower than today, though with surprising parallels. History rhymes.

Although there was also a trade route to Hengistbury Head in Dorset, you would probably have crossed from Gaul, as we still do, where the channel is narrowest. Even the Greek geographer, Strabo, who certainly never visited Britain, knew that *Cantium* in the eastern corner of *Brettanike* was visible from the Continent. You would probably have tried to land, where Caesar first tried to land, in Dover. The legions were dissuaded, as Caesar put it, by 'the forces of the enemy drawn up in arms on all the hills' with 'the sea . . . confined by mountains so close to it that a dart could be thrown from their summit upon the shore.'

This was a little off-putting. Caesar sailed north and probably landed at Pegwell Bay on the Isle of Thanet. You don't need to. Dover was the obvious place to disembark if people weren't shooting arrows at you, and it was definitely much used by the Gauls in their frequent cross-channel and two-way interchange of goods and people. (Gold, metal, amber, pottery, swords, horse gear, salt, wine, hunting dogs, corn, slaves, words, technology and expertise had all been traded for many centuries throughout the Celtic-speaking world and certainly between Kent and Gaul). Dover, like Kent, London and the Thames, is another rare English place name with pre-Roman origins. It comes from the Celtic word for water, something like *dwfr*.

From Dover the road headed inland, keeping to ridges and dry land, passing forests but also pasture and farmland growing wheat and barley. Kent was probably the most farmed part of Britain. Julius Caesar was to write: 'The most civilised of all these nations are they who inhabit Kent, which is entirely a maritime district, nor do they differ much from the Gallic customs. Most of the inland inhabitants do not sow corn, but live on milk and flesh.'

The Roman writer, Tacitus, agreed that the Celts living in Britain were very similar to those in Gaul. The name of the tribe through whose farmlands you are journeying was the Cantiaci.

The Cantiaci had four kings, in reality little more than tribal warlords, about whom we know nothing other than their names and that they were able to ally together to oppose Caesar's invasion. Segovax, Carvilius, Cingetorix and Taximagulus may sound like men from an *Asterix* adventure, but they were real enough. We don't know which kings ruled the land around the road inland, but they may not have been doing a very good job at keeping the peace. For although the land was 'thickly studded with farms', an increasing proportion were protected.

By 60 BC the British population was probably over a million

and there seems to have been pressure on land and resources. More homesteads were fortified. Some kept piles of sling stones in readiness. Others were burnt or had their cattle stolen. Violence, if not ubiquitous, was widespread in pre-Roman Kent. You would have had to keep your wits about you as you marched north.

You would probably have passed Druids on the Old Kent Road. Britain was the heart of the Druidic religion and the Romans believed that those from the wider Celtic diaspora wishing to learn more about Druidic lore travelled to Britain. The increase in violence and presence of Druids might have led to gruesome sights as you travelled north over the Medway towards the Thames.

Writing at about the same time as our journey from Dover to London, the Greek geographer Strabo wrote that Celts had the custom of 'hanging the heads of their enemies from the necks of their horses when departing from battle and nailing the spectacle to the doorways of their homes upon returning. The heads of those enemies that were held in high esteem they would embalm in cedar oil and display them to their guests.'

Would we have seen heads hanging from doorways in ancient Chatham or Deptford? Very possibly. Historians, always looking for established apple carts to overturn, have expressed scepticism about Roman and Greek descriptions of the Celts as bloodthirsty barbarians. But they are probably wrong. The archaeological evidence is starting to corroborate the ancient writers. Not far from Kent on the other side of the channel, archaeologists have found a site at Ribemont containing the remains of over 500 young men who were butchered, decapitated and left exposed in neat piles on the ground. There were no skulls.

But the Old Kent Road was probably busy enough to be comparatively safe most of the time. Many would have walked.

Those who could afford it used horses, chariots or carts. (Horse harness, cart fittings, chariots and iron bits have all survived in hordes and burials.) Women rode as well as men. And horses may have had little bells on, which would have jingled as they travelled. It would be hard to hear bells jingling on the Old Kent Road today.

Women you saw on your journey may well have been painted in woad, which was as near to black as it was to blue. Pliny described this and indeed it is possible that the most ancient name for Britain, *Brettanike*, means 'painted' in Celtic. Many whom you passed on this ancient Kentish road to the Thames, certainly anyone of wealth or status, would have worn neck rings, known as torcs. These were made from intertwined 'ropes' of twisted wire normally of gold, bronze, iron or silver. The ends could be twisted apart to place it around a neck.

In pre-Roman Britain, skilled goldsmiths knew how to make beautifully elaborate torcs in gold and legend has it that the magnificent golden Great Torc, made in about 75 BC and unearthed by a ploughing farmer in 1950, was tried on for size by King George VI. As treasure trove, he was told, effectively it belonged to him anyway. This was fittingly regal. Boudicca was said to have worn a torc and virtually every surviving statue of a Celtic warrior or god features a torc. Sometimes it was all they wore. Ancient writers are agreed that the bravest Celtic warriors went into battle naked and the evidence from surviving statues agrees.

If you were travelling in a group or had friends in Kent, you might have had fun on the way. To the Romans, no slouches in this department, the Celts had a reputation for sexual licence. Julius Caesar, who had a penchant for other men's wives, reported that, 'ten and even twelve have wives common to them, and particularly brothers among brothers, and parents among their children.'

The Roman historian, Cassius Dio, related the reply of a captured British queen to the Empress Julia Augusta who was teasing her 'about the free intercourse of her sex with men in Britain. She reportedly responded tartly: "We fulfil the demands of nature in a much better way than do you Roman women; for we consort openly with the best men, whereas you let yourselves be debauched in secret by the vilest." Such was the retort of the British woman.'

As the road from Kent approached the Thames and ran over the land now known as the Old Kent Road, it would have had to pick its way through the wide marshes and mud flats that spread to the south of the river. Perhaps, as now, there were places to drink along the way as the Old Kent Road approaches the river. According to ancient Greek writers, the Celts certainly liked a drink and were keen to buy it. As Diodorus Siculus wrote about the time of our visit: 'They are extremely partial to wine and glut themselves with the unmixed wine brought in by merchants. Their desire makes them guzzle it and when they get drunk they either fall into a stupor or become manic.'

Other than one Asda superstore, there is not much wine to buy on the Old Kent Road these days. But what there is, is still undiluted.[3] And what would you have found by the much wider and shallower river Thames? It is impossible to be certain. The route now followed by London Bridge certainly was a crossing point, the last one before the sea as the likely pre-Roman name, *Lundonjon*, indicates. And it was a natural point of confluence, for the meeting of trackways, for trade and barter, feasting and drinking.

The crossing was probably a mixture of fords, banks, islets and short sections of bridge; that the Celts could and did build wooden bridges and causeways is certain. Maybe you hired a guide. Probably it was only fordable at low tide. You would have seen forges manufacturing metal tools by the river. We have found the evidence and indeed flint tools had been made in Southwark for thousands of years.

There were also shrines. A stone carving from Southwark shows a Celtic hunting god standing between two hounds. There may even have been sacred rooms built on wooden piles built over the water where the weapons and mutilated bodies of defeated enemies were displayed; such a building has probably been found in a Celtic site in Switzerland. Almost certainly you would have prayed to or made offerings to the Thames as you crossed. Prehistoric Britons regularly made votive offerings to local river fertility goddesses and the Victorians found two splendid Bronze Age shields near London Bridge.

Once you had crossed the river, the land to the north, notably the twin hills of Ludgate Hill and Cornhill, was much higher than Southwark, Lambeth or Bermondsey. As Simon Jenkins has observed, the best way to appreciate the hills today, partly buried beneath millennia of stone and tarmac, is to ride a bicycle, preferably by night, west from the Tower of London. But in 60 BC, the topography would have been much clearer. Both hills would have risen forty or fifty feet above the wide Thames and were separated by the valley of the Walbrook stream that now tinkles through London's drains.

On those hills London existed well before Londinium, as the archaeology is showing with increasing confidence. For thousands of years it has been a busy and a holy place. Stone Age rubbish dumps with hundreds of pottery fragments recall a place of feasting and ceremony. It is highly likely that there were places to trade bronze, iron, corn, wine, pottery and slaves. It is also probable, though it will never be proved due to the subsequent city, that there were earthwork and wooden palisade defences on the hills north of the river crossing.

At any rate it was common practice in Celtic, and even Stone Age, culture to reinforce hills beside roads, above all when they crossed strategic points. In short, as you journeyed along the causeway that was the prehistoric Old Kent Road from Canterbury to London, you were travelling to somewhere worth visiting, no matter how successfully subsequent ages have erased nearly all its physical traces.

After the Roman invasion you would have journeyed along broadly the same route, though straightened in places, and you would have walked not upon earth but upon the stone of a legion-built Roman road. The Roman name of the Old Kent Road is lost, but it was almost certainly the first imperial construction, linking the newly conquered province to the Continent. At Canterbury it split into four branches heading to Richborough, Dover, Lympne and Reculver. It was built by men from one of the Second, Ninth, Fourteenth or Twentieth Legions, probably by Italians but possibly by Spaniards or Germans.

If it obeyed the Roman Laws of Twelve Tables, it would have been at least eight Roman feet wide in all places. Just south of the Roman London Bridge it met the Roman road heading to Chichester (now Kennington Park Road and the Clapham Road). The meeting point itself (known as Southwark or the southern fort since the eleventh century) was busy and bursting: it included a port on the south of the wide Thames, shops, bars, brothels (lots of brothels), workshops, temples and homes.

By the late Roman Empire, as the Old Kent Road headed further away from the city, it was flanked by three centuries' worth of tombs, which the Romans traditionally place outside the city gates. Sarcophagi and funerary monuments (including a head of the god Pan) have been found by this and other roads heading out of the city in recent years. It is curious to think of the contemporary Old Kent Road, which is not an elegant space, as a memorial highway flanked by classical urns and statues but, for a stretch at least, it seems to have been so.

In the Roman Empire, maintenance of roads was the responsibility of the provinces. At some stage in the late fourth or early fifth centuries as Roman provincial government collapsed, this ceased. However, the highway was still used during the 'Dark Ages' as it remained both direct and more passable than alternative routes. It became known as *Casingc Stræt* or Key Street.

Who called it Key Street? Britons as well as Anglo-Saxons it seems. We were once taught that 'waves' of Anglo-Saxons 'pushed' the Britons back into Cornwall and Wales. However, modern DNA evidence suggests that there was far more interbreeding and intermingling between Anglo-Saxon settlers and indigenous Britons than was once imagined. About 75 per cent of the ancestors of modern Britain and Ireland arrived in the Stone Age, before even the start of farming. So the farms along the Dark Age road from London to Kent had just as many farmers with a British as an Anglo-Saxon heritage. They also made far more use of existing infrastructure and settlements than once realised.

As with other former Roman roads, ease of passage seems to have attracted Saxon villagers – perhaps often with Roman or British precursors. It is remarkable how many of the Anglo-Saxon villages in Kent, Surrey or Middlesex mentioned in the Domesday Book were on or close to the network of Roman roads that span out of the ancient city. As you travel into London on the modern A2, you pass through or near the Anglo-Saxon villages of *Darent Ford* (Dartford), CrayFord, Welling, Eltham, *Blachehedfeld* (Blackheath), *Grenwic (Greenwich) and Depeford (Deptford)*. Only the Anglo- Saxon village of *Hacheham* has entirely lost its name to New Cross – after the name of a coaching inn. All owe their existence, and often their name, to their location on or by the road from London to Kent.

The Kent Road itself remained largely rural with occasional watering troughs for horses or inns for humans. A lepers' hospital was built near Southwark to keep the contagious out of London. Chaucer's pilgrims travelled along the Kent Road and the archers of Agincourt returned along it. Both apparently rested at what is still known as the Thomas a Becket pub, beside which, certainly by the sixteenth century, cadavers of executed felons rotted slowly in metal gibbets. The pub, now an Edwardian extravaganza of Dutch gables and red brick, has been a boxing nursery, a grill, and more recently a Vietnamese restaurant. But it is still said to be haunted by nuns or criminals depending on whom you believe.

The Old Kent Road is probably older than London. It is the route along which invaders have come and the defeated fled. It is the route that invading Germans would have taken in 1940. The surviving plans for Operation Sealion show that the 16th German Army under General von Rundstedt would probably have approached London on or near Watling Street. But the Old Kent Road was also the road of pilgrims, travellers and tourists. The Thomas a Becket pub still stands forlornly opposite the drive-to warehouses and beside a second-hand tyre shop. Anyone driving from central London to get to the Eurotunnel will pass it, just as Chaucer's pilgrims did.

If you start the history of London not with the Roman city but with the Celtic, Roman and Anglo-Saxon roads that led to it and through it, you realise that most of the neighbourhoods in which modern Londoners live and the daily journeys they take are defined not by the Romans, but by the Celtic roads that preceded them and the Anglo-Saxon villages that followed them. London starts not with Londinium but with *Lundonjon*. It does not begin with city walls but with streets.

The oldest surviving human skull in Britain was found in the Kentish village at Swanscombe, only a stone's throw from the Watling Street along which Caratacus retreated and Aulus Plautius and Constantius Chlorus advanced. Of course it was. When you drive to Dover for your summer holidays, you are travelling through time as well as through Kent.

Chapter 2

STRAND

London reborn on the Saxon shore

These wall-stones are wondrous —
Calamities crumpled them, these city-sites crashed,
    the work of giants
Corrupted. The roofs have rushed to earth, towers in ruins.
Ice at the joints has unroofed the barred-gates, sheared
The scarred storm-walls have disappeared —
The years have gnawed them from beneath.[4]
Anon., *The Ruin*, Anglo-Saxon poem

The one street that can claim to be the start of the continuous history of London as a trading entrepôt is in neither the City of London nor Westminster. It is the street that links them: the Strand. The clue to its history, and physically why London's story restarted here, lies in the name. For 'strand' is an Anglo-Saxon word which means shore or beach (as it still does in German). And it was on this northern Thames shore, sloping steeply upwards to safe, dry land from the Thames, that Anglo-Saxon traders or settlers pulled up their boats.

They could not do it to the south, for the land was low-lying and marshy, and they could not do it to the immediate east, into the old Roman city, for the wharfs had been blocked by a late Roman river-facing wall, now collapsing lumpishly into the river. Even if they could, old Roman waterfronts did not suit shallow Saxon vessels. But their ships could travel right up to this shore, below the old Roman road, on an incoming tide. So this is what they did and it was where London was reborn.

The Dark Ages in England were truly dark. In much of Europe the end of the Roman Empire was less a disaster than a decline, more of an ill-conceived changing of the guard. In France most bishoprics, cities, towns, villages and even farming villas had a continuous existence, a history marked today by place names and street patterns that in many cases can be traced directly back to their Roman origins. In Britain, urban civilisation crumbled, and her streets and buildings crumbled with it. What few evidential shards of fifth-century construction survive are of blocked-in gates and ramparts repaired, or of crude huts squatting in the ruins.

One surviving letter to the Continent pleaded for help, speaking of 'the groans of the Britons'. You cannot blame them. The fate of Roman London, certainly, is clear. It shrank to a small kernel in the city's south-east. Much of Londinium became gardens or open ground; layers of deep, dark soil surround Roman buildings in the archaeological strata. The defences were possibly, just about kept up. As late as 457 the Britons of Kent are recorded, like Caratacus, as fleeing to London after their defeat by the Anglo-Saxon leader, Hengist.

However, at some point probably in the second half of the fifth century, the city ceased to be governed or inhabited in any systematic way. There no doubt remained a few residents within the old walls, but they were farming or scratching a living, overshadowed by the 'wondrous wall stones' about them, the brooding presence of a richer inheritance. The street pattern was largely lost. London Bridge collapsed; low-lying districts flooded and reverted to marshland. There is almost none of the flotsam of everyday life (pottery and glass, buckles and coins) that inhabited settlements leave in their wake. And the tiny number of finds are suggestive.

Archaeology is an impersonal science. but occasionally it speaks to the heart. At some point in the 400s, a Saxon wandering in the ruins of Londinium dropped his brooch on top of the fallen-in tiles of an old Roman bath house. Whether he was scrabbling over the ruins or helping demolish the building we do not know. But at any rate no one ever bothered to clear up the tiles, which remained as they had collapsed with his brooch on top of them until unearthed by archaeologists over a millennium later in 1969. London had fallen.

Fittingly given her subsequent history, London's revival seems to have been due to maritime trade. Possibly aided by fluctuations in the Thames's tidal head, Saxon or Frisian sailors could travel on an incoming tide past the remains of London Bridge, beyond the mouth of the river Fleet and right up to the beach below where the Strand now runs. From there they could pull their shallow-draft boats safely up the steep bank rising to the old Roman road. And from there, goods and people could travel deep into the Anglo-Saxon kingdoms of Mercia or Wessex via the old Roman roads.

At an uncertain moment in the sixth or early seventh centuries, this is what started happening and a small market and settlement was re-established around the Strand. It was possibly seasonal at first. But it grew. It was called *Lundenwic* and this name should be just as famous as Londinium, for London has had a continuous existence ever since. The Romans came and left. The Saxons conquered and stayed. *Wic* came from the Latin *vicus* and seems to have come to mean trading settlement or market. It may have had a connotation of being beside a larger settlement, near a church or close to Roman remains, with their 'wondrous' wall-stones. Seventh-century York was called *Eofowic* and was also about a kilometre away from the old Roman fort.

Lundenwic was perfectly positioned: on the periphery of competing kingdoms and controlled by none; readily accessible to both riverine and maritime travel and to roads heading east, west, south and north. The main English exports were probably wool and slaves – though it is impossible to be certain. But exports there certainly were, because someone was paying for them. Many of the coins and about one in five of the pottery fragments that were dropped into the mud or rolled under Lundenwic's huts came from the Continent. By the late seventh century, Lundenwic covered about 150 acres stretching all along the Strand and for nearly half a mile to the north.

By about 730 the monk Bede, writing as far away as Northumbria, could call Lundenwic a 'mart of many nations'. He was right. Goods travelled from far and wide: pitchers from Ipswich, brooches from Germany, amber from the Baltic, a lead seal from Byzantium, all found their way to Lundenwic. The kings of Kent sent senior officials, known as reeves, to London to oversee their transactions. London was at the crossroads of land and sea and between the competing kingdoms of the East Saxons, the Mercians and of Wessex, all of whom sought to control it at different times.

What would it have been like to walk along the Strand? It would have been busy (London's population was probably about 7,000). It was Lundenwic's main road stretching from the roofs 'rushed to earth' of Roman London all the way to the fields surrounding the current site of St Martin-in-the-Fields, where homes were encroaching upon an ancient cemetery and where there was possibly already a small church. You may have had the remnants of the Roman road beneath your feet. The Elizabethan historian, John Stow, claimed they were still buried under the Strand's pavement in the sixteenth century.

To your south, ships were pulled up on the sandy beach immediately below you – the shoreline was 50 metres further north than now. A rare surviving charter describes it precisely as 'where the boats land on that river, towards the southern side, beside the public road'. In parts, the beach was embanked with stone rubble and old tiles pillaged from the Roman city, together with stakes and oak planks holding them in place. You might have seen customs officials imposing tolls (probably 10 per cent) on visiting merchants. Some transactions probably took place on the beach itself.

To your north, where tourists now throng London's former fruit and vegetable market at Covent Garden, was a busy, smelly and noisy market town in precisely the same place: single-storey buildings of wood, wattle and daub (a mix of soil, sand, clay and dung), some whitewashed, few more than 12 metres by 6 metres, with dirt floors and thatched roofs. They were arranged along gravel-lined streets with wooden drains and a nexus of alleys meshing outwards. Some were clustered around courtyards.

The huts held homes, shops, traders and manufacturers. Lundenwic was awash with cottage industry: weaving cloth, carving pins, combs and knife handles from horns and antlers, glass-working or leather-working. Further out there was iron smelting and farms. Somewhere there was a mint producing the gold and silver *scillings* (another Old English word) with which rich, mercantile London was awash.

Somewhere you would have seen the slave market. Captives from all over England were brought to London to be sold abroad. A tale survives of one Imma, taken in battle near the river Trent in 679, who was brought nearly 200 miles to be sold to Frisian merchants. He escaped, but most were presumably not so lucky.

Who else would you have met on the Anglo-Saxon Strand besides slaves and slave traders? Merchants and officials certainly, perhaps in fur jackets and gold chains if they could afford them. The richest merchants probably had their storerooms here, as close as possible to the beach. Kentish or Mercian kings had halls here to protect their interests. People came from all round the country and beyond: the Bishops of Hereford and Worcester owned land here, and so did the abbey of St Denis near Paris. We know that the Mercian king Coenwulf visited London, as did the churchmen Theodore and Hadrian, who initially came from Turkey and North Africa.

We also know a very few, tantalising rare names of ordinary Anglo-Saxon Londoners whom you might have met upon the Strand. At one of the farms on Lundenwic's fringe, two men carved their runic names onto a bone. One was Tartberht. The other, with less good writing, was Dric, possibly short for Daegric.

The Strand would have smelt. Rubbish was piled in pits, ordure was left in cesspits, and there were tanneries to the east. Cattle, pigs and sheep were bred within the town for their meat, and some were butchered right by the Strand. Piles of bones indicate that at least some locally had very meat-rich diets. Other eighth-century Londoners ate figs, grapes or lentils from the warmer parts of the Continent, but most food came from the surrounding farms and villages.

Some of these villages would be visible on the widely wooded land rising to the north and south as you walked down the Strand. Most were accessible by the remnants of Roman roads stretching in all directions in what are now the suburbs of south and north London. *Neasdun, Padintune, Tottenheale, Cloppanham, Brixges Stane, Stretham* and *Totinge* are all Anglo-Saxon villages near Roman roads. It is these villages, mere coagulations of farms, distended and distorted by a thousand years, which form the network of physical places that defines modern greater London, its local centres, high streets, and many of its train and Tube stations.

The end of the Strand's role at the heart of London came with Viking attacks in the ninth century. London was savaged, sacked and occupied by the Norsemen in 842, 851 and 872. When King Alfred reconquered London in 886, he moved the city firmly and clearly within the old city walls, which were repaired, whilst the bridge was rebuilt and the port restored. Deeper-drafted ships began to moor at the old Roman docks at Billingsgate. Lundenwic, no longer safe, or the easiest place to moor ships, appears to have been rapidly abandoned and returned to agriculture or grazing.

When much of the land was granted to Westminster Abbey in about 959, there was no evidence in the deeds at all that it was anything other than farmland. Lundenwic, the market that grew from the beach, was abandoned. Some vestigial memory must have remained, however, for the Strand kept its name as did a Wych, or market, Street, running north-west. One thousand years later an archaeologist, Martin Biddle, travelling down the Strand on a red London double-decker bus, suddenly realised what the name must signify. Within a few years, archaeology had proved him right. Names matter.

With the erection of Westminster Abbey on Thorney Island in the eleventh century and the subsequent growth of the royal palace, the Strand was no longer just the road west. It was also the link between court intrigue in Westminster and commerce in the City. For 500 years, therefore, the Strand became a street of palaces. For those who wished to be in the middle of it all, for royal brides or favourites (Anne Boleyn, George Villiers), for Lord Protectors of various hues (John of Gaunt, Edward Seymour, Oliver Cromwell), and for countless courtiers (Robert Devereux or Lord Burghley) and benches of bishops, it was *the* place to live.

Their titles and bishoprics still survive in the names of hotels, government offices, or the streets descending to the Victorian embankments below. However, despite the Strand's role linking the Cities of London and Westminster, for much of its history it has actually been a back alley rather than a highway. It was not paved until 1384, had cottages and fields to the north into the seventeenth century, and in 1765 the middle of the street was still 'constantly adorned with a liquid, noxious mud', according to one French visitor, Pierre-Jean Grosley.

The Strand was a muddy mess because those who could afford it travelled not by street but by boat. London's palaces, like Venetian palazzos, looked to the river not the road. The medieval Lord Mayor of London travelled to Westminster by barge. The livery companies followed in careful order of precedence. Queen Elizabeth also travelled to her palaces by barge, and maybe Shakespeare had her in mind when he described Cleopatra's barge 'like a burnished throne, burn'd on the water'. Something of the symbolism of the river as highway survives even today. Churchill's funeral cortège travelled down the Thames – just as Nelson's had – and Queen Elizabeth II feted her 2012 Diamond Jubilee by barge.

As court and fashionable society moved west, the palaces of the Strand were sold up and pulled down. First to go was the most famous of them all, the Savoy, torched by rebels incensed by its luxury during the Peasants' Revolt in 1381. York House, gifted by James I to his favourite George Villiers, Duke of Buckingham (known as 'Steenie' after St Stephen, who apparently had the face of an angel) was sold by his son, also called George, a spendthrift rake of whom Dryden wrote, 'in squandering wealth was his peculiar art'.

The only proviso put on the developer, the dastardly Dr Nicholas Barbon, was that every part of his name should be remembered in the ensuing streets. Running down to the river where Saxon boats beached, we therefore still have George Street, Villiers Street, Duke Street, Buckingham Street and York Place. Best of all was Of Alley, though this was sadly subsumed by York Place by an unromantic twentieth-century Westminster Council.

Somerset House was rebuilt as government offices by William Chambers, and Durham House was redeveloped as a set of sumptuous new terraced streets by the Adam brothers, touchingly named the Adelphi in honour of their fraternal partnership and love, Adelphi being Greek for 'brothers'. By the eighteenth century the whole area was thick with prostitutes and demi-monde. In the 1760s, diarist James Boswell used to pick up cheap whores, 'threepenny uprights' in the slang of the time, on the Strand. On the site of Cecil House and the Savoy Palace, theatres and hotels rose up. Last to go was Northumberland House, which was replaced with a new street, Northumberland Avenue.

Briefly, the Strand was fashionable. Benjamin Disraeli called it 'perhaps the finest street in Europe'. Music hall songs exhorted revellers to 'go down the Strand . . . the place for fun and noise' – and light: the Savoy Theatre was the first public building to be lit by electricity. The Savoy Hotel was in turn built with the profits that theatre empresario Richard D'Oyly Carte made from the Gilbert and Sullivan operettas. It had seventy bathrooms at a time when many hotels had none. Supposedly, the builder asked if the hotel was for amphibian guests.

The hotel's first manager, César Ritz, was sacked for embezzlement but bounced back all right. Oscar Wilde conducted parts of his affair with Lord Alfred Douglas at the Savoy (in Room 346). But glamour was brief. The Strand was where the satirical 'Burlington Bertie from Bow' sauntered in the 1915 music hall song:

> I'm Burlington Bertie, I rise at ten-thirty
> and saunter along like a toff
> I walk down the Strand with my gloves on my hand
> Then I walk down again with them off.

Imperial replanning transformed the area's scale and street pattern in the early twentieth century, both demolishing and rediscovering tradition. Wych Street was destroyed. However, the name Aldwych, or old market, which had been used until the sixteenth century, was disinterred and given to an entirely new crescent at the end of the Strand lined with huge, steel-framed stone offices: Bush House, Australia House and India House. Modern traffic rushes past them, but the street's name is still Saxon.

The Strand is no longer on the shore of the river. You cannot even see the Thames. It is neither fashionable nor salaciously unrespectable. It has changed utterly, crammed with buses and embanked by abandoned Victorian pleasure palaces rather than mud-splattered cottages and palace back doors. Covent Garden immediately to its north may no longer be a market for food and produce, as it was in Anglo-Saxon London and from the seventeenth to the twentieth centuries; but it is still a market. Savoy Palace no longer exists, but its sumptuous luxury, so noxious to fourteenth-century peasants, is matched by the Art Deco glamour of the Savoy Hotel. Frisian trading boats may no longer be beached on the riverbank to buy English slaves, but Lamborghini supercars park in Savoy Court instead.

The Strand has transmogrified. And yet it is still here.

Chapter 3

FLEET STREET

From friars to filth

No one ever went broke underestimating the public taste.
Rupert Murdoch

Pity poor Fleet Street. It is the only *Monopoly* street within the City of London. Yet for much of its history it has been a place of frontiers where dirty trades can be practised, 'night soil' emptied, and where the city's writ ran weak; a place of filthy waters and disease-filled prisons. The area just south of Fleet Street was one of the most violent and least sanitary parts of London, known as Alsatia after the disputed territory between France and the Germans; indeed, for 200 years 'Alsatia' had the same meaning that the word slum does today.

Printing was practised on Fleet Street from 1500, when William Caxton's assistant, the appropriately named Wynkyn de Worde, opened a print shop. The presence of much of the British press on or near Fleet Street for most of the twentieth century gave the street another reputation as, depending on your point of view, either the Fourth Estate tirelessly defending the man on the Clapham omnibus or as the shameless purveyor of hidden agendas and lurid sensationalism; 'power without responsibility, the prerogative of the harlot down the ages', as Stanley Baldwin complained.

However, to think of the history of Fleet Street merely in terms of the 'Fleet Ditch' (as the river was commonly called from at least the seventeenth century), or the gutter press, is to miss its early history as a bridge over a bucolic 'river of wells' and a pleasant, extramural suburb of 'spring waters' overlooked by castles, palaces and friaries, which have passed from London's memory of itself as thoroughly as Lundenwic on the Strand.

London is where London is because it is the last point before the sea where the Thames could be forded or bridged. But why did the Romans build, and King Alfred's men repair, London's walls precisely where they did? They did so because of natural moats. The best defences channel water to their aid. It is no coincidence that just to the east of the ancient city walls were the marshes of Wapping and to the west was the river Fleet, which rose in the hills of Hampstead and Highgate.

In the eleventh century, the Fleet flowed freely through the wood and dales of *Ken Ditch* ('ditch of a waterway', now transformed into the Kentish of Kentish Town) and *Holu Burna* (Old English for 'stream in the hollow', now transformed into Holborn), before disgorging in the Thames in the London Fen – an impassable marshy delta that nevertheless had at least one navigable channel. Medieval ships certainly used the river as a harbour. The word 'Fleet' means a tidal inlet in old English; a Viking anchor was found in the river's mouth and another medieval anchor as far north as Kentish Town Road.

When William the Conqueror approached London after his victory over King Harold at the Battle of Hastings on 14 October

1066, he did so cautiously and circuitously despite the approach
of winter, heading first north to Canterbury, then west through
Surrey, before crossing the Thames in Berkshire and circling
back to approach London from the north-west. Londoners had
selected Edgar Aetheling, grandson of Edmund Ironside, as
their king, but for whatever reason London chose to submit to
the Norman pretender, who was crowned in Westminster Abbey
on Christmas Day.

William, determined to exert a tight grip on the city, instructed
the creation of two castles at strategic key points: the smaller,
overlooking the marshes to the east, was the first incarnation of
the Tower of London. The second, half as large again at 15 acres,
was to the west and overlooked the mouth of the river Fleet.
Both castles relied on a mixture of the surviving ancient walls
and freshly built, wooden bailey walls and keep. Wood is not the
friend of urban longevity and the western, larger fortress may
have burnt down.

At any rate by the 1170s, Thomas a Becket's secretary, William
Fitzstephen, could write that the west of London had not one
but 'two towers very strongly fortified', presumably Norman
keeps similar to the White Tower of the Tower of London.
These two lost London landmarks, Montfichet's Tower and
Baynard's Castle, were only about 400 feet apart and must
have been an imposing site: the twin towers of west London.
Rising over the city walls by up to 60 feet, they dominated the
river Fleet and the bridge and street that ran over it for nearly
two hundred years.

What of Fleet Street and the valley of the river Fleet itself? It
was initially delightful. Writing in the late sixteenth century, John
Stow recalled that the Fleet used to be called the 'river of wells' as
it headed towards the Thames with, as William Fitzstephen put
it in the twelfth century, 'sweet wholesome and clean water that

flows rippling over the bright stones, among which Holy Well, Clerken Well and Saint Clements are held to be of most note; these are frequented by greater numbers and visited more by scholars and youth of the city when they go out for fresh air on summer evenings. It is a good city indeed.'

One can picture Londoners in tunics and hose heading west over the bridge and causeway crossing the river Fleet and the London Fen to the orchards, meadows, pasture and arable land on the far bank and beyond, much of which was owned and carefully tended by Westminster Abbey.

The street itself was raised on piles out of the damp and, by the late twelfth century, was lined with shops and gable-ended houses. It was busier and more populous than the Strand immediately to the west. Some shops sold luxuries to their rich neighbours or the king's court and goldsmiths worked there. In 1321, a Fleet Street bootmaker sold Edward II 'six pairs of boots, with tassels of silk and drops of silver-gilt, the price of each pair being 5s'. At the western end of Fleet Street, a chain or bar was raised between a row of posts to signify the limit of the City's authority. It was promoted to a wooden archway by 1351.

Unsurprisingly, those who could afford it, rich men or well-endowed institutions, chose to live and work by Fleet Street outside the increasingly crowded city. Those who did enjoyed 'spacious and beautiful gardens' that were 'planted with trees', in contrast to the increasingly crowded, narrow and insanitary city. Many monasteries and friaries were established just inside or outside London's walls and by the thirteenth century a halo of religious institutions encircled the city.

In 1223 the Dominicans, or Black Friars, created a priory north of Fleet Bridge. By 1247 the Carmelites, or White Friars, had done likewise a few hundred yards away south of Fleet Bridge Street. Their friary had gardens running down to the

Thames, through which the friars could stroll and meditate; the area is still called Whitefriars. Immediately to the west, the Knights Templar also had buildings and gardens stretching from the west of Fleet Street down to the Thames.

In 1276, Edward I gave the Dominicans permission to move their priory within the city walls, and what remained of west London's twin towers, Montfichet's Tower and Baynard's Castle, was demolished for the creation of the huge priory of Blackfriars, whose towers and steeples were to overlook the river Fleet for three hundred years.[5] The Fleet had become both a river of friars and of wells.

However, in a pattern that is as old as cities and will be repeated for all time, those seeking bucolic repose from the city quickly destroy what they love. Fleet Bridge Street may have started as a pleasant route to western orchards, but it did not stay that way for long. The Fleet was too useful and the pressures of population too great. Stone went up the Fleet in the early twelfth century to help rebuild St Paul's. We also have records of corn, hay, coal, wine, firewood, Welsh cheese, stone, herrings and oysters all being landed on the Fleet – and no doubt much more besides. But the main problem for the Fleet was less the merchandise going up the river than the refuse going into it.

Butchers threw their offal and garbage into the Fleet, tanners rinsed their tannic grime into the river, and cutlers polluted it with the water used to harden knives. Property owners extended their buildings over it, and larger property owners (the Templars) built mills in it to power the grinding of their daily bread. Everywhere, everyone emptied their ordure and 'night soil' into the 'river of wells' with predictable results. By 1290 the White Friars' gardens just south of Fleet Street were overwhelmed by the 'putrid exhalations' of the river, which not even their incense could mask.

According to John Stow, in 1307, the Earl of Lincoln complained in Parliament that in former times:

> the course of water running under 'Holeburne' Bridge and Fleet Bridge, into the Thames, had been of such breadth and depth, that ten or twelve 'naves' (ships) were wont to come to Flete Bridge, and some of them to 'Holeburne' Bridge, yet that by the filth of the tanners and others, and by the raising of wharfs, and especially by a diversion of the water in the first year of King John (1200), by them of the New Temple, for their mills without Baynard's Castle, and by other impediments, the course was decayed, and ships could not enter as they were used.

Worse was to come. The Fleet had started its descent from river to ditch, drain and sewer. Filth brought disease. A sixteenth-century physician, Dr Jones, wrote that in the area's 'stinking lanes, there died most in London'. When the plague struck, it hit hardest and deepest by the Fleet. Commissioners of Sewers recorded that 'in every parish along the Fleet, the Plague stayed and destroyed.' Perhaps when Henry VIII dissolved the friaries on either side of the Fleet in 1538, the friars were secretly pleased to go; the number of brothers living there had fallen before dissolution.

King Henry would probably have understood. In one of his many odd decisions, he was briefly their neighbour. In 1512, when fire had destroyed the royal apartments in both the palace at Westminster and the Tower of London, he ordered the construction of a new palace beside the Fleet on land reclaimed from the eyots (small islands) and rivulets of old London Fen. Bridewell Palace was lyrically named after one of the many wells that had fed into the river and was presumably the least olfactorily pleasant of his royal residences. At any rate, Henry only used Bridewell for seven years, from 1522–9, before he abandoned it in favour of Whitehall, seized from the disgraced Cardinal Wolsey.

Nevertheless, it was here that many of the twists and turns of the momentous decision to divorce Catherine of Aragon were plotted and where much of Shakespeare's *Henry VIII* is set. Abandoned, Bridewell became first a residence for the French ambassador (Holbein's brilliant, anamorphic and richly metaphorical portrait *The Ambassadors* was painted there) and then an orphanage and a prison. For many years Bridewell was a slang term for jail across the English-speaking world.[6]

Despite this fleeting royal presence, with ordure and offal floating by, those who were able to lived mostly elsewhere. The river's stench was inflicted mainly on those who could afford nothing else. Parts of Fleet Street become notorious for crime, violence and affray. One Henry de Buke murdered a man by Fleet Bridge and the poet Chaucer was said to have beaten up a 'saucy' friar on Fleet Street. The White Friars complained of the gross number of prostitutes in the area – though as one Victorian writer primly put it, 'sirens and Dulcineas of all descriptions were ever apt to gather round monasteries.'

Poor governance did not help. Clandestine marriages without licence (so-called 'Fleet marriages') were common, performed by clergymen imprisoned in Fleet Prison for debt but allowed to live nearby. Some taverns even bore signs depicting male and female clasped hands above the words 'Marriages Performed Within'. Fleet Street was a Liberty of London, an extension of the City, exempt from the king's feudal dues but it would seem less tightly governed by the Lord Mayor.[7]

The south side was worst. Inhabitants of land within the former Carmelite friary claimed, in 1580, to be exempt from the City's jurisdiction. Elizabeth I allowed the claim and James I confirmed this by charter in 1608. The result was crime and chaos. Daniel Defoe, wanted for sedition, sought refuge here. At any attempt to enforce the law, 'bullies with swords and cudgels, termagant hags with spits and broomsticks poured forth by the hundred.' In 1621, local apprentices abused the Spanish ambassador and were rescued from punishment by the mob, who turned on the marshalmen in Fleet Street and beat them up.

Some crime was more private. Across the centuries, criminal dens, including that of the eighteenth-century criminal overlord, Jonathan Wild, looked out on the river and made full use of it.[8] One supposedly 'stood alongside the brook, whose rapid torrent was well adapted to convey away everything that might be evidence of crime' including trapdoors for escape and the disposal of evidence. 'Once a sailor was decoyed there, robbed and thrown naked out of a window into the stream, and was taken up at Blackfriars bridge a corpse.'

Many modern writers bemoan the culverting of London's lost rivers. We know that rivers and canals in well-managed and modern cities are associated with happier residents and higher prices. However, you can hardly blame the early modern authorities for taking the opposite course. The Fleet was filthy and dangerous, and like the nearby streets, it needed control. The Fleet was scoured in 1502, 1606 and 1652. After the Great Fire, Christopher Wren beautified and deepened the Fleet Ditch, creating a 'New Canal' worthy of Venice at a cost of £50,000 (nearly £6 million today) with baroque arches and an elegant new bridge celebrating the Lord Mayor. Down the road, the wooden medieval entrance to the City (the Temple Bar) was replaced with an ornamental arch.

However, it was no good. Londoners kept throwing their offal and waste into the river and it bunged up again, malodorous and unnavigable. Jonathan Swift described the river Fleet in 1710:

> Sweepings from butchers' stalls, dung, guts and blood,
> Drown'd puppies, shaking sprats, all drenched in mud,
> Dead cats, and turnip tops, come tumbling down the flood.

Denied trade to its wharfs, the 'New Canal' rapidly went bust. It survived just long enough to permit a gloriously implausible painting by the maritime painter Samuel Scott of the mouth of the river Fleet, worthy of Canaletto in its Adriatic sunshine. But there was more need for streets than unusable open sewers. The Fleet was covered over north of Fleet Bridge and turned into a market in 1733, and south to the Thames in 1766. The newly created streets, Farringdon Road and New Bridge Street, meet Fleet Street at what is now Ludgate Circus, named after the western of the two hills that had first attracted the Celts to London.

National and City Authorities took a firmer grasp of the whole neighbourhood. The Fire of London was halted here.[9] Alsatia's right of sanctuary was abolished in 1697 and Fleet Marriages were declared void by the 1753 Marriage Act. Fleet Street became safer and cleaner, though prosperous, boisterous and busy rather than genteel; the haunt of showmen and shopkeepers, doctors, grocers, goldsmiths and book printers. London's richest self-made man, Hugh Audley, who eschewed all trappings of nobility, lived here.[10] The Rainbow Coffee House on Fleet Street was a mecca for quacks.

The first daily newspaper, the *Daily Courant*, was published on Fleet Street in 1702. Boswell said he liked the cheerfulness of Fleet Street 'owing to the quick succession of people'. There are reports of freak shows, the exhibition of huge animals and, in

1718, of a fire-eater who 'ate burning coals, swallowed flaming brimstone and sucked a red hot poker five times a day'.

Anyone following Dr Johnson's suggestion, 'Come and let us take a walk down Fleet Street,' would have had to be careful. Crowds jostled sedan chairs, carriages threw up mud, there were no pavements, and young lawyers and apprentices were rowdy and raucous. Houses were gable-ended, as they had been in 1400, and the busy shops were 'rendered picturesque' as one Victorian writer put it, 'by the countless signs, gay with gilding and painted with strange devices, which hung above the shop-fronts . . . lions blue and red, falcons, and dragons of all colours, alternated with heads of John the Baptist, flying pigs, and hogs in armour.'

Even these could be dangerous in high winds. In December 1718, a Fleet Street signboard suddenly gave way and fell down, bringing the house down with it, and killed four people including the Queen's jeweller.

In the 1760s, the city began to take a still keener interest in the street's management, building pavements (reportedly English and Scottish construction teams raced each other to see who could build more), and banning protruding signboards in the interests of public safety. There was a city watchman at Temple Bar to keep the peace.

The City of London also built up a considerable freehold ownership of the dangerous streets to the south of Fleet Street that ran through former palace, friary and gardens. This simple landownership pattern with its longer, straighter streets and larger blocks was perfect for new office buildings and printing presses, which needed more space than the twisting alleys of the city's medieval street pattern could permit.

The first large printing press was opened in 1824 in Bouverie Street just south of Fleet Street, very close to where Charles Dickens would open the *Daily News* in 1845 and to where the

Sun and the *News of the World* would later have their head-quarters. Excavations have revealed a Carmelite crypt beneath 30 Bouverie Street, the former offices of the *News of the World,* the twentieth-century's most sensational and commercially successful newspaper.

With a pleasing irony, the tabloid purveyor of sex and scandal to the millions, ultimately brought down by its own poor taste in bugging the public's phones, was planned and plotted where once White Friars sought refuge from the 'putrid exhalations' of the Fleet river. History as metaphor.

Chapter 4
WHITEHALL
Forgotten palaces

You must no more call it York Place, that's past;
For, since the cardinal fell, that title's lost:
'Tis now the king's, and call'd Whitehall.
William Shakespeare and John Fletcher, *Henry VIII*

Before daybreak on 25 January 1533, a young English gentle-woman rose early in her chambers near the Thames, was dressed by her attendants and walked down a long Tudor gallery with linenfold panelling, blue and gold moulded ceilings, carved doors, and rush mats upon the cold floor. The gallery led to a 'darke passage over the streete' from which she took a winding stair in one of four small towers up to 'the highest chamber which is over the West Gate', a large and well-furnished private study with sumptuous oriel windows to north and south. Had it not been a mid-winter dawn, light would have streamed in as she entered.

The young gentlewoman was not conventionally beautiful, medium height at best with olive skin and 'a bosom not much raised'. Even her admirers admitted she was not the handsomest woman in the court. But she did have very striking dark eyes, an elegant figure and an instinctive confidence and grace that clearly had the power to enchant or, as her critics would later put it, to bewitch. At any rate, she had captured more than one heart in her twenty-six years.[11] Anne Boleyn was unmarried, four months pregnant and about to marry the father of her child, King Henry VIII, who used this room as one of his innermost sanctums.

Odd though it seems to us today for a royal retreat, it was a room in a gatehouse, spanning the public highway, rather as if Buckingham Palace spanned the Mall from which the King could watch the cars go by. The gatehouse was demolished in 1759 to help the flow of traffic (some urban pressures are immortal). However, anyone can visit the wedding site. If you catch the 3, 11, 12, 24, 87, 88 or 159 buses heading north along Whitehall to Trafalgar Square and sit on the top deck, you won't be more than a few yards away from the place where England's most consequential marriage was consecrated secretly, at dawn on a winter's morning.

The story of Whitehall is one of ancient rights of way and lost palaces, of how streets last longer than buildings, and of how a street can totally change physically and yet still be playing the same role.

Like the Strand and Fleet Street, the road that is now called Whitehall owes its form to the need to connect the king's palace at Westminster with the City of London. The rutted medieval track heading north to the hamlet of Charing was originally called King Street. Its proximity to power attracted courtiers and bishops eager for homes near the king's court. Henry II's treasurer Richard FitzNigel lived here. He was the first to use a chequered cloth to count the king's taxes, which is why the chief finance minister is still known 900 years later as the Chancellor of the Exchequer.

Hubert de Burgh also lived here. He was King John's closest advisor and persuaded him to sign *Magna Carta*. Hubert gave his home to the Archbishop of York and, as York Place, it became the London home over 290 years to thirty-two successive Archbishops of York. It was also used by Edward I after a fire at Westminster Palace. 'The King's chamber' was painted green, episcopal papers record. Whether Edward stayed there for long or whether it was the King's chamber in the way that many stately homes have a 'Queen Victoria's bedroom' in which she only slept once, is unknown.

Worthy of a king it may have been, but York Place was part of a bustling neighbourhood not a palace. King Street and the network of alleys and yards leading off it in 1500 was a fizzing mix of tenements, civil servants' houses, brewhouses, shops, workshops and inns. The Archbishop of York's treasurer, Dr Richard Duck, lived off King Street. Next door at the sign of the Bell (London shops had signs not numbers, for the less literate), lived Richard Russell with his two sons, one a carpenter, one a chandler (or candle maker). Nearby lived the Tulls, the Wyatts, the Dixons and the Lyttons.

Narrow alleys led down to the river. In Endive Lane was a butcher, a baker, a pin maker, a cobbler, a tiler and a spurrier (or spur maker), alongside porters and watermen – as ubiquitous as taxi or Uber drivers are today. In Lamb Alley were the Lamb and Red Lion brewhouses. Everyone's main client was doubtless the court.

Most of this prosperity was swept away within fifteen years. The last and greatest of York Place's episcopal residents was Thomas Wolsey: the brilliant son of an Ipswich butcher who rose through industry, intelligence, administrative ability and sheer cunning to be the greatest power in the land in the early sixteenth century. Whitehall's first lost palace was the expanded York Place that he created.

Amassing a huge fortune (about £11 billion in today's money), Wolsey could certainly afford it. He bought land to the south from Westminster Abbey, and he bought to the north 'a parcel of land, formerly belonging to the King of Scotland' (whence 'Scotland Yard', though the location has moved). On his expanded home, however, he did not build a huge new hall or a soaring perpendicular chapel – to match Henry VII's newly completed Lady Chapel mausoleum at Westminster Abbey. Instead, he shouted more elegantly of his wealth by fitting fashionable bay windows, planting an orchard, moving the chapel and, best of all, creating a 250-feet-long gallery built out over the river with unparalleled views of the Thames through mullioned and leaded lights.

The Venetian ambassador, who presumably knew a thing or two about palaces with good river views, was seriously impressed by the 'windows on each side looking on gardens and rivers'. Londoners have not normally made the best of the river Thames. Thomas Wolsey, it seems, was an exception. He had turned York Place into the finest residence in London.

Hardly surprisingly, when the cardinal fell from grace, the king nabbed the lot. It was better than the stench of the Fleet at Bridewell. Wolsey's gentlemen-usher, George Cavendish, who was probably in the room at the time, recalled Wolsey's submissive, if tart, reply to the king's messenger requesting York Place:

> I will in no wise disobey, but most gladly fulfil and accomplish his princely will and pleasure in all things, and in especial in this matter . . . Howbeit, I pray you, show his

Majesty from me that I most humbly desire his Highness
to call to his most gracious remembrance, that there is
both heaven and hell.

Subtle satanic threats were lost on Henry, who wasted no time.
Within ten days of Wolsey's departure, he arrived by barge with
Anne Boleyn and toured his new palace. He was apparently
stunned by the wealth of tapestries, vestments, and gold and
silver plate to be found within: 'such a quantity of plate of all sorts
as was almost incredible'. Emulating Wolsey, masterminded by
Thomas Cromwell, and buoyed by a 500 per cent increase in his
disposable income thanks to his dissolution of the monasteries,
Henry bought 60 acres of neighbouring land and began to build
a palace complex on both sides of King Street.

Whitehall's second lost palace is the palace that Henry VIII
built. Two gatehouses to connect the palace's two halves without
needing to cross at street level, with on the river side enlarged and
elegant river-facing quarters for Anne Boleyn, a new Privy Gallery
for the king with bedrooms and meeting rooms, and a new
garden planted with herbs and decorated with heraldic beasts. On
the landward side, a Henrician sports complex with two indoor
tennis courts and two outdoor courts, a cockpit for cockfighting
and a tilt yard for jousting, display and bear-baiting (where Horse
Guards Parade still stands in direct descent). The Henry who
built this sport-obsessed palace was still, or still wanted to be, the
strapping bluff King Hal of youth, not the grotesque, ulcerated
and varicose-veined obese he was to become.

The buildings to the west were mainly in thin red Tudor bricks;
the gatehouses and the buildings to the east were mostly in a
chequered pattern of dark flint juxtaposed against lighter stone.
Ironically, this was a style copied from Thomas Wolsey's original
buildings and used materials (such as flint) that were sourced

en masse from Wolsey's native Suffolk. It may have been the white stone that gave the palace its new name, although White Hall was a name generally given to festive halls (there were others in Kenilworth and Cheam). Either way, the palace had divided King Street into three sections. The public highway within the palace became known as 'The Street'. The wider road running north of it to Charing Cross became known as Whitehall.

As Henry grew old, bitter and very fat, one of his favourite places seems to have become the gatehouse study in which he had married Anne Boleyn and was also to marry Jane Seymour. He kept a wheelchair or 'tramm' in a 'chairhouse' (probably a turret room within the gate) and increasingly moved no further than his bedroom, his favourite gatehouse, and the gallery from which he could observe the tilt-yard jousting in which he could no longer participate. At his death, books from his great library, maps, a globe, nine terracotta statues, armour, a secret jewel house, a private wardrobe and 'instruments of astrology hanging upon the wall' were left in his gatehouse chambers.

During the next sixty years, fewer external changes were made to the palace. Henry VIII liked to chuck his money about. His daughter, Elizabeth, was far more parsimonious. Apart from a banqueting house built in 1572 to celebrate her never to be solemnised nuptials, Elizabeth changed little, even though it was her principal residence. She lived in some style, however. One visitor, a Moravian baron, wrote of 'the magnificence of its bedrooms and living rooms, which are furnished with the most gorgeous splendour'.

James I was unconvinced, even though Whitehall was ten times bigger than Stirling Castle, the biggest castle in his native Scotland. He was contemptuous of Elizabeth's banqueting house, calling it an 'old, rotten, slight-builded shed'. He swept it away, but not before it had hosted the first recorded performances of

The Merchant of Venice, The Merry Wives of Windsor, Measure for Measure, Othello and *King Lear*. James I and his son Charles I wished, like Augustus though with less perfect self-assurance, to find Whitehall made of brick and to leave it made, if not of marble, then certainly of gleaming white stone. What else befitted the palace's name and their own divine right to rule? Whitehall also needed to be in the latest style, using Vitruvian proportions, not decorative brickwork or curvilinear gables.

There was only one man for the job. The former set and costume designer, Inigo Jones, recently returned from trips to France and Italy and newly appointed Surveyor General of the King's Works, had transformed himself into the most supremely able and efficient mimic of Palladian classicism. He was not solely the architect but the civil servant, the manager of masons and the instructor of sculptors – Wales's most influential architect.

Over a few short years, his ability to capture accurately both the letter and the spirit of classical design gave English architecture a stylistic plunge bath from which it did not fully emerge until the 1950s. Ultimately Inigo Jones would design a new palace complex for Whitehall arrayed around eleven interconnected circuses and courtyards with a chapel of episcopal proportions and a riverfront inspired by the Alhambra in Granada.

The palace that James and Charles did not quite build is Whitehall's third palace.[12] The problem was lack of funds. Unlike Henry VIII, they had not pillaged the monasteries and 500 years of carefully marshalled monastic treasures. Instead James and Charles failed to work effectively with Parliament. And Charles I, particularly, blew his ready money on stuffing Whitehall Palace's long galleries and privy chambers with the most stupendous art collection: 460 paintings including twenty-eight Titians and nine Raphaels.

All that actually got built was the Banqueting House, a stately essay in good taste and Palladian proportions, topped off with a heady mix of pilasters, balustrades, sumptuous swags and a ceiling painting of unprecedented complexity and cost, Rubens' *The Apotheosis of James I*. Due to a mistranslation of staggering stupidity as to the length of English and Dutch feet, Rubens' original work was too large and had to be cut to shape; several heads were lopped off in consequence.

Much of the building's detailed design and project management was probably done by a comparatively little-known mason, Nicholas Stone. But, whoever did the hard graft, the Banqueting House celebrated the display of public kingship. The masses were permitted to enter the gallery and observe ceremonies such as the 'touching' for the King's Evil.

Thankfully, the Banqueting House still survives, though so altered externally as to be unrecognisable from the building that dazzled Horace Walpole and foreign ambassadors. The windows were bricked up not glazed, there was an external staircase for the people to use and it was covered in three strata of differently hued stones; yellow Oxfordshire limestone, tobacco-coloured Northamptonshire stone and white Portland stone. In the most dramatic of its redesigns over the years, in 1830 John Soane clad it entirely in dazzling white Portland stone.

Whitehall Palace survived most of the seventeenth century, though Charles I's art collection did not – sold off by Oliver Cromwell. During the Commonwealth, Oliver Cromwell lived in Whitehall in part of the palace (commuting to Hampton Court for the weekends) with the rest transformed into a complex of parliamentary offices. However, the palace increasingly fell into disfavour as 'nothing but a heap of houses, erected at divers times and of different models'.

After the restoration of the monarchy, Charles II and then his brother James II dreamed of pulling it all down. The diarist John

Evelyn recorded that on 28 October 1664, Charles II borrowed a pencil and paper off him, sat by the window and 'with his own hand, designed to me the plot for the future building of Whitehall'. Sadly, the sketch does not survive, though Christopher Wren's comprehensive rebuilding plans the same year do – Whitehall's fourth lost palace. But they still did not have the money. They were reduced to inserting better modern building cheek by jowl with the old – a fitting metaphor for their lack of real power compared to European monarchs.

Charles II commissioned Christopher Wren to create new apartments nearer the river and away from the people. James II went further, erecting a Catholic chapel for his queen (to widespread disapproval) and pulling down the Tudor Privy Gallery and replacing it with Christopher Wren's designs of brick, stone and marble. Here is another lost palace: a crowded combination of the Tudor and the correctly classical. Meanwhile, grace and favour apartments for dukes, mistresses and royal bastards were stuffed into the old cockpit, gatehouses or tennis courts.

Charles II's mistress, Barbara Villiers, lived for a while in Henry VIII's old favourite gatehouse, and the diarist and naval administrator, Samuel Pepys, may briefly have lived in part of the other gatehouse. On 21 May 1662, he saw her underwear hanging out to dry on the rose bushes of the Privy Garden.

Hundreds of new residents multiplied the number of stairways, entrances, kitchens and, fatefully, fireplaces. There were fires in 1651, 1661, 1667 and 1691, and strict instructions were given that there should be as many 'boquetts' full of water as fireplaces. But it was not enough. At about four o'clock in the afternoon of 4 January 1698, a Dutch maid to one of the palace's tenants, Colonel Stanley, left linen to dry by an open fire. 'Such was the fury and violence' of the 'dreadful and dismal conflagration' that followed, it killed not only the poor maid who had started it, but also 'reduced to ashes all that stood in its way from the Privy Stairs to the Banqueting House and from the Privy Gardens to Scotland Yard'.

Only the Banqueting House, the two gatehouses (now known as King Street Gate and the Holbein Gate), and the former sports complex side of the palace survived. It was the end of the line for Whitehall Palace. William III had never liked it (for it made his asthma worse) and he fled to the newly built Kensington Palace, only three and a half miles away but safely rural. 'I cannot live there,' he wrote. The association between residence at Whitehall and the governance of the country was broken.

Christopher Wren proposed at least two plans for Whitehall, yet more of the street's lost palaces. Had they been built, a veritable Versailles for London, Christopher Wren might be known not as the architect of St Paul's but as the architect of the Whitehall Palace. London, maybe even British democracy, might be symbolised not by the Gothic wonder of Charles Barry and Auguste Pugin's Westminster, but by the baroque cupolas of Wren's Whitehall.

History turns on a pin. Instead, archery was practised in the ruins, and the area occupied by the palace was leased out as a prestigious neighbourhood for the great and the good to live and entertain in. Aristocrats built mansions: Pelham House, Gower House, Fife House, Pembroke House, Grantham House and Montague House. Though on a different pattern, the streets, yards and alleys that predated Thomas Wolsey were recreated – best known today is the replacement of Axe Yard (site of yet another former brewery) by Downing Street, developed by the canny and perfidious courtier and official, Sir George Downing.

A new main road, Parliament Street, was created in 1750 running through the old Privy Garden and bowling green. Whitehall was widened and the two gates were demolished to ease the traffic – though the destruction of Henry VIII's former rooms was resisted at first by the architect Sir John Vanbrugh, a preservationist before the name. In parallel, ministers started using some buildings as government offices. The first purpose-built government office was the Admiralty, whilst many other departments, far smaller than their equivalents today, worked out of town houses and back alleys.

Only when private leases fell in towards the end of the nineteenth century was this second incarnation of streets and alleys cleared away to permit the construction of the temples to Victorian governance and civil service reform, the Cabinet, Foreign, Indian, Colonial and Home Offices. These erased what remained of King Street, south of the site of the former palace.

They in turn might have been swept away by Sir Leslie Martin's grotesque 1960s proposals, eagerly championed by the Royal Fine Art Commission, to demolish most of Whitehall and replace it with twelve huge slab blocks and elevated roads. Thankfully common sense prevailed as modernism's contempt for traditional street patterns began to be seen for what it was.

The street running from Westminster to Charing Cross has altered course very slightly and had various names at different times. King Street and The Street have been lost, but Parliament Street and Whitehall have been retained. The salient fact is that the ancient right of way has survived the willpower and the purses of ten generations of palace builders and politicians. Nearly all the buildings that surround the street have not. Tourists milling artlessly outside Downing Street may feel that they are communing with history, but they are merely looking at its most recent manifestation.

Modern Whitehall is almost entirely a Georgian and Victorian creation. It can seem an impersonal place to the outsider, locked out by high security from the modern temples of ministerial office. But it was ever thus. The Tudor gatehouses were built to prevent courtiers needing to meet the people, just as a triple archway links the Treasury and the Foreign Office today.

It is still a place of power, symbolism, money and intrigue, as it was for Cardinal Wolsey, Charles II or Sir George Downing. The Horse Guards still guard the higher, drier land where Henry VIII jousted. There is a still a Red Lion pub selling beer only a few yards away from where the Red Lion brewhouse made ale in the fifteenth century. Officials, journalists and advisors still gossip in it as Pepys did in the Leg Tavern on King Street.

As the font of power, Whitehall is also a magnet for regicide and assassins. Having walked through the very same Privy Gallery and Holbein Gate that Anne Boleyn did en route to her fatal marriage, Charles I was executed on 30 January 1649 'in the open street' outside the Banqueting House. The location was chosen by Oliver Cromwell partly because it made for easy crowd control, but also because it symbolised the odd combination of arrogance and self-indulgent frippery of the Stuarts.[13] When an IRA murder squad planned the assassination of the British government in 1991, they fired their mortar shells at Downing Street from a van parked a few yards away from the site of Charles I's execution and right next to the door by which he probably exited the building.[14]

Whitehall is changed completely and yet it is still the same.

WATER WORKS

*Fifty years ago, nearly all London had every house
cleansed into a large cesspool . . . Now sewers having
been very much improved, scarcely any person thinks of
making a cesspool, but it is carried off at once into the
river. The Thames is now made a great cesspool instead
of every person having one of his own.*
Thomas Cubitt, 1840

History is not a straight line. It does not run as a simple course from bad to better to best. Sometimes things get better, sometimes they get worse. The history of London's water supply is such a tale. Initially, it was a simple matter to bring water to London's streets and homes. However, under the pressure of a growing population and, ironically, technological innovation, the drinkability of London's water supply got steadily worse from the Middle Ages until the nineteenth century. Only from the 1850s and 1860s did the safety of London's water start to improve again and become as potable as the water that was drunk in Londinium or Lundenwic.

Besides the ease of crossing the Thames, an important secondary attraction of London's site to Celt or Roman was the presence of readily accessible, drinkable water from either the Walbrook river, running between the hills of Ludgate and Cornhill, or through the Fleet running to Ludgate's west. The

Romans used clay pipes to carry the waters of the Walbrook to public conduits and to public baths such as those discovered in Upper Thames Street. Water, and its use, was a public matter, not a private one. Water ran to the standpipe, the public fountain or the communal bath. It did not run to the private home. Even public lavatories were communal with reusable sponges.

It is customary to contrast the superlative plumbing of the Romans with the shoddy standards of the Middle Ages. This is slightly unfair. When it came to the critical business of sourcing clean water, medieval towns were better than we usually imagine. London was so small that wells and rivers were able to meet most of their needs: Clerks' Well (Clerkenwell), Holywell (near Blackfriars), and St Clement's Well were all in easy walking distance. Many fetched their water themselves. Others paid water carriers to do it for them and in 1496 water carriers formed their own guild – the Brotherhood of St Cristofer of the Waterbearers. They used pipes too – of lead or elm.

As London grew, clean (or at least cleanish) water had to be sourced from further afield. From 1237, water was being channelled in lead and elm pipes from the springs of Mary le Bourne (now Marylebone) under the streets to conduits on Cheapside. The water was free, but some Cheapside merchants, 'brewers, cooks and fishmongers', paid a voluntary subscription. No doubt clean water outside their shops drove good passing trade. In 1439, the Abbot of Westminster permitted the City to extract water from the Abbey's land at Paddington.

It was still insufficient for the growing city. In 1613 the entrepreneur, Hugh Myddelton began constructing a canal, the 'New River', to bring water 38 miles from Amwell in Hertfordshire to a reservoir at Sadler's Wells to meet the growing city's inexhaustible thirst for clean water. It is still a source of the city's water supply today.

Medieval London was less good at removing waste. The few sewers that existed were intended for surface water only, not for sewage. The contents of chamber pots went into cesspits. This was clearly smelly and unpleasant, and it could cause disease or death. In 1326, Richard the Raker fell into a cesspit and 'drowned monstrously in his own excrement'. However, it did work, after a fashion. There was regulation on the quality of cesspit construction. The first Mayor of London, Henry Fitzalwyn, decreed that a 'necessary chamber' should be two and a half feet from a neighbouring building if it was made of stone and three and a half feet if made of other materials.

There was also a vibrant market in recycling waste. 'Rakers', 'gong merchants', 'night men', or 'night soil men' could make a very good living emptying cesspools and selling the contents to tanners in Southwark, or as fertiliser to farmers whose fields were only down the road. Advertisements talk of 'night men' who kept 'carts and horses for emptying bog houses, drains and cesspools'. It was a dirty trade but they were paid well to do it. In the thirteenth century, rakers could earn 6d a night – many times a labourer's normal daily wage. From the sixteenth century, saltpetre men extracted nitrogen from excrement for making gunpowder. The cannonballs fired at the Spanish Armada were propelled, in part, by London's dung.

In short, medieval and early modern London took a very different approach to their management of water and waste. Clean water was piped to the street. Waste was earthed and recycled. People may have understood no more about microbes than they did about the far side of the moon, but there was an instinctive understanding that drinking or using dirty water was a bad idea. Even children knew what was good for them. An account of a schoolboy's preparation for school in 1573 records him telling the household page to bring him water to wash, but warns: 'I will have no river water for it troubled [dirty]. Give me well or fountain water.'

Did people throw waste out of the window and into the street? Probably less than *Blackadder*-style history would suppose. It must have happened, but was something shameful to be done after dark. Jonathan Swift's satirical *Directions to Servants* advises, 'Never empty the chamber pots until they are quite full. If that happeneth in the night, empty them into the street; and if in the morning, into the garden.' Apart from anything, urine had value. It was needed to tan leather, make soap and finish textiles. Why throw it away when there were eighty tanneries in London who needed it.

However, as London's size and population grew, this approach became inadequate and increasingly insanitary. There were too many people, too close together, and too much excrement to manage. On 20 October 1660, Samuel Pepys recorded 'going down to my cellar . . . I put my feet into a great heap of turds, by which I find that Mr Turner's house of office is full and comes into my cellar.' Regulations on cesspool quality or forbidding the casting of garbage into sewers were repeated ad nauseam – doubtless because they were not being adequately followed.

It was to get worse. The first great mistake in the history of London's water supply was made in 1582. For the first time, drinking water was permitted to be sourced from the Thames. A Dutchman named Peter Morice bought a 240-year option to construct and manage a waterwheel in the first arch of London Bridge to draw water from the Thames and pipe it to private residences in the City. The Thames may not have been as filthy as it was to become, but with offal and effluent clearly being dumped into the river Fleet, and no doubt elsewhere, this meant that for the first time water consistently tainted by sewage was being piped for general use.

Worse was to follow during nearly 300 years of declining standards. In 1723, the Chelsea Water Company was established to draw water from the north bank of the Thames. Their slogan was: 'Water three times a week for three shillings a quarter.' Six other companies followed over the next 122 years.

Many people instinctively realised this was all very foolish and didn't drink the stuff. Foreign visitors were consistently amazed at the volume of alcohol that Londoners drank. One French visitor, César-François de Saussure, wrote in the eighteenth century: 'The lower classes, even the paupers, do not know what it is to quench their thirst with water. In this country, nothing but beer is drunk . . . Small beer is what everyone drinks when thirsty; it is used even in the best houses and costs only a penny a pot.'

David Copperfield drank it as a child. Housewives brewed it themselves or bought it from the local 'brewhouse'. Those who could afford higher duties drank strong beer, wine or brandy or, when global trade permitted, coffee, tea or chocolate. The key was not to drink the water. Perhaps it is no coincidence that one of the attractions of the newly fashionable suburbs of west London was that they had their own water supply distant from the river Thames. Once upon a time there were springs in Piccadilly and Bloomsbury.

Pamphleteers agreed. In 1827, one complained that water piped from the river was 'a fluid saturated with the impurities of fifty thousand homes – a dilute solution of animal and vegetable substances in a state of putrefaction – alike offensive to the sight, disgusting to the imagination and destructive to the healthy.' In 1850, Charles Dickens called the Thames a 'system of drainage' and his journal, *Household Words*, asked, 'How many companies take their supplies from the Thames, near to and after it has received the contents of the common sewers?' He was not given a clear answer.

Experts argued that there was nothing to worry about. 'The free currents of air which are necessarily in constant circulation for their proximity to the majestic Thames,' wrote one scientist, Professor Booth, 'have been considered (and not improperly) as the great cause of the salubrity of the metropolis.' As too often, non-empirical 'expertise' trumped common sense.

The second great error in the declining quality of London's water was in permitting (from 1815), and then requiring (from 1848) waste to be flushed into the public sewers and thence into the Thames. One can understand why the error was made. Pressures of density and population meant that cesspits could no longer cope with the vast volumes of excrement. One Whitechapel medical officer reported in 1858:

> Wherever there is a cesspool, the ground in its vicinity is completely saturated with the foul and putrefying liquid contents, the stench from which is continually rising up and infecting the air which is breathed by the people, and in some instances, poisoning the water which is drawn from the public pumps.

As London grew it became harder, and more expensive, to transport night soil to the farms of Middlesex or Hertfordshire. The physical volume of the stuff was also becoming nauseating. Night soil men kept it in giant heaps, known as laystalls, in their yards before transporting it to their agricultural customers. One witness wrote of 'table mountains of manure . . . extensive and deep lakes of putrefying night soil . . . dammed up with the more solid dung'.

Worse, as the nineteenth century economy globalised, the bottom fell out of the market for poo. In 1847, South American guano (solid bird droppings) became available as a cheaper fertiliser. What to do with all the newly unsellable waste? With no market for excrement, too much was simply left to fester, particularly in poorer neighbourhoods that could not afford to pay the declining number of night soil men. Hector Gavin, a doctor who worked at Charing Cross Hospital, recorded in 1848 that the residents of Bethnal Green were compelled to get rid of waste 'by throwing it on the gardens, yards or streets'.

The obvious solution to overflowing cesspools was the flushing lavatory, so that waste could be washed far away. Their widespread introduction in the early nineteenth century without an adequate sewerage system to support them was the third great error in the history of London's water works. Sir John Harrington had invented the water closet in the sixteenth century. He tried it out on his godmother, Queen Elizabeth, at Richmond, though she reportedly did not like the fact that the noise revealed to the wider court that she was at her privy.

The invention was ignored for 200 years until a series of improvements at the end of the eighteenth century and the creation of several firms to manufacture and market water closets. From about 1810, flushing lavatories, or pan closets, began to be installed and critically connected to sewers in large numbers in London's wealthier districts. The London builder, Thomas Cubitt, estimated in 1844 that the number of flushing lavatories had increased tenfold over the previous twenty years.

This was a veritable revolution in daily life. Previously homes had relied upon the chamber pot of pewter, faience or porcelain stored in the scullery and tucked under the bed or in dining room sideboards – perhaps to be used in full view of others during a late-night drinking session. Only the ducal or regal had possessed a private close-stool room. (The French nickname for the *lieu d'aisance* was *le lieu*, from which comes the English derivation 'the loo' – still posh lingo after 300 years). Now the piping of water closets created the need for segregated bathrooms more widely, and what started as luxury for the rich in time became a commodity for everyone.

In 1851, 827,000 people used WCs at the Great Exhibition – most probably for the first time. They had to 'spend a penny' to use them, a lavatorial euphemism that is still understood 170 years later. Further flushing public conveniences followed – at first exclusively on *Monopoly* streets. The first flushing 'halting station' was built in 1851 on Fleet Street, the first women's flushing public lavatory was built a year later on the Strand.

From the 1850s, flushing lavatories began to be installed in newly constructed middle-class homes as London spread east, west, south and north. For water closets to work hygienically and be able to flush out the basin, they required non-porous clay pipes, piped water and rooftop cisterns. This is what builders began to build. The accompanying key technical advance was the new flush mechanism of Thomas Crapper – 'A certain flush with every pull.' The newly possible pedestal lavatory designs had fruits, leaves, birds, shells and even, for the patriotic visitor, views of Windsor Castle.

During the second half of the nineteenth century, water ceased to be a public utility and became a private necessity. Turkish baths (as used by Pepys) closed and domestic hot water pipes took their place; first fitted into more expensive homes in the 1840s and in middle-class homes from the 1870s. In the 1890s the shower arrived. One first-time user commented, 'When I attempted to take one of these new-fangled things, the hose leapt out of the bath and turned itself on me. Definitely prefer the old way of bathing in a hip bath.'

The problem was where the water from the bathrooms and the water closets went. Older and small sewers had been built to cope with surface water, not effluent. New sewers were bigger and connected 11,200 out of 16,200 houses by 1852. But both deposited their contents firmly into the river Thames from which so much of London's drinking water now came. By mid-century, around sixty sewer outlets spewed their contents into the river and the consequences for public health were disastrous. In 1816, it was still possible to catch salmon in the Thames – a sure sign of clean water. None were caught in 1820. It was not only the fish who died: mortality from cholera and water-borne diseases exploded. The first epidemic, in 1832, killed 5,275. The next, in 1848–9, killed 14,789.

It is normal in history books to poke fun at the Victorian proponents of the miasma theory, which assumed that diseases were airborne not water-borne. ('From inhaling the odour of beef, the butcher's wife obtains her obesity,' wrote one professor of chemistry in 1844.) In fact, they simply had the wrong disease. Some diseases (cholera) are spread by foul water, others are airborne. The Spanish flu pandemic of 1918 and the Covid pandemic of 2020 were both spread by droplets in the air – if not by a miasma of meaty smells. But many others *did* notice what was going on.

By 1849 standard advice, as published in a guidebook of that year, was to avoid 'the unwholesome water furnished to the tanks of houses from the Thames'. The statistician, William Farr, wrote that the 'appearance of epidemic cholera and . . . the striking increase of diarrhoea' coincided with 'the introduction into general use of the water closet system'. Some Victorian cities, including Manchester, even tried to ban the use of WCs, 'because of the strain their outpourings imposed on the drainage and sewage system.'

However, impelled by 'the Great Stink' of 1858, when the foul state of the Thames prevented Members of Parliament from using those rooms that overlooked the river, the route taken for London was not to ban the WC, but to build the drainage London needed. Benjamin Disraeli's 1858 Local Management Amendment Act gave the Metropolitan Board for London the authority and money they needed. And, as is well known, they took it.

The programme of their chief engineer, Sir Joseph Bazalgette, was one of the high-water marks of Victorian confidence, a happy collusion of engineering, sanitation, municipal reform and beautification. Main sewers were not merely built for the 1860s, but for the next century. The Thames was not simply embanked, it was enriched. Abbey Mills pumping station was not just built, it was beautiful. For the Victorians, form did not follow function. They were too wise and public-spirited.[15]

And it worked. London's last cholera outbreak was in 1866. Ninety-three per cent of the 4,363 deaths were in the area supplied by the East London Water Company, which was still using improperly filtered water from the Thames. Towns had always been more lethal environments than the countryside, but by the 1920s the 'urban penalty' had been removed for the first time in human history. However, improvements were slow in poorer neighbourhoods.

Water remained a publicly accessed utility into (just) living memory. In 1934, one year before Victor Watson and Marjory Phillips's day trip to London to scout out London street names, half of London's working-class housing still had no water supply and had to rely on local standpipes, as their predecessors had to do for a thousand years.

Chapter Five

PALL MALL

The spymaster as property developer

*Among all the exercises of France, I preferre none before
the Palle-maille, both because it is a Gentleman-like sport,
not violent, and yeelds good occasion and opportunity of
discourse, as they walke from the one marke to the other.
I marvell, among many more Apish and foolish toyes, which
wee have brought out of France, that wee have not brought
this sport also into England.*
Robert Dallington, *A Method for Travell: France as it
Stoode in the Yeare of our Lorde 1598*

Some men of power blaze across history, meteors in the firmament. Others exercise their influence quietly in dark and secret places, retreating from the spotlight but guiding, informing, controlling none the less.

Henry Jermyn, Earl of St Albans, was such a man. By turns spymaster, diplomat, linguist, courtier, *bon vivant*, architectural aficionado and sycophant, he was a father figure to Charles II and a confidant and possibly lover to Charles I's widow, Queen

Henrietta Maria. His papers, which would be an historical El Dorado, were burnt or lost and his name is now remembered due to the streets he built, not the secrets he wielded. For Henry Jermyn was also one of the very first of that perennial London type, the aristocratic property developer, as mindful as the shopkeeper or the street trader on making a buck, but needing to do so behind the veil of courtly decorum.

Appropriately for a French-speaking counsellor to kings, the neighbourhood where Henry Jermyn made his princely fortune bordered Pall Mall, that most regal and most Parisian of London streets. It was named after a sixteenth-century French courtly pastime, the game of *palle-maille*, which was all the rage in the Francophile Stuart courts and which is now forgotten, other than the minor matter that it is one of the ancestors of modern golf.

Had you journeyed west from the village of Charing Cross at any time until the 1660s, you would have taken a highway, probably Saxon in origin, that very rarely for London, no longer exists. It ran through church-owned farmland just south of modern Pall Mall and north of the modern Mall. From the thirteenth century it passed a leper hospital (St James's Hospital) and then turned north-west to reach what is now Hyde Park Corner.

From the 1530s, a high wall ran along the southern side of the road. That most effectively acquisitive of monarchs, Henry VIII, had bought or seized all the land around the highway. He enclosed the marshy land to the south, now St James's Park, which served as his rather boggy private deer park. St James's Hospital itself was converted into a secondary palace for the heir to the throne – a purpose it has normally served ever since.

Meanwhile the land to the north, where Pall Mall now runs, was known as St James's Field. It was leased as meadows to farmers serving the endless London market for milk to drink and animals to eat, and sometimes soldiers mustered there. Every summer, apprentices and partygoers, tinkers and pedlars, merchants and stallholders congregated in these meadows for one of the great raucous London fairs, St James's Fair, a high-summer opportunity, sanctified by tradition, to indulge, drink and misbehave. Whores and 'infamous persons', including one year a man called 'Tory Rory', were arrested for indecent conduct. Unsurprisingly, that infamous killjoy Oliver Cromwell banned it in 1651 and it did not occur again until after the monarchy's restoration.

But it wasn't only the common Londoners who enjoyed themselves in St James's Fields; so did monarchs, with a royal tennis court and physic garden. The most prominent activity they chose to indulge in was a game played in a freshly planted avenue of elm trees just north of the ancient road heading west. Rather oddly, its arrival in London was a direct consequence of the failed dynastic politics of sixteenth-century Scotland. This fashion came, via Edinburgh, from Paris.

Mary, James I's mother and Elizabeth I's cousin, is known to most of us as Queen of Scots. She is better understood as a French princess. Daughter of a French mother, raised from the age of five in the Valois court, and married to the teenage French king, Francis II, who promptly died of an ear infection, her return to Edinburgh was less a coming home than a leaving of it. She never learnt the knack of handling the violent Scottish nobles who played the game of Scottish renaissance politics roughly and with murderous intent.

But one thing she did bring back with her from France was a taste for the fashionable court game, *jeu de mail*, known in the original Florentine Italian as *palla a Maglio* (from the Italian *palla*, a ball, and *maglio*, a mallet) and in English as 'pall mall'. Indeed, her liking for the game was one of the reasons she was forced to flee Scotland and seek sanctuary with her cousin, Elizabeth, who was ultimately to behead her. One of the points made in the 'book of articles' accusing Mary, probably falsely, of complicity in her second husband's murder was that shortly afterwards she was seen at Seton with his murderer, Lord Bothwell, playing 'one day richt oppinlie at the fieldis with the pal mall and goif'.

Mary never saw her son, James VI of Scotland and James I of England, beyond the age of ten months. But either the taste for the game was genetic or it became sufficiently common in the Scottish court for James to share his mother's appetite. In 1599, he advised his son that he should engage in 'running, leaping, wrestling, fencing, dauncing, and playing at the caitche or tennise, archery, palle maillé, and such like other faire and pleasant field games'. The Stuarts brought the game to London, where it was played at the English court throughout the seventeenth century, before falling out of fashion in the eighteenth.

A combination of golf and croquet, pall mall was played in a long, cockleshell-strewn court enclosed by a wooden fence. Players used croquet-like mallets, which were wielded as you would now hold a golf club. The aim was to hit the ball along the court towards a target hoop. Once near the hoop, rather as a modern golfer swaps over to their putter, players changed implement to a stick with a spoon-shaped end for lifting the ball up accurately into the hoop. Those who hit their ball out of the court were 'out of bounds'. The aim was to reach the hoop in as few goes as possible. History does not record if the king always won.

Where did the king and his courtiers play pall mall? Rather than encroach upon the precious hunting ground of St James's, the court encroached upon St James's Field north of the highway. Sometime before 1630, when state papers refer to 'St James's field where the pallmall is', an alley for pall mall was set up along the south side of St James's Field – running north and parallel to the historic highway. By the 1640s, a line of 140 elm trees were maturing nicely 'in a very decent and regular manner on both sides of the walk'.

Monarchy was more public. Despite the fence surrounding the court and a 1630 order that all ways into the field from the public highway be closed, those leaving London on the public highway were able to observe the king and his courtiers at play immediately on their right as they marched west. The traveller and merchant, Peter Mundy, observed Charles I 'playing att Palle Malle by St James' in 1639. It is rather as if we could observe the royal family playing tennis while we drive behind Buckingham Palace.

Such fripperies did not impress the parliamentary republic that cut off King Charles's head down the road in Whitehall. By 1650, a mean wooden building with 'two small drinkinge rooms' had been built (it is not clear by whom) near the pall mall court and in 1651, a former royal servant, Hugh Woodward, bought St James's Field (becoming known as Pall Mall Field) for £2,000.

Woodward was not in it for the agriculture. He wanted to turn the land into cash – and he did not hang around. He formed a syndicate of carpenters, bricklayers and other builders, to whom he sold off or subleased plots for development. Within just over a decade there were 250 houses and sheds 'of all sorts' around Pall Mall Field. These included a row of houses south of the pall mall alley facing the ancient highway to the south. They turned their backs to the court and were possibly responsible for the destruction of some of the wooden fence and around twenty of the double avenue of elm trees.

The alley as an appropriately attractive and sequestrated court for royal relaxation was ruined. It is hard to be courtly when you are cheek by jowl with the servants' quarters round the back of some speedily built speculative housing. What to do? It is at this point that the strange story of Henry Jermyn and his intensely close relationship with the king's French mother enters the story, not merely of Pall Mall, but of the creation of London's entire West End.

The scion of Suffolk gentry, at the time of the monarchy's restoration in 1660, Henry Jermyn had served three generations of the Stuart dynasty as courtier, diplomat, spy and financier of last resort for nearly forty years. Aged only nineteen, he had travelled in the entourage sent by James I to Paris to arrange the marriage of Henrietta Maria, King Louis XIII's fourteen-year-old sister, to the future Charles I. Henrietta Maria's subsequent relationship with her husband was rocky, particularly to start with. But she did become close to the handsome, fluently French-speaking Henry Jermyn, who was only five years her senior and who rose rapidly as her gentleman usher, vice-chamberlain and master of the horse.

In the tortuous years preceding the English Civil War, Jermyn was a backstage power broker in the complicated intrigues within the king's court and the queen's court and an advocate of pre-emptive action against those who wished to curb the king's authority. In 1641, he was forced to flee for France after his plan was revealed to seize the Tower of London and liberate the king's supporter, Lord Strafford, from imminent parliamentary execution.

During the Civil War, Jermyn accompanied the queen and ensured her safety before again fleeing with her to France and helping arrange the safe escape of her family. Inevitably, tongues wagged and contemporary gossip recounted that the queen and her elegant master of the horse were lovers. Some or all of her children, including Charles II, were even rumoured to be his bastards. This seems unlikely.

But we do know that Henry Jermyn never married anyone else

(though he had affairs in his youth) and that Henrietta Maria and Henry Jermyn's lives were entwined for forty years. During the long years of the interregnum, he was her closest companion, ran multiple clandestine correspondences on her and her son's behalf, and raised 647,416 *livres tournois* (about £20–25 million in today's money) to support the Royalist cause. The huge debts he incurred in the process were crippling.

It is hardly surprising that on the Restoration, Charles II raised him to the Earldom of St Albans, promoted him to Lord Chamberlain, and showered him with land and manors in America, England and, critically for our story, London. The Bailiwick of St James's, which included the pall mall court and St James's Field, had been made over by Charles I to his wife in 1629. Thirty years later, she must have been delighted to help arrange its transfer to the new Earl of St Albans. Between them Henrietta Maria and Henry Jermyn proceeded to plan out the whole neighbourhood.

The spoilt pall mall court was moved south into St James's Park – where it ran along the northern part of the current Mall. Charles II enjoyed pall mall and was good at it. The poet and politician, Edmund Waller, described him hitting the ball so hard that no sooner had he struck it than:

'Tis already more than half the mall,
And such a fury from his arm has got
As from a smoking Culverin 'twere shot.[16]

However, dust blowing off the old highway on the higher land parallel to the court was 'very troublesome' and spoilt the king's game. According to a conversation that Samuel Pepys recorded with the groundsmen, the cockleshell covering already had a tendency to turn 'to dust' and deaden the ball, so this was no good. It was therefore decided 'to barre up the old way' with posts and rails and divert traffic down the old, disused pall mall alley.

This was very annoying for those living in the row of houses that had been built to the north of the old highway. Suddenly their back gardens were facing the street and their front doors were facing a blocked-off road. They petitioned for the right to augment their gardens onto the old road. They were successful. And thus, the change in route from the ancient road west to the new line of Pall Mall became irreversible and permanent.

Surprisingly few ancient roads have been erased in the creation of contemporary London, but the courtly pleasures of pall mall accomplished one such loss. The king wanted to call the new road Catherine Street after his wife. However, Londoners would have none of it. The new street had already become known as 'Pall Mall' and Pall Mall it has remained.[17]

Meanwhile Henrietta Maria and Henry Jermyn got to work. Henrietta Maria employed her compatriot, the landscape architect André Mollet, to formalise the marshy St James's Park through which the river Tyburn flowed. The river was culverted into a canal and exotic waterbirds were installed. They are still there. Charles II then opened the park to the public who loved it – sometimes a little too much.[18]

The Restoration rake and poet, Lord Rochester, told how after dark:

Nightly, now beneath the trees' shade
Are buggeries, rapes and incests made,
Under this all sin-sheltering Grove
Whores of the Bulk and the Alcove.[19]

Lord Rochester liked this sort of thing, so it is unclear if his lines are reportage, autobiography or fantasy. More prosaically, nearby, Henry Jermyn had a plan to make a lot of money. He may have been busy with countless diplomatic intrigues (he was a constant advocate of alliance with the French), but he was no fool. He had spotted a 'gap in the market'. He had noticed that the wealthy increasingly wanted to live nearer the court and away from the overcrowding, noise and smells of the City of London. In 1614, only seventy-one people with a claim to gentility lived in the nearby parish of St Martin. By 1640, this had risen to over 750. Meanwhile most financiers remained resident near their counting houses in the City. Only 4 per cent of a seventeenth-century directory of 2,000 bankers and merchants lived in the West End. Might more want or, after the Great Fire of 1666, need to leave?

In a complex series of transactions and petitions, Henry Jermyn and his lawyers persuaded the king to lengthen his leasehold of St James's Field and convert some of it into a freehold, so that Jermyn could build 'great and good houses' as 'dwellings of Noble men and other Persons of quality'. In turn, plots were then sold on or subleased either to builders or to future owner-occupiers. Throughout the 1660s and 1670s, Pall Mall was developed as a mix of taverns, shops and houses.

Meanwhile a network of elegant streets and squares to its north were laid out and then developed as a residential neighbourhood with clear quality stipulations on what was permissible: St James's Square, King Street, Duke Street, Charles II Street, Duke of York Street and, tucked in at the north end of the former St James's Fields, the street that 350 years later would be Henry Jermyn's most lasting legacy – Jermyn Street.

An Act of 1662 required owners of houses in Pall Mall to contribute to the cost of paving the street. Unsurprisingly, Jermyn was one of the commissioners who oversaw enforcement, but he also invested in the neighbourhood's future himself. He used his considerable influence at court to ensure that a new parish (St James's) was carved out of the historic parish of St Martin and he then proceeded to pay for a new church. He was granted letters patent to hold a market and built the marketplace for it, abutting Pall Mall.

The historic and time-honoured St James's Fair was notionally moved to this marketplace, for '15 dayes at least' annually, but in fact suppressed. No mention is made of the ancient fair after 1665; what Henry Jermyn wanted, he seems to have got. He even got lucky when a new water supply was found just north of his land.

The City of London were opposed to the new development, as they feared its consequence for their water supply. But for all their wealth, they were powerless. Samuel Pepys recalled that 'my Lord Mayor told me . . . that this City . . . dare not oppose it.' They were wise to pick their battles. Jermyn's connections were second to none. Gossips continued to speculate about the nature of his relationship with the queen mother. Pepys wrote that Henrietta Maria 'being married to my Lord St Albans is commonly talked of; and that they had a daughter between them in France, how true, God knows.'

Jermyn's connections were architectural and not just courtly. He knew all the best men to advise him on town planning and Queen Henrietta Maria was a lifelong architectural patron. Inigo Jones had worked extensively for her in the 1620s and 1630s, and on the Restoration she was appointed High Steward of Greenwich. As her Lord Chamberlain, Jermyn oversaw the demolition of the old Tudor palace (where Henry VIII had been born) and commissioned the first phase of the new Baroque Greenwich Palace. Eighteenth-century sources assert that Henry

Jermyn was a freemason alongside Sir Christopher Wren. Maybe, maybe not, but he did commission Wren to build St James's Church – one of London's very finest. Nothing but the best for the denizens of Pall Mall.

Anyhow, the new neighbourhood of St James's was a commercial and social success. Some of the best houses were in St James's Square, where Jermyn himself moved into a house and which Pepys described as 'most noble'. Others agreed. Before 1675 Lord Bellasis, the Earl of Arlington, Viscount Halifax and the French ambassador, Monsieur Courtin, were all neighbours.

If anything, the houses along the south side of Pall Mall were even smarter. One clergyman recorded in 1720 that they 'have a Pleasant Prospect into the King's Garden; and . . . to many of them there are raised Mounts, which give them the Prospect of the said Garden, and of the Park.' The king's mistress, Nell Gwyn, was one resident. It is not known if she liked standing on the little hill at the bottom of her garden to admire St James's Park.

Living in the new street of Pall Mall in Restoration London definitely meant that you were as close to the courtly apex of wealth and power as it was possible to be.

By the time he died in 1684, Henry Jermyn had certainly rescued his own finances. His estate owned the freehold of nearly half of the newly built and fashionable parish of St James's and controlled or profited from a series of leases from the Crown on much of the rest. Jermyn was not the very first aristocratic property developer, but he was the first West End developer who set the pattern the entire West End was to follow. Legal agreements in neighbouring estates explicitly demanded that they should follow the model of Pall Mall.[20]

Henry Jermyn, Earl of St Albans, Baron Jermyn of St Edmundsbury and Knight of the Garter was probably not the father of Charles II, as some gossips would have it. (Although intriguingly after Jermyn's death, Charles II created his own illegitimate son by Nell Gwyn, the Duke of St Albans.) Indeed, Jermyn had no legitimate sons, only nephews, to whom he might leave his considerable estate. Such was the price of his undoubted lifelong devotion to Queen Henrietta Maria. But with robust royal support and his many and multifarious connections with both architects and builders, Henry Jermyn undoubtedly *was* the father of the West End.

And Pall Mall was where it all started.

Chapter 6
LEICESTER SQUARE
The triumph of the commons?

Wealth however got, in England makes
Lords of mechanics, gentlemen of rakes.
Antiquity and birth are needless here;
'Tis impudence and money makes a peer.
Daniel Defoe, *The True-born Englishman: A Satire*

Our ancestors' lives were lived to an interwoven rhythm of the seasons and of festivals that we have lost: Michaelmas, Candlemas, Lammas Day and a communion of saints' days. Even their names are leaving our language, save for the unthumbed pages of church calendars or the term names in some of our older schools or universities. Yet these feasts and festivals marked not only the lives of the saints or of Our Lord, but also the changing year and the obligations and rights that it brought as days waxed or waned. Some of these ancient rights affect our lives still, even if we have never heard of them.

It is a safe bet that very few of the thousands of tourists who daily throng through Leicester Square have ever celebrated

Lammas Day. However, were it not for ancient rights associated with this Anglo-Saxon feast, Leicester Square would not exist in the form we know it today.

Had you walked north from Charing Cross village at any time until the late seventeenth century between 12 August and 6 April, you would have seen parishioners of St Martin-in-the-Fields (and it still was mainly in the fields) exercising their ancient rights to dry clothes and pasture their cattle on the common land. In fact, you can still see them today. The National Archives in Kew, the Pepys Library in Magdalene College, Cambridge, and the London Metropolitan Archives in Clerkenwell all contain copies of a map, often called the 'Woodcut' or 'Agas' map, which was printed in 1633, but was based on earlier copies from the 1550s and 1560s.

On these maps, a little north-west of the medieval parish church of St Martin, you can see a large field. On it, frozen for eternity, a lady stoops beside drying tunics to lay down her laundry, while nearby a solitary cow grazes beside two chatting parishioners. St Martin's Field had so-called Lammas rights, which entitled commoners to pasture and use the land between harvest, or Lammas Day, and spring. Lammas is an Anglo-Saxon word meaning 'loaf mass'. By the seventeenth century, the commoners' rights in St Martin's parish were possibly a thousand years old.

This was a problem for Robert Sidney, 2nd Earl of Leicester. A near contemporary of Pall Mall's Henry Jermyn, Robert Sidney was an intellectual aristocrat, 'rather a speculative than a practical man', according to one contemporary, 'very conversant in books, and much addicted to the mathematics'. About the same time as the surviving 'Woodcut' map was printed, he bought four acres of the common land. He was not primarily trying to make money; he wanted to build a house. The problem was the people.

The land on which Lord Leicester wanted to build his house was well chosen, looking down the fields sloping gently towards Charing Cross and Whitehall. Airy and healthy, it would have had a pleasant view of Westminster and the Thames. However, it also lay within the common field and building on it would deprive the inhabitants of St Martin's parish of their Lammas common and other ancient rights.

The differences between the Earl of Leicester and the inhabitants of the parish of St Martin reached the Privy Council and Lord Leicester was obliged to compromise. The limits of his home were set by the Privy Council and much of the Lammas common remained open to the parishioners: 'the nether part' of the field, which became known as Leicester Field or Fields, 'being equall in quantity and better ground then the other part', was ordered to be:

> turned into Walkes and planted with trees alonge the walkes, and fitt spaces left for the Inhabitantes to drye their Clothes there as they were wont, and to have free use of the place, but not to depasture it, and all the foote wayes through that Close to bee used as now they are.

In short, the commoners were still able to use Leicester Fields, their ancient common land, and to dry their clothes, but they lost the right to pasture. Lord Leicester was obliged to pay the parish three pounds per year in compensation and for relief to the poor. (How well the vicar, William Bray, administered this is not recorded.)

Lord Leicester got his house, but the parishioners were not entirely dispossessed. They got some guarantees and remaining rights over the rest of the land, and these guarantees were to have a very long tail. Forty years later, a rather elderly Lord Leicester started looking with envy at the success of his Pall Mall neighbour, Henry Jermyn. He wanted some of it for himself. He didn't even need to commission Christopher Wren to build a new parish church, as ancient St Martin-in-the-Fields lay just to his south down St Martin's Lane.

However, what to do about Leicester Fields over which the parishioners had such firm rights? The obvious answer was to turn them into a public square. In February 1670, Lord Leicester obtained a licence from the king to build. No mention was made of the former agreement with the parishioners; however, limits were set to the houses to be erected and these left Leicester Fields open, as it had to be. Under the terms of their leases, the contractors who built the square's houses were obliged to set up rails and posts enclosing the centre and to plant it with 'young trees of Elm'.

The square was clearly modelled upon the successful St James's Square down the road, with Lord Leicester's own mansion on the north side supplying aristocratic dignity. The difference was that in St James's Square, and in many of the aristocratic squares that were to follow over the next two centuries, the landlord was able to restrict the right of access to the square to tenants. Leicester Square had to remain open to all, which was to help set a very different course for Leicester Square's history over the centuries to come. For whereas most of London's squares have remained residential and exclusive, Leicester Square became a place of theatres, music halls and cinemas, temples not of aristocratic reserve, but of plebian entertainment. It's all in the land.

Leicester Square's evolution into a more middle-class and raucous place began quickly. Lord Leicester aspired to create houses like those in St James's Square down the road. However, they ended up being rather more modest, despite their potentially exclusive location. The design and proportions of London's streets was far more strictly regulated in the late seventeenth or eighteenth centuries than it is now, with a set of house types laid down by law. Surviving contracts and engravings show the houses to the south, east and west of Leicester Square were 'second rate'. That meant they had three storeys, a basement and an attic, with the ground and first floors at least ten feet high.

Lord Leicester's more modest strategy was possibly to permit faster subletting of plots and quicker building, because the square certainly went up in a rush. A surviving map shows it already complete in 1676. Perhaps it was because he was advised that the 'open to all' nature of the square (still revealingly called Leicester Fields) would limit the development's attraction to the more genteel. Either way, the consequence of these more modest plots was that Leicester Fields almost immediately became a far more socially 'mixed' community than we might imagine.

Many of us think of the past as a world of fixed hierarchies, of the washed and the unwashed, the haves and the have nots. It was certainly hierarchical, but the elite was very open to talent and energy. Families moved up and down. The elite also led lives that intersected with their fellows far more than would normally be the case in a modern 'exclusive' suburb. Neighbourhoods could be astonishingly variegated: aristocrats, professions and 'trade' living cheek by jowl. Leicester Fields was such a place.

Take, for example, the west side of Leicester Fields: the house (subsequently No. 43) in the square's south-west corner started life as the Sun tavern, before becoming a goldsmith's shop (under the sign of the Black Lion), then a tavern again (this time called the Hoop), before being joined with the house next door and becoming the home of George III's physician, Dr (later Sir) Noah

Thomas. Next door (No. 44) was also occupied by doctors for over a hundred years.

No. 45 had a rather plusher start. Its first resident Sir John Reresby was another Royalist who had spent the Commonwealth abroad at the court of Charles I's widow, Queen Henrietta Maria. Subsequently it became an apothecary's shop and then home, successively, to an upholsterer, an artist and a doctor, before becoming a hospital for diseases of the skin.

Two doors up, the largest house in the terrace was occupied by a Member of Parliament and then the Swedish envoy, before becoming home to the portrait painter, Sir Joshua Reynolds, who fitted a 'commodious and elegant room for his sitters'. Next time you look at any painting by Reynolds after 1760, consider that it was probably painted in Leicester Square. The square was popular with artists. William Hogarth lived there, so did Michael Dahl, who painted Mary Davies, the dynastic progenitor of Mayfair, in his Leicester Square studio in 1700.

Further up the west terrace were homes occupied by earls, barons, baronets, MPs, generals and diplomats, but also by painters, engravers, auctioneers and victuallers. Round the corner, Lord Leicester's grand house still took up most of the square's north side and from 1742 was leased to none other than the Prince of Wales. For over thirty years, Leicester House was a royal residence, home to the heirs to the throne. The phrase 'Leicester House faction' even entered the lexicon, meaning those who supported successive princes in their frequent opposition to their respective fathers.

Despite the presence of royalty, the square still remained socially mixed. Thomas Bird, who was born in Leicester Fields in 1718, became a common soldier and was executed for robbery. Leicester House itself was partly hidden behind shops and taverns, and in 1749 there were at least sixteen tradesmen living in the square. Leicester Square was organically the type of 'mixed community' that utopians envisage and normally fail to create.

The demi-monde nature of the neighbourhood, well connected and serious but also lascivious and sensual, is caught in the life of Sir Thomas de Veil, who lived on the south side of Leicester Fields in the 1720s and 1730s. Thomas de Veil was a Huguenot by birth, who had made his fortune as a soldier. He then worked as what we now call a political lobbyist before becoming a magistrate. Operating initially from Leicester Fields, he was the most important figure in early eighteenth-century law enforcement, personally investigating cases, interviewing suspects, protecting witnesses and breaking up criminal gangs. Whilst living in Leicester Square, he was the subject of two consequent assassination attempts.

Thomas de Veil lived hard as well as working hard. He was a freemason – in the same lodge as his neighbour William Hogarth, who satirised him. De Veil married four times, fathered twenty-five children, and was rumoured to have accepted sexual favours from prostitutes in exchange for judicial leniency. Even a supportive anonymous biographer (possibly de Veil himself) conceded that 'his greatest foible, was a most irregular passion for the fairer sex.'

Still called Leicester Fields into the nineteenth century, the garden on which the square's other blue-blooded and blue-collared inhabitants looked out was probably still open to all, but it was not very genteel.[21] In 1698, a group of aristocratic young thugs after a night's drinking and gambling went 'by break of day to decide their differences in Leicester fields, where a pretty young man, Coll. Richard Coote's son of Ireland, was killed dead upon the place.' It is possible that the public right of access was partly lost during the eighteenth century, victim to an urbanising neighbourhood's more transient population; however, it seems unlikely.

Certainly, the more mixed nature of the square's residents constrained the exclusivity of its garden. The neighbourhood acquired a reputation as a place of 'great mischiefs', which it never quite shook off. Records and engravings show gangs fighting and muggings in the square.

A critical memory of the common land's ancient rights also survived in successive legal contracts, which were fundamentally to shape the neighbourhood's history. Jocelyn Sidney, the last Earl of Leicester, died in 1743 and the family estate was broken up forty-five years later: the Sidneys had been an argumentative and thin-breeding family with the title passing as frequently between brothers as to sons. The ownership of the garden was inherited by a merchant family, the Tulks, but with one crucial, restrictive covenant:

> The Owners and Proprietors . . . shall for ever afterwards at their own sole and proper costs and charges keep and maintain the said Square Garden or Pleasure Ground and the railing round the same in sufficient and proper repair.

The key phrase is 'pleasure ground'. The capital's pleasure gardens were not private but public places, either free to access (as was the most famous, Vauxhall), or priced to sell. In short, the Lammas Day rights of Leicester Fields had not quite been forgotten.

In 1808, Charles Tulk sold the garden for £210 to Charles Elms, a dentist living in the square, to whom the obligation to maintain the garden 'uncovered by any buildings' was transferred. Foolishly, the garden's maintenance thus ceased to be the responsibility of the ground landlords of the surrounding houses, who had the strongest incentive to keep the garden in good order. The garden therefore became a liability, not an asset.

During the nineteenth century it became 'a neglected and dirty place', in which 'the unwashed Arabs of Westminster disported themselves at their own wild will among the putrefying remains of dogs and cats.'

From its first construction, there had always been taverns in Leicester Square. Well located but not exclusive and with the garden itself increasingly ill-managed, the square became more attractive as a place to work or offer entertainment rather than to live. The first of many Leicester Square circus masters was Ashton Lever, a landed gentleman and naturalist, who had collected over 25,000 fossils, shells, insects and stuffed animals.

Overwhelmed by visitors wishing to see his collection at his mansion home near Rochdale, he brought the collection to London, rented Leicester House when the royal family surrendered their lease, converted its principal rooms into galleries, then put 'the elephant and the zebra' in an outhouse and opened to the paying public as the 'Holophusikon' (the phrase has not caught on). From royal residence to paying museum in one jump. The admission price was five shillings and three pence, or two guineas for an annual ticket.

The spectacle was initially a success. Receipts were £2,253 in 1782, but interest subsequently waned. Despite his attempts to impress and educate visitors, Sir Ashton was obliged to cut his prices (to two shillings and sixpence) before going bust in 1784 and disposing of the collection by lottery. It is a tale of spectacle, transient success and disaster, which Leicester Square has witnessed many times since.

Following Ashton Lever's first essay, spectacles, entertainments, theatres, hotels and cinemas have been opening and succeeding, failing and closing for over 200 years. First up, the Italian theatre manager, Giovanni Gallini, and the Irish law student, Richard Bray O'Reilly, attempted and very nearly succeeded in raising the funds and securing permission to build an opera house on Leicester Square. They had sumptuous designs worked up by John Soane, which you can still see in the John Soane museum. It is one of London's more intriguing 'what ifs'.

Two museums did manage to open a few years later, the National Museum of the Mechanical Arts and the Royal Panopticon of Science and Art, but both failed quickly. More successful was Miss Linwood's gallery of needlework pictures at Savile House, which somehow survived for forty years, and Robert Burford's semi-circular rotunda in the square's north-east corner, which showed off the painter Robert Barker's London panoramas from 1794 to 1861. They were so good that the words 'panorama' and 'panoramic' have entered the language. It cost three shillings to enter.

Even more dramatic was the Great Globe built within Leicester Square itself, possibly illegally, by the geographer, entrepreneur and map seller James Wyld, to rival the 1851 Great Exhibition. It was a purpose-built hall containing a giant hollow globe over 60 feet in diameter. Inside, the public could mount a staircase and, from a series of platforms, view the Earth's surface on the concave interior. Mountain ranges and rivers modelled in plaster were all to scale.

It was a runaway success. Over a million visited in each of the first three years including Prince Albert, the Duke of Wellington and the King of Belgium. But visitors tailed off, James Wyld had a very shaky legal right to build on the square, and he was obliged to demolish the globe and sell its contents for scrap.

Simultaneously came a rush of hotels, normally with evocative French names such as the Sablonière or the Cavour, Turkish baths, oyster bars and, above all, theatres and music halls: Daly's, the Empire, the Hippodrome and the Alhambra, which was particularly arresting. Over £25,000 was invested in its decoration, complete with minarets and Moorish excess. It was aimed at the mass market and yet Queen Victoria brought her family to see 'Black Eagle, the Horse of Beauty'. According to one report, 'the great majority of the people at the Alhambra were respectable tradespeople and mechanics with their families, looking at the dancing.' Bass pale ale was the favourite drink, followed by brandy and soda.

The square changed physically. Leicester Square's austere Georgian houses were, little by little, converted into the Moorish facades and Corinthian pilasters of Victorian and Edwardian commercial exuberance. Its demi-monde nature lost its aristocratic admixture, but gained a flavour as a demesne where refugees and foreigners lived. Karl Marx briefly lived round the corner and Thackeray called the square a 'dingy modern France'. When revolution broke out across Europe in 1848, one English chartist recorded that 'great was the clinking of glasses that night in and around Soho and Leicester Square.'

The square also gained a reputation as a place where more raucous, potentially risqué, entertainment was available. For all the mechanics drinking pale ale, in 1870 the Alhambra lost its dancing licence in a row over the can-can. In 1871, two middle-class transvestites, one a stockbroker, the other a solicitor, were ejected for causing a disturbance. The Alhambra's owner defended it by asserting (how could he know?) that only 3 per cent of its audience were prostitutes. By the early twentieth century, Leicester Square was celebrated in the music halls and the marching song 'It's a Long Way to Tipperary' during the First World War as the heart of London's pleasure-seeking district – 'Goodbye Piccadilly, farewell Leicester Square!'

Meanwhile what of the garden around which this cornucopia of entertainment was growing? When a former shoemaker and biscuit baker turned builder and amateur architect, Edward

Moxhay, bought the garden, he had a very clear intent to build upon it. However, in a landmark legal ruling he was prevented from doing so. Even though he had bought the land *without* a restrictive covenant, the earlier Leicester Fields covenant was judged to 'run with the land' or, in other words, to bind future as well as current landowners. It is a ruling that is still cited today wherever the writ of common law runs.

In direct consequence, the eccentric fraudster and serial company promoter, Albert Grant, was able to buy Leicester Square garden for £11,060 in 1874. Grant was an enigma. Irish-born, he had changed his name from Abraham Gottheimer, somehow secured (most likely by purchase) an Italian hereditary barony, and styled himself Baron Grant. He was probably the inspiration for Anthony Trollope's crooked and megalomaniac financier, Melmotte, in his 1874 novel, *The Way We Live Now*. With what must have been exquisite if mendacious salesmanship, Grant had raised and promoted a long series of companies, nearly all of which went bust, wiping out his investors, but from which he emerged financially enriched.

He was elected twice to PARLIAMENT. At the first time in 1865, he was accused of being a 'fraudulent adventurer'. At his second time, in January 1874, he was proven so to be, and he was unseated for bribery and corruption within six months. At precisely the same time as he was facing these charges, and presumably as an exercise in reputation management, Grant bought Leicester Square garden, renovated it to his own design (including statues of famous residents such as William Hogarth and Joshua Reynolds) and presented it as a public park to the Board of Works. It was the one public-spirited act of his life. Leicester Square has been in public ownership ever since and is now managed by the City of Westminster.

And thus, via good luck and ill, the un-sequestrated rights to the common land of St Martin's Field, obscured but not lost for over 200 years, were unambiguously rediscovered. Some-times, history takes the long road to get back to the right place.

Streets and squares matter. But so does the ownership of the land that surrounds them. Despite its location and its princely patronage, Leicester Square never became as exclusive as St James's Square; its owners never really tried. Common rights as old as England, forgotten but translated into legal covenants, forbade it. Some lords were able to escape their obligations to age-sanctified traditional liberties. Henry Jermyn was able to make the ancient St James's Fair disappear into history, though he was much helped by Oliver Cromwell's suppression of such high jinks.

The 2nd Earl of Leicester was not such a man, and the deal he did with the Privy Council to permit his developments contributed to the ultimate failure of Leicester Fields as an exclusive enclave of the aristocratic. It is also cheaper on the *Monopoly* board. Leicester's heirs and squabbling successors may not have been delighted, but generations of Londoners, from Edwardian theatregoers to contemporary revellers, have reason to be grateful to the Anglo-Saxon feast of Loaf Mass Day, or Lammas Day. If only they knew.

Chapter 7

BOND STREET

'The World is Not Enough'

Orbis non sufficit: The world is not enough
Motto of Sir Thomas Bond, developer of
Old Bond Street

If you want to reach for a ready cliché, complain about the modern world's 'consumer culture', about the prevalence of capitalism or commercialism, of advertising or shopping centres. But cross your fingers as you do, for you will be talking verifiable nonsense. Shopping is as old as cities – which makes it at least 14,000 years old and counting. The most common catalyst for the creation of most English towns was the granting of a medieval market, and London's first shopping centre, the City's Royal Exchange, was opened 450 years ago in 1571.

It is not only shopping that is ancient. So is enjoying it and using it to show off your relative success, visiting not the local high street but London's West End, buying not English beer or wool, but teas or silks, sugars or calicoes from the wide world. Few London streets have been associated with luxury shopping as firmly as Bond Street, New and Old, but by the time it was first laid out in the late seventeenth century, going shopping in London was already nearly two millennia old and counting.

London has always shopped. It has all the ingredients: a good harbour, a strategic bridge, a major road junction, fertile hinterland, and many people to buy and sell. There is clear evidence of the rapid creation of bakeries and shops selling household goods before the Boudiccan revolt destroyed Londinium in AD 60. Later, Roman shops clustered densely around the Forum, and markets abounded in medieval London: at Smithfield, Newgate, Leadenhall, Cornhill, Gracechurch, Eastcheap, Queenhithe and Billingsgate.

Visiting markets could be fun, as one medieval writer made clear:

In those places of display the varied decorations for wedding entertainment and great feasts so pleases the gaze of those going by that, having looked down half of one row, the force of desire soon hastens them to the other . . . And then, insatiate, causes them almost infinitely to repeat their inspections.[22]

Even better were itinerant fairs. There were probably over 2,700 fairs in fifteenth-century England and Wales and something of the excitement of their arrival and their amalgam of shopping and enjoyment is captured, even today, in the transition of historic trading fairs into modern funfairs. Medieval Londoners used permanent shops too. Cheapside was the Bond Street, Regent Street and Oxford Street of medieval London all combined.[23] By 1400, it contained over 400 shops selling not just staples, but luxuries, armour, swords, jewellery, textiles and girdles.

Most shops were tiny, less than 2 metres wide and between 2 metres and 4 metres deep. One, in 1299, was only 0.9 metres by 1.2 metres, no more than a market stall with walls. Goods were sold not *in* the shop but *out of* it, literally over the counter, which was opened into the street. (This was forbidden in narrow, though not main, streets from 1666.) Most medieval shops had open-fronted, unglazed windows, often in pairs and with arched tops. They were shuttered overnight, with the shutters normally hinged horizontally not vertically, so that the bottom shutter might form a stall-board for displaying goods and the top shutter a canopy for keeping goods cool or dry. Many were crammed; in 1322 the shop of a London mercer, Richard de Elsyng, held 1,750 items in stock.

As London grew, so did the size and number of her shops and stalls. By 1400 some shops were up to 37 square metres, and by 1688, the seventeenth-century statistician Gregory King could estimate that England had 50,000 shopkeepers and tradesmen. Sixty years later there were probably 142,000, with 21,000 in London alone. If these estimates are correct then Adam Smith, the true originator of the phrase that England is a 'nation of shopkeepers', was exaggerating. Only about 2.5 per cent of Englishmen were.

Shopping was moving west though, following inhabitants and fashion. New markets for food opened over the newly enclosed Fleet ditch, at Covent Garden, at St James's and Bloomsbury. Noble landlords were eager to play the role of retail property developers. Following the example of Sir Thomas Gresham's 1571 Royal Exchange on Cornhill, Robert Cecil, chief advisor successively to Elizabeth I and James I, bought an old stable and developed it into the New Exchange on the Strand. The Middle Exchange and the Exeter Exchange followed in the 1670s.

These Exchanges along the Strand, long since demolished

and forgotten, were the fashionable malls and galleries of their day: with plate glass windows (not medieval wooden lattices), the latest, slightly gauche, Jacobean classicism, pilastered arcades onto the street, niches and statues. They created a concentrated space, open to the street but cleaner and safer, in which the rich and fashionable from the new West End or the old City could see, shop and socially intermingle.

The New Exchange permitted only haberdashers, stocking sellers, silk mercers, linen drapers, girdlers, milliners, seamsters, goldsmiths, jewellers, perfumers, stationers, booksellers, confectioners, and those who sold china, pictures, prints or maps. In summer, the shops were open from 6am to 8pm and in winter from 7am to 7pm.

Samuel Pepys mentions the New Exchange 132 times in his 1660s diaries, particularly after the Great Fire destroyed the Royal Exchange in 1666. He observed the improving facilities: 'I walked in the Exchange, which is now made pretty, by having windows and doors before all the shops to keep out the cold.' He went there to shop (with or without his wife), meet people, discuss business ('while my wife was buying things I walked up and down with Dr Williams, talking about my law business'), drink whey (briefly fashionable and, salted, probably comparable to Indian lassi), catch boats down the river, hail carriages and ogle shop girls.

His favourite was Dorothy Stacey, 'pretty Doll', who was his wife's milliner and whose good looks could put him off his shopping. He wrote wistfully on 6 September 1664:

> Having called upon Doll, our pretty 'Change woman, for a pair of gloves trimmed with yellow ribbon, to [match the] petticoat my wife bought yesterday, which cost me 20s; but she is so pretty, that, God forgive me! I could not think

it too much – which is a strange slavery that I stand in to beauty, that I value nothing near it.[24]

But fashion was fickle. Maybe the New Exchange was mismanaged, or perhaps it got a bad reputation, for in 1699 the writer Ned Ward referred to its 'seraglio of fair ladies' and the rival Middle Exchange became known as a 'whores nest'. It could simply be that the modish lure of Henry Jermyn's St James's was too great. Certainly, by the early eighteenth century, references to the New Exchange in contemporary manuscripts almost completely disappear, and in 1737 it was demolished to build five new narrow Georgian terraced homes.

Meanwhile Bond Street had been created, the thoroughfare that for over 200 years has best replicated the New Exchange's role as the pinnacle of expensive shopping. Appropriately for London's scrappy history, Bond Street was built not in one burst but in two halves, thirty years apart, and it was named not after a king, prince or duke, but after a self-made banker, courtier and developer who made a good marriage.

Bond Street's eponymous Sir Thomas Bond has achieved a curious fake fame in modern Britain, as the real-world ancestor of Ian Fleming's fictional spy, James Bond. His coat of arms featured on the first 1963 edition cover of *On Her Majesty's Secret Service*, the tenth novel in the series. His family motto, translated into English, was the name for the nineteenth James Bond film, *The World is Not Enough*. In reality, Thomas Bond was a seventeenth-century south London boy from semi-rural Peckham, who made good by following Charles II into exile, marrying the queen mother Henrietta Maria's French maid, and being very skilled at making money.

When Henry Jermyn took control of the ownership and development of St James's, Bond saw his chance. He created a syndicate to buy Clarendon House, the sumptuous 15-bay-wide mansion of the disgraced Earl of Clarendon, and, even though it was less than twenty years old, promptly demolished the lot. Jacobean property development was merciless. The plan was to create and lease out three streets running north from Piccadilly through the remains: Dover Street, Albemarle Street and Bond Street. However, Bond died before they could be properly exploited. He left a son to inherit his baronetcy, but his death delayed the completion of Bond Street until the 1720s. The distinction between the 1680s and 1720s street (Old and New Bond Streets) survives in formal nomenclature to this day.

Bond Street immediately became a fashionable place for the *ton* to live and saunter. Unlike the medieval city or the seventeenth-century Strand, Bond Street was paved and lit, safe and regulated, and it was pleasant to walk outside. So-called 'Bond Street loungers' strolled down the street and, at one time or another, Jonathan Swift, Edward Gibbon, Laurence Sterne, James Boswell, William Pitt the Elder and Lord Nelson all lived upon it.

In eighteenth-century London, unlike modern America, the rich and fashionable had no problem with living above the shop, as long as the shops were genteel and in the right place. Bond Street quickly became a very refined place to shop, particularly for jewels (echoing Cheapside's goldsmiths) or paintings – though the Bond Street society chemist, Savory & Moore, was also famous for its laxatives.

Bond Street's windows got steadily bigger as taxes reduced and glass-making technology improved. The 1851 abolition of window tax began the gradual substitution of plate glass for small panes, and by the 1860s, individual windowpanes could descend to the pavement. Meanwhile stores' rears were increasingly lit by elaborate skylights; Daniel Defoe had observed them as early as 1726. Later, the arrival of electricity permitted deeper and better lit sales rooms and, ultimately, the department store.

London's finest shops were helped by another improving technology – faster transport. Increasingly the rural rich could send to London for their luxuries. A Mrs Purefoy in Buckinghamshire, wanting a sedan chair that would be 'strong and tite', did not seek it in Oxford or Bicester, but sent directly to London. Tea, coffee, sugar, chocolate, Indian calico, French silk. All became available, if you had the means. Indeed, as improving transport expanded the role of the West End as the place where middle-class women, and some men, came to shop, as 'town' in popular parlance, Bond Street became firmly established as *the* pinnacle of West End retail, even a suburban reference point.

The *Bayswater Chronicle* praised west London's Whiteley's department store in 1879 as giving Westbourne Grove 'quite a Bond Street air'. Magazines and wives' and daughters' diaries are rich with references to Bond Street or West End shopping trips. In 1877, Florence Sitwell 'went to a shop or two, lost ourselves and finally got home'. Suggested shopping itineraries in 1888 began in Old Bond Street before snaking through Mayfair and St James's, and after 1900, the Central Line ran past the north end of Bond Street with approximately 100,000 people a day riding between Shepherd's Bush and Bank.

One very practical consequence was the problem of where to go to the loo, as pubs and inns were increasingly judged inappropriate for nice young ladies coming to town. The answer was the female club. In the last decades of the nineteenth century, a number of ladies' clubs were opened between Regent Street, Oxford Street and Bond Street to give shopping ladies somewhere to rest, luncheon, go to the loo and pick up their parcels: the Empress, the Pioneer, the Ladies' Army & Navy, and many others all changed the nature of the feminine West End shopping trip.

Investors, managers and committees were often female, too. A Miss Cohen, for example, opened the Ladies International Club on Old Bond Street itself and the same was true of many of the managers of Bond Street's shops or the tea rooms that began to supplant clubs in the early twentieth century. Lucy Christiana, later Lady Duff-Gordon, was the most famous British fashion designer of the late nineteenth and early twentieth centuries,[25] and according to *Queen* magazine, there were at least five female-owned and managed tea shops in Bond Street in 1902. Not all women historically were quite as oppressed as we now like to pretend.

Rich customers were not an unmitigated advantage for Bond Street's shopkeepers. For, in an age before cheques and electronic money, the rich hated paying cash, as they felt it was beneath them. Eighty per cent of all sales in elite West End shops were therefore offered on credit. As Lady Jeune put it in the 1870s, 'No well thought-of firm ever demanded or expected more than a yearly payment of their debts.' One shopkeeper recalled, 'The richer people are, the more difficult it is to get them to pay their bills.' However, as one draper explained, it was difficult to turn away the 'carriage custom' of the rich, because of the size of their budgets and the 'lustre' they bestowed on the shops.

The consequence, of course, was much higher risk for the merchant and higher prices. One way in which new department stores such as Fenwick's, which opened on Bond Street in 1891, were able to lower prices was by refusing credit.

THE BURLINGTON ARCADE

In August 1815, two months after the Battle of Waterloo, and while the world was still wondering whether peace had finally been achieved after a generation's warfare, the 61-year-old George Cavendish bought Burlington House on Piccadilly from his nephew, the Duke of Devonshire. He intended to live there; however, he immediately discovered a problem. The back windows and gardens on Bond Street's east side overlooked his land and the inhabitants were in the habit of chucking oyster shells and other rubbish into his back garden.

His architect, Samuel Ware, proposed a solution: build a covered and arcaded shopping street on the edge of his land behind Bond Street linking Glasshouse Street (now Burlington Gardens) with Piccadilly, 'a Piazza for all Hardware, Wearing Apparel and Articles not Offensive in appearance nor smell" This was smaller than the forgotten Royal, New, Middle and Exeter Exchanges in the City and on the Strand and very similar to the Royal Opera Arcade, which was already being built down the road between Charles II Street and Pall Mall. Such a solution would have the added advantage of turning a liability (gardens need gardening) into an asset.

The initial plans were to achieve a £3,690 income off an initial expenditure of £20,000 – a handsome near 18.5 per cent annual return. So far, so straightforwardly commercial. However, from such simple motivations Samuel Ware was to craft an arcade of delicacy and poetic rhythm. Modern shopping malls descend into long lines of sheer glass with flashing lights or mannequins behind.

The 196-yard Burlington Arcade is spared this fate by a beautifully conceived melody of gently varying shopfronts within a pattern.

As the Survey of London has observed, the shop fronts' rhythm can be described as: 'd-aba-c-aba-c-aba-c-aba-d', where each hyphen is an enriched arch, each 'a' is a double shop flanked by doors, each 'b' is two smaller separate shops, each 'c' is a heightened version of 'a' and each 'd' is a single shop and one double shop splayed back from the street entrance. It is almost as if the authors are describing the rhymes of an elaborate sonnet or Keatsian ode.

There are even more nuanced touches, not immediately apparent to the non-searching eye, but which augment pedestrian appeal: the tent-like ceiling, the variations in height, the glazed rooflights, the undulating pattern of projecting and recessed windows, and most subtly of all the slightly oblique doorway angles to accentuate the display windows.

The charm worked. The jewel-like arcade with its varying pattern of arches and windows was rapidly and densely let to the purveyors of luxuries to London's richest. It had the advantage of a modern shopping mall, you could not get wet, but also the advantage of a street: it went somewhere. The estate rapidly achieved its financial targets and income only increased. By 1828 the arcade's 55 shops included eight milliners, eight glovers, five linen shops, four shoemakers, three hairdressers, three jewellers or watchmakers, and two each of lacemen, hatters, umbrella and stick sellers, case makers, tobacconists and florists.

The rest of the shops were composed of a shawl seller,

ivory turner, goldsmith, glass manufacturer, optician, wine merchant, pastry cook, bookseller, stationer, music seller and engraver. So attractive and fashionable did Burlington Arcade become that shopkeepers were able to sublet their tiny, first-storey back rooms. In 1850 the estate was receiving £4,000 in rent, but the actual income from the arcade, including subleases, reached £8,640. At least some of the subtenants were prostitutes of the highest class – and price.

It is not clear how obvious or prevalent was Burlington Arcade's illicit secondary market. Victorian London's great biographer, Henry Mayhew, who observed their presence over 'a friendly bonnet shop', commented that men who wished to avoid 'publicity in their amours' avoided the arcade at certain hours. A Member of the Board of Works, proposing a similar arcade nearby, perhaps self-interestedly, disagreed saying he 'had never seen anything dreadful there'.

Over the last 100 years the Burlington Arcade has been fortunate in its history: skilful additions in 1911 and 1931 added offices above the Piccadilly frontage and opened the arcade more obviously to the street. Its northern stretch was badly bombed in 1940, but then perfectly restored in the early 1950s, its commercial owners being unseduced by traffic-modernist fantasies of the 'end of the street'.

Since Lord George Cavendish's descendant, Lord Chesham, sold the arcade in 1926 for £330,000, it has changed hands multiple times. It is now a very investible asset in the property empires of equity funds and the global elite: '37,000 sq ft of retail space' unlike any other and with 4 million visitors per year. Protected by its Grade II listing, is hard to develop fundamentally, but is it is capable of hard management and rich returns. Prudential Assurance, Thor Equities and, reputedly, the Reuben brothers, have all been owners, with the value for such a non-fungible luxury asset rising to £300 million by 2018.

Build it in arches and Regency stucco, and even poetry, in the right place, can make you rich.

Today, the finest design that money can buy is still poured into Bond Street, which preserves its role as an exclusive promenade for fine art and rare jewels. Although part of a conservation area since 1967, change still happens – though only of the most costly timbre. In 2011, a late Victorian building was demolished and replaced by the architect George Saumarez Smith, with one of the finest street buildings created in London in the last fifty years. Boasting three Odyssean bas-reliefs by the artist Alexander Stoddart, it is an almost unique creation in the modern city, as Saumarez Smith both understands the classical tradition and is self-confident enough to play within it. Appropriately, it houses an art gallery.

In 2017, Westminster City Council, conscious that Bond Street's tarmac and higgledy-piggledy street signs were tatty and cluttered beside the elite streets of Davos, Paris or New York, commissioned a 'no-expense spared' rebuild of the street's surfaces with York Stone, Portuguese silver granite, green and black stone paving, and streamlined road signs. It is an undoubtedly pleasant place to walk, though an expensive one to shop. Bond Street even has a website that gushes, in the curiously placeless English of luxury marketing, of 'art, fashion, shopping, glamour and style'.

It is a street for all time. It is the only Mayfair street that cuts directly from Piccadilly to Oxford Street. Its proportion, the ratio of its height to its width, provides precisely the sense of enclosure that most humans find reassuring without being toweringly oppressive. And its design, outside and in, is the retail equivalent of new wine in old bottles: Georgian and Victorian exoskeletons entirely transformed within by Edwardian excess or modern minimalism as luxury brand or season's colours dictate. Bond Street's prices may be exclusive, her fashions may be fleeting, but the joy of shopping and the ceaseless search for the latest look is timeless and ecumenical.

Chapter 8

OXFORD STREET

Going west

His heart's not big that fears a little rope.
Seventeenth-century ballad

Oxford Street was not originally a street and it did not go to Oxford. Like the Old Kent Road, which it best resembles among the *Monopoly* streets, Oxford Street was a road out of the city, not a street within it. Its original destination was not a university town on the Isis, but a Roman provincial town in Hampshire, *Calleva Atrebatum*, now known as Silchester. The line that the modern Oxford Street follows is certainly that of the Roman *Via Trinobantina*. However, like the Old Kent Road, it is probably much older. For its destination, *Calleva Atrebatum*, was in origin not a Roman fort but, like London itself, a Celtic settlement where British earthworks surrounded farms and homesteads.

Where Londoners now shop on Oxford Street, legions marched and pre-Roman Britons probably travelled. Streets have this habit of hanging about, the most ancient and timeless features of our urban infrastructure. But whereas we now think of Oxford Street as a street to shop in, desirable or tacky according to taste, for hundreds of years it was the road to execution. Over the centuries, Oxford Street has been called the Uxbridge Road, the Oxford Road, the King's Highway and the Worcester Road, but its most common and consistent name for at least 500 years has been the Tyburn Road.

'Going west' in English slang still means going to your death, following the raucously ceremonial route west that many thousands of men and women took on their last journey from prison at Newgate along the Tyburn Road to their public execution by hanging or burning at Tyburn, near where Marble Arch now stands and where the traffic rushes past unheedingly. Oxford Street's most consistent theme is not the ritual of the shopping trip, but that of public execution. Perhaps even more surprisingly, its role as the highway to execution helped lead directly to its modern role as a place of entertainment and of shopping.

Imagine the hubbub of going to a football match today, to a school sports day, or to a funfair or village fête; the crowds thickening as you approach the site, the street stalls selling sausages, burgers or balloons, and the everyman nature of the crowd – families with children, elderly bachelors, thin and thick, the young and the old. As you get nearer the fête or the fair or the turnstile gates, the hubbub increases and maybe some elements of the festivities become audible before they become visible: a tout's cries, a fairground ride, or that strange background hum that a large crowd creates as it chatters and breathes.

On 16 November 1724, those walking to and along what we now call Oxford Street would have had that experience. For that was the day that the authorities hanged, publicly and with great fanfare, the notorious villain, escape artist and popular hero,

Jack Sheppard. As Friedrich Engels was to write 120 years later, 'Some children have never heard the name of Her Majesty, nor such names as Wellington, Nelson . . . [but] there was a general knowledge of the character and course of life of Jack Sheppard, the robber and prison-breaker.'[26]

Jack Sheppard's last journey, as it had been one week before for 'Julian' (a sixteen-year-old arsonist from Madras), Joseph 'Blueskin' Blake (a burglar and Sheppard's one-time confederate), and Abraham Deval (a forger), and as it was to be for 2,168 executed felons between 1715 and 1783, was down Tyburn Road.

Jack Sheppard's fame was certainly justified. Born in Spitalfields shortly before his father's death, his widowed mother placed him in the Bishopsgate workhouse. There he managed to pick up enough education to begin an apprenticeship as a carpenter to Mr Wood of Wych Street (one of London's surviving Saxon streets until the replanning of the early twentieth century).[27]

All went well for five years until Sheppard started hanging out with prostitutes and criminals in local taverns. He began stealing from his clients and then robbing and burgling. He was very good at stealing, but not so good at subsequently not being caught.[28] Betrayed, he was arrested and then began a cycle of arrests and increasingly spectacular escapes. He was strong, small (5 feet 4 inches), and presumably his carpentry training came in handy.

It was rumoured that the devil came in person to help him. Certainly, his final escape borders on the supernatural. Handcuffed and chained via leg irons to the wall, Sheppard used a nail he found on the floor to unfasten the handcuffs and detached his leg irons from the wall. Still in irons, he entered the chimney, removed an iron bar blocking his way by picking out the mortar and then climbed to the next storey. Here he broke through or picked the locks of a series of five doors all locked from the other side. He opened the last by removing the hinges and opening it 'in reverse'. Finding himself at the top of a high wall from which he could escape the prison, he returned to his cell, retrieved his blankets, turned them into a rope and vanished into the night. Of course, he was recaptured again within a fortnight.

London's printers and hack writers (including Daniel Defoe, no longer seeking sanctuary in Alsatia, south of Fleet Street) rushed out hyperbolic pamphlets to marvel at Sheppard's increasingly impressive escapes, advertising them with language only a breath away from modern tabloids, their true spiritual successors. One described his successive escapes as 'wonderful . . . miraculous . . . surprising,' and of his last jail break, 'the most astonishing and never to be forgotten'.

Hanoverian London's publicity machine was every bit as effective as the modern one. About 200,000 people were said to have thronged the streets to watch the procession on the morning of his execution. This must be an exaggeration, as it would have been nearly a third of London's population, but the crowd was clearly immense.

The day started when a guard called Watson found a knife in Sheppard's pocket; the guard cut his hand in doing so. Sheppard had been planning a final escape from the scaffold, but it was not to be. His tumbrel left Newgate Prison (where the governor had been enjoying a 'Governor's Execution Breakfast', probably of devilled kidneys) at about 7am.

Although only one man that day was to 'dance the Paddington frisk' (contemporary slang for hanging), the procession that was to head down Oxford Street was substantial. It was headed by a City Marshall wielding a silver mace, extensively guarded by liveried and mounted Javelin men and accompanied by Sheppard's coffin, the hangman who would put him in it, and his 'ordinary' (the term for the prison priest, Reverend Wagstaff), who would read Sheppard his last earthly prayers.

Surrounded by huge and growing crowds, the procession paused outside the church of St Sepulchre, where the bell was tolling and the traditional prayer was incanted:

> All good people, pray heartily unto God for these poor sinners who are now going to their death. You that are condemned to die repent with lamentable tears. Lord have mercy upon you.

Further stops were made at inns along the Tyburn Road. At the City of Oxford tavern, where Wells Street crosses the modern Oxford Street, Sheppard drank a pint of sack – roughly equivalent to sweet sherry though possibly not as strong – with the champion bare-knuckle boxing hero James Figg, who ran a fighting school at the tavern and who had been to visit him in prison a few days before.[29] The heady mix of crime and sport that was to find echoes in 1960s London was present in the 1720s as well.

Women were probably prominent as the procession made its slow progress down Oxford Street; they certainly were at most. One witness recalled, 'Sometimes the girls dress in white, with great scarves, and carry baskets full of flowers and oranges, scatting these favours all the way they go.'

At Tyburn itself, at the end of the modern Oxford Street, the crowds were enormous and raucous. If contemporary engravings are anything to go by, there would have been many children amongst the masses and hundreds of touts, tinkers, pedlars and salesmen of every possible description. It was quite literally a carnival, with a popular villain being hanged in the middle of it all. Sheppard's ghost-written confession, printed at Blackfriars on the morning or on the day before, was widely sold to the crowd. Then, as now, crime paid best for those who wrote about it.

Everyone came to the execution from the very lowest to the

very high. It was far more ecumenical than modern football. Those who could afford it bought wooden seats in the pews nearest the gallows. These could cost up to £10, an incredible sum the equivalent of £2,335 today and which only the very richest could afford. James Boswell confessed that he was 'never absent from a public execution' and that 'I had a sort of horrid eagerness to be there.' The MP, George Selwyn, was criticised for being 'not merely silent but nearly always asleep' in the House of Commons but was such an assiduous connoisseur of executions that he corresponded with judges about the best vantage points from which to watch them.

At about ten o'clock, Sheppard's procession reached the end of modern Oxford Street, near the modern Primark store. It drew up at the 'Tyburn Tree', a wooden triangle on three legs known as a 'three-legged mare' a few yards to the east. The 'tree' was large enough to hang over twenty felons at once. But it rarely saw such custom. Back in August 1724, six had been hanged at once, including three highway robbers, a forger and a fraudster. But today, it was only one.

In the middle of the swirling crowd, guarded by the Javelin men, Sheppard's tumbrel was backed under the 'tree' and the rope round his neck was thrown up by the hangman, Richard Arnet, to his assistant sitting on the beam. The assistant tied it on to the beam, the ordinary said a final prayer, the horses were whipped, the cart pulled away and Sheppard was left 'dancing the Tyburn jig' (another contemporary phrase), as his legs twitched and convulsed.

Poor Jack Sheppard, who had processed along Oxford Street in such state, did not die quickly. Because he was so small, the fall did not break his neck and it took him some minutes to lose consciousness. His ghost writer, Daniel Defoe, and publisher, John Applebee, had hoped to rescue his body quickly and try to resuscitate him. But, just like Sheppard's plans to cut himself down, the scheme failed. The crowd surged forward to pull his legs and end his agony. And when the hearse that Defoe and Applebee had ordered advanced to try and rescue him, the mob believing them to be surgeons seeking the body for dissection (a common fate for criminals' cadavers) surged forward and pelted the driver with stones. Jack Sheppard was truly hanged by the neck until he was dead. His memory was to live on in operas, ballads, novellas, engravings and folk custom for over a century, but his body was buried that night, near midnight, in the churchyard of St Martin-in-the-Fields.

What of Oxford Street itself, along which this macabre carnival had processed? On the winter's day when Jack Sheppard was executed, the road itself was not in a good state, being 'a deep hollow road, filled with sloughs', bordered more by hedges than by houses. It was surfaced in gravel, badly maintained, and apparently 'carts were daily overturning'. A conduit ran alongside the road carrying water from Paddington to the City. There was also a pound for stray animals. The street must have been in an even worse state than usual afterwards. Did the conduit survive the crowds surging past unscathed, or did it require emergency repairs?

Oxford Street was not a fashionable place to live. This is hardly surprising given the noisy mob that periodically charged down it, a gibbet at one end and a slum at the other – St Giles, where Hogarth's famous *Gin Lane* morality tale was set. Engravings and maps from the 1730s and 1740s still show it as a back land, almost rural. The great landlords, including the Earl of Oxford, focused on smart residential streets to north and south. They left Oxford Street (the name increasingly used during the eighteenth century, in reference to the Earl more than the destination) to piecemeal development by leaseholders and gardeners, brewers and builders.

In order to profit from the coaches that headed west along the road or the crowds that passed through, these smaller developers focused on building taverns, coaching inns and shops, thus starting the continuous tradition of Oxford Street as a place of commerce and passage that continues until this day.

One of the earliest buildings built on Oxford Street, near the junction with Tottenham Court Road, was the Castle Inn, later the Boar and Castle. Probably named after a small fort that stood nearby during the Civil War, it was a coaching inn that was ideally positioned to profit from the growth of the carriage trade and of the West End. By 1780 it had twenty-six bedrooms, stabling for sixty-five horses, and sixty wagons a week were claimed to depart from it.

Five windows wide and with a yard behind, one writer later recalled, 'Here West End passengers, who had booked their places at the Bull and Mouth in the City, joined the vehicle, and here the coachman and the guard received their last commissions, reckoned their passengers, tightened the straps of the luggage, and prepared for a brisk drive to Hounslow, where the first change of horses took place.'

During the nineteenth century, as the carrying trade declined, it became more of a place to drink in than to travel from. In 1861 a music hall was built on the site, though a new pub next door kept the historic name until it was also demolished thirty years later.

As for the street surface itself, it improved. A turnpike trust was established in the 1730s to charge a toll and look after the west of the road properly. Their tollgate, near where the Tyburn Tree stood, survived into the nineteenth century and was one of the 'entrances' to London, now expanded well beyond its historic city walls.

The St. Marylebone Paving Commissioners took over maintenance of much of the rest of the road in the 1770s, which led to a marked improvement. This in turn encouraged further investment in new shops and taverns. In 1783, executions at Tyburn stopped. The authorities were increasingly concerned by the popularity of the spectacle and judged that executions were more readily managed from the prison yard.[30]

Three years later, a German visitor to London, Sophie von La Roche, recalled of Oxford Street:

> Just imagine . . . a street taking half an hour to cover from end to end, with double rows of brightly shining lamps, in the middle of which stands an equally long row of beautifully lacquered coaches, and on either side of these there is room for two coaches to pass one another; and the pavement, inlaid with flag-stones, can stand six people deep and allows one to gaze at the splendidly lit shop fronts in comfort . . .
>
> Up to eleven o'clock at night there are as many people along this street as at Frankfurt during the fair, not to mention the eternal stream of coaches. The arrangement of the shops in good perspective, with their adjoining living-rooms, makes a very pleasant sight. For right through the excellently illuminated shop one can see many a charming family scene enacted: some are still at work, others drinking tea, a third party is entertaining a friendly visitor; in a fourth parents are joking and playing with their children.

Sophie von La Roche may have been impressed, but Oxford Street was never truly fashionable. Over time, drapers, furniture shops, inns and market stalls gave way to music halls, theatres, department stalls and souvenir shops. The aim was consistently to attract the many not the few, particularly those coming up to London to do their shopping. The Vere Hall Rooms were opened in 1878, 'furnished as private rooms, with letter-paper and every convenience for writing and resting'. This was Victorian code for ladies' loos, once again an important need for those up in town to visit Oxford Street's drapers and milliners.

If Jack Sheppard was one iconic figure of Oxford Street's history, the other was surely the genius American businessman, Harry Gordon Selfridge, who brought department store shopping to Oxford Street's unmodish West End in 1909, when Selfridges opened with huge public fanfare worthy of the publicity surrounding Sheppard's execution. The narrow bays of Georgian inns and shops were swept away to be replaced by three-storeyed Ionic columns marching down the street.

Inside the steel-framed store, one of the first in London, Selfridges essentially kept up the same tradition of the public executions – of entertaining the masses: over its first thirty years the store hosted the first plane to cross the channel, terraced gardens, cafés and restaurants, string quartets, a mini golf course and an all-girl gun club. As Harry Selfridge may have coined and certainly said, 'The customer is always right.' But he never forgot to put high-margin products in prominent places so that the customer could be right profitably.

Oxford Street has changed beyond recognition since Jack Sheppard was driven to his death along it, from rural road to urban street, from coaching inns to music halls, from rutted mud to level tarmac. Its role as the road to Tyburn and to the public fair of execution is forgotten by the tourists and shoppers who still throng there. But the legacy of its role 'going west' to death or to public spectacle lives on in its physical form and the uses to which it is put today. Jack Sheppard's life was very short. But, in a manner of speaking, he has cast a long shadow.

GO TO JAIL

*By reason of the foetid and corrupt atmosphere that is
in the heinous gaol of Newgate, many persons are now
dead who would be alive.*
Richard Whittington, Mayor of London, 1419

Where do people go to prison? Over the centuries the nature and experience of going to jail has changed from being something local to something remote; from one of partial sequestration from everyday life to one of near complete divorce; from a world in which wives and children could stay overnight to one in which the incarcerated might be hundreds of miles away. Prisons have become incalculably cleaner and safer, less lethal and less corrupt, but they are also more disruptive of the pattern of everyday life. London's prisons used to be around the corner and down the street; in short, they were part of the city. Now they are a place apart.

As in so many things, the folk memory of London's prisons is Dickensian, an amalgam of grey stone, straw beds, Fagin's incarceration, Pip's visit to Newgate and, above all, Charles Dickens's own childhood experience of Marshalsea Prison relived in *Little Dorrit* and *The Pickwick Papers*. One of his earliest published articles was a record of an 1835 visit to Newgate, where he visited the condemned cell:

it is a long, sombre room, with two windows sunk into the stone wall, and here the wretched men are pinioned on the morning of their execution, before moving towards the scaffold . . . their doom was sealed; no plea could be urged in extenuation of their crime, and they well knew that for them there was no hope in this world. 'The two short ones,' the turnkey whispered, 'were dead men.'[31]

This folk memory of difficult conditions in dirty jails is not entirely wrong. Until the nineteenth century, London's prisons were effectively private and prisoners who were not able to bribe the 'turnkeys' might starve to death. Newgate Gaol was described by Daniel Defoe as 'an emblem of hell itself' and one eighteenth-century warden of the Fleet Prison, Thomas Bambridge, was so venal and cruel that a parliamentary commission was set up into his monstrosities.

However, there is another side to the story. This involves not only the conditions of the prisons themselves, but why people went to prison, and how this and their location influenced their relationship with the streets and buildings that surrounded them. Like so much of the wider history of our streets, it is a surprisingly unstudied subject. It is hinted at by the story of Ranulf Flambard, the first Londoner whose name we know who had to 'go to jail'. Flambard was a Norman-born royal administrator and churchman who fell rapidly out of royal favour on the succession of Henry I, was accused of corruption, imprisoned in the Tower of London, and promptly escaped and fled to Normandy.

The story goes that his friends smuggled a rope hidden within a flagon of wine, that Flambard intoxicated his guards with the wine, and then escaped out of the window to his waiting comrades. So even though Flambard was imprisoned in the Tower of London, his friends were only around the corner and his incarceration was informally managed. The same pattern would hold true until the nineteenth century.

All jails were around the corner in medieval London. We know that one of the Norman towers of west London, Baynard's Castle, had a prison. Probably Montfichet's Tower did as well. South of the river in Southwark, the Bishop of Winchester, who governed the manor, had a prison (known as the Clink) attached to his palace since at least 860. But these were royal or episcopal prisons. Where could the city authorities lock up felons? The answer was on their doorstep and spanning the public highway, in the city's fortified gates.

From at least the twelfth century, and probably before, Newgate and Ludgate, the two gates heading west, were converted into jails. Both gates were misnamed. Newgate was assumed to be new, but was in fact of Roman origin. Ludgate was supposed to be named after London's mythical British founder, King Lud, but it was probably a corrupted derivation of Fleet.

Not mythical, however, were the prisoners within the city gates. Newgate was the dangerous prison and Ludgate was the posh one. The infamous Venetian libertine Giacomo Casanova visited London in 1763 and described Newgate as 'an abode of misery and despair, a hell such as Dante might have conceived'. The landscape architect, author and gardener Batty Langley's brother, William, worked as a turnkey at Newgate. Langley explained how 'it is customary when any felons are brought to Newgate to put them first in this condemned hold, where they remain till they have paid two shillings and sixpence, after which they are admitted to the masters' or common felon's side.'

Ludgate, in contrast, was used for freemen of the city and

clergy who were imprisoned for debts, trespasses and fraud. It seems to have been a fairly lax regime. There was a roof to walk on and a 'large walking place' within a ground floor yard, and it was clearly possible for prisoners to pay directly for good food and good conditions. Many did not want to leave. The Mayor of London complained in 1419 that 'many . . . have been more willing to take up their abode there, so as to waste and spend their goods upon the ease and licence that there is within.' A prison where people want to remain is hardly performing its primary function.

In fact, imprisonment for crime was far less common in the past. It cost too much money. The city authorities preferred to fine malefactors (which was profitable) or to flog them, execute them, or place them in the town stocks (which, if not profitable, was at least quick and cheap). You needed guards for a day, not for a decade.

In 1582, the English lawyer and historian William Lambard categorised the three forms of punishment as infamous, pecuniary and corporal. Infamous punishment was for treason and was execution by hanging, drawing and quartering. Pecuniary punishments were fines for swearing or failing to go to church. Corporal punishments were either capital (hanging, burning, boiling or pressing) or not capital (cutting off the hand or ear, burning, whipping, imprisoning, stocking, setting the pillory, or ducking). Later, transportation to America and then to Australia would be added to the list.

Imprisonment was one, and only one, of a long list of options, many far more terrible and torturous. Prison was a place where people were sent when they were arrested, as they awaited trial (which were then much quicker and shorter) and, normally, as they awaited some other form of punishment. This is why London's criminal prisons could be so small and local. Newgate,

London's largest prison, had a capacity of only 150 until the late eighteenth century.

If, however, you were less likely to 'go to jail' for crime, you were far more likely to 'go to jail' for unpaid debts (appropriately for *Monopoly*). Until the laws changed in 1869, debtors who were adjudged to owe money that they could not pay were sent to prison until they did. Eight of the prisons scattered all over London were entirely or partly for debtors: the Fleet, the Marshalsea, the King's (later the Queen's) Bench, and Whitecross Street were the largest. They were managed by private individuals, who had normally purchased the office at great expense and had no duty to feed or look after their prisoners. Instead, they needed a return on their investment. Conditions therefore depended on where you were and what you could afford to pay for board and lodging with funds kept hidden from creditors.

On the one hand, poorer debtors desperately needed help to stay alive. In Elizabethan London, men marched the streets begging for 'food for the poor prisoners' with a box on their backs to put it in. On the other hand, when the Exchequer official, Richard Stoneley, was briefly imprisoned for debt in 1596, he was able to pay 15s a week for his chamber and clearly lived well. His private diary records dinners of calf's head, roast veal, boiled beef, a woodcock, cheese and fruit, accompanied by claret and sack to drink.

Nor was the barrier between jail and prison absolute. Those imprisoned for debt were able to invite their wives, families and friends to visit, dine or even stay with them. Richard Stoneley's wife and daughter regularly came to dinner. Other families 'lived in'. Over 200 years later in 1824, when Charles Dickens's father was imprisoned for debt, his wife and youngest children lived with him and the twelve-year-old Charles came to spend the day on Sundays.

On payment of a fine, debtors were even able to go for a walk. Richard Stoneley paid 10d to the 'Warden of the Fleet for half a day abroad', paid 2s 8d to be able to visit his home, and 3s 4d for 'one week's liberty abroad by the Warden's agreement'. Some prisons even spread out into the surrounding streets. leet Prison had expanded out beyond the walls over about one acre. Those who could afford it paid the Warden to be able to live in more comfort in the 'Liberty of the Fleet', a tight network of surrounding streets. As we have seen earlier, those who did were able to earn money on the side to ease their circumstances. Most notoriously some imprisoned clergymen performed marriages without licence (so-called 'Fleet marriages') in the prison's chapel or in a network of surrounding taverns.

The Clink prison in Southwark had special grates, so that poorer prisoners could beg from passing pedestrians, and a brothel on the premises with a cut of the profits going to the gaolers. Luckily for the gaolers and turnkeys, most of those imprisoned for debt were middle class and easier to exploit. The modest debts of the poorest were not normally worth the cost of court action.

Thus, for much of London's history, its prisons were awful, dangerous places, but they were far more part of city life. If you were a criminal, you would probably not spend that long in them, and if you were a debtor, you might still be living with your family or visiting them every week. However, if you were rich but unable to meet your debts, you might spend years in a debtors' prison. The first Grosvenor baronet, of the family that were to create Mayfair, spent the best part of a decade in Fleet Prison.

Prisons were everywhere. One seventeenth-century verse recalled:

In London and within a mile I weene
There are layles or Prisons full eighteene
And sixty Whipping-posts and stocks and Cages.

Prisons haunted the imagination. Pip, in Dickens's *Great Expectations*, worries that with 'Newgate in the next street', his returned convict benefactor Abel Magwitch could be seized at any moment. If the most famous prisons were Newgate, Ludgate, the Fleet, the Tower of London and, more briefly, Bridewell, there were dozens of others at one time or another: Bread Street, Giltspur Street, Wood Street, the Clink, the King's Bench, Marshalsea, Colbath Fields, Whitecross Street, the Gatehouse, Tothill Fields and the roundhouse in St Martin's Lane. By 1800, there were nineteen jails in all for prisoners to 'go to'. Echoing Matthew Arnold and William Morris, London's 'biographer', Peter Ackroyd, has gone so far as to write of 'the city as prison'.

However, everything changed during the nineteenth century. Whipping, executing and transporting people fell out of fashion as barbaric or simply hard to do (the American Revolution did not help either). Prison became a more common punishment. In parallel the 'abandon prisoners to the whims of the warder' approach, which had typified penal history, was rejected as both cruel and ineffective. Prisoners should be punished and recuperated, not just left to their fate.

The utilitarian prophet, Jeremy Bentham, proposed a 'pan-opticon' plan with a star of separate wings converging at a central point, where guards might efficiently keep watch. Millbank Prison, where the Tate Britain now stands, was the closest that practical prison design ever got to such philosophical urgings.[32]

Meanwhile, the filthy state of the old prisons, particularly the treatment of women, came in for increasingly harsh criticism.

The Quaker philanthropist, Elizabeth Fry, found the female wards at Newgate 'filthy to excess and the smell was quite disgusting . . . They slept on the floor, at times one hundred and twenty in one ward, and without so much as a mat for bedding.' Prisons should be clean but hard; unpleasant but not disgusting. They should be run professionally by salaried officers, not turnkeys on commission. This was hard to do in the fetid caverns of antique prisons.

At the same time, there was the eternal pressure on some historic central sites to clear them away for other more profitable uses. The Giltspur Street compter (small prison) was sacrificed to 'road widening' in the 1850s, and Whitecross Street prison was replaced with a railway goods yard in 1870. Finally, as Victorian suburbs grew around the nexus of medieval villages and roads, they created both the need and the opportunity for new suburban prisons on the expanding edge of town. During the nineteenth century, therefore, Victorian prisons migrated out from the centre and became both larger and far fewer in number; all of the historic prisons were closed.[33]

By 1901, when Newgate was demolished, London had only five prisons: Brixton, Pentonville, Wandsworth, Holloway and Wormwood Scrubs. All were new or extended, and they were enormous compared to their predecessors. None sat in the city, but were instead lost in 'great suburban parks with monstrous walls wrapping much in mystery.' Many prisoners were sent even further away to prisons in the far west or north. In these new bureaucratic prisons, the poor were less likely to die due to their inability to pay a bribe, but anonymity, the spartan treatment, and the work and treadmills were, if anything, more incessant and unrelenting.

The old jails had been corrupt, unfair, sometimes filthy and often dangerous. But they were of the city, particularly the debtors' prisons. The new system had its advantages: prisoners could be taught and might work, and some earned up to 8d a week. The great chronicler of Victorian London, Henry Mayhew, observed that 'almost every gentleman placed in authority over the convicts appears to be activated by the most humane and kindly motives towards them.'

However, if Victorian prison could not quite plumb the corrupt depths of the old, for some prisoners it may have been worse. Prisoners were kept isolated, stripped of their identities and forced to work, not left to lounge. They were sequestrated from friends, family and fellow inmates, isolated from the city, surrounded by high walls and wide grounds. In 1844, Dr Carus, the personal physician of the King of Saxony, visited the model prison of Pentonville, 'a trial of the complete system of solitary confinement'. Its clinical precision appalled him:

> Order is preserved . . . with military strictness; and when
> the prisoners assemble, either in church or for instruction,
> or to walk . . . absolute silence reigns. Besides this, they
> wear a peculiar sort of cap, the shade of which falls over
> the face, and being provided with two holes for the eyes,
> forms a sort of mask, rendering all mutual recognition
> impossible . . . no names exist, but each prisoner is denoted
> and called for by the number of his cell.

The average age of the nineteenth-century's estimated 6,000 prisoners was between fifteen and twenty-five. Not surprisingly, suicides rose within the 'separate system' practised at Pentonville and elsewhere. With the 'penal' very prominent in penal servitude, late Victorian prisoners may have been cleaner, but they may not have felt much better off than their filthier, beer-swilling predecessors.

Chapter 9

BOW STREET

Cries and coffee shops

Whereas many thieves and robbers daily escape
justice for want of immediate pursuit, it is therefore
recommended to all persons who shall henceforth be
robbed on the highway or in the streets, or whose shops
are broken into, that they give immediate notice thereof
with as accurate description of the offenders as possible
to JOHN FIELDING Esq, at his house in Bow Street.
Notice in the *Public Advertiser.*

Modern London is a city of zones. We live in one part of the city, work in another, and are entertained in yet another. Maybe that is now changing slightly after the Covid pandemic, but to revert to the sheer intensity of living in historic London would be a revolution indeed. It is hard now to imagine the complex and connected lives that could be lived in a comparatively small number of public and private places. One street that demonstrates the sheer vitality and diversity of London's historic street life is Bow Street, near Covent Garden.

No more than a tenth of a mile in length, it curves gently like the longbow after which it was named, yet this brief street has packed more life into it than many acres of low-density suburbs. Coffee houses, street sellers, theatres, taverns, brothels, an opera house, a police station and a magistrates' court have all lived here cheek by jowl for centuries. From Bow Street, equidistant between court and counting house, the king could be served, money made, or the myriad cries of London heard and recorded.

Bow Street was the home and the office of two of the most remarkable brothers England has ever produced: Henry Fielding, who has a better claim than any to be the father of the English novel, and Sir John Fielding, who, not content with being a successful entrepreneur and publisher, both created modern law enforcement and paved the way for the very concept of the police in the English language. He also happens to be arguably the most influential blind man in English history.

In the history of our streets, fleeting decisions concatenate down the centuries. At some point between 1610 and 1613, the 3rd Earl of Bedford, a descendant of Dorset merchants who had made their first fortune trading with Gascony and whose grandfather and great-grandfather had risen to great estate under Henry VIII and Elizabeth I, built a wall. It ran north-east to south-west through the eastern portion of the formidable landholding his forebears had been granted just north of the Strand, where Saxon traders had re-established London when they pulled their ships up the Thames's muddy banks.

He would not have known that, but he did know that the 2nd Earl had granted the land east of his wall on a long lease to Sir Edmund Carey and, for some reason, he wished to sequestrate the land he managed directly from that of his lessee. Another parcel of land to the south, and extending slightly further west, was leased out to another tenant.

The effect of these apparently inconsequential Elizabethan and Jacobean land management decisions was that when the 4th Earl of Bedford chose to develop what became the Covent Garden ESTATE together with Inigo Jones in the 1630s, the obvious line for a street to the east of Covent Garden had a kink in it. It was shaped rather like that most English of weapons, the longbow. So Bow Street it became, presumably in obedience to inescapable common parlance rather than through aristocratic preference: all the estate's other streets have far more courtly titles, such as King Street, Russell Street and Southampton Street.

The ubiquity of the longbow is now hard to grasp. Gentlemen fought on horseback, but for at least 350 years all peasants and yeomen had been archers. Since 1252, all Englishmen between the ages of fifteen and sixty had been obliged to equip themselves with bows and arrows, and since the fourteenth century, Sunday archery practice had been obligatory. Every Butts Close in the country records the fact; they are named after medieval archery grounds. What could be more natural than the builders or first tenants of a street shaped like a bow should name it thus?

As it was called, so did it live. Bow Street was the tradesmen's entrance to the Covent Garden Estate. Peripheral, facing a blank wall, and leading nowhere to the north (the back of the previously developed Long Acre blocked it off), Bow Street could not command the same princely rents as the immediately fashionable Covent Garden. Among the early tenants were a developer who had 'gone to jail', a carpenter, a schoolmaster and a profusion of doctors.

But if Bow Street was cheap, it was not without pretensions or potential. As with all the developing London estates, lower rents did not discourage the estate from being very exacting in its development terms. The pre-lease articles of agreement required that the roof timbers, first floor and external woodwork should be of oak, not the cheaper deal. Room heights were also stipulated: 10, 10½ and 9 feet for ground, first and second floors respectively. Correct classical proportion, note the *piano nobile*, was the path to an elegant future, which also happened to make very efficient use of available street frontage. Bow Street was well situated; within easy walking distance of both the Cities of London and Westminster and the superhighway of the river Thames.

In short, as London grew, Bow Street went up in the world. It quickly became a place for the artistic, the literary, the scurrilous, the immigrant and the upwardly mobile. By the 1690s, the Dutch-born sculptor Grinling Gibbons lived here. So did the Yorkshire-born Dr John Radcliffe. They were both the best in their business, respectively the 'King's Carver' and the king's physician. (The luscious swags and garlands that typify Gibbons's genius are best seen at St James's Piccadilly, commissioned by the Earl of St Albans; whilst John Radcliffe's success paid, inter alia, for the divine Radcliffe Camera in Oxford.)

Down Bow Street lived John Ayres, who was born into rural poverty and had started life as a footman, but whose industry and intelligence briefly turned him into one of the most famous advocates of Restoration-era self-help. His bestsellers, in large part penned in Bow Street, had titles such as *The Youth's Introduction to Trade*, *The Writing Master* and *The Penman's Daily Practise* [sic]. The desire to 'get on in the world' is ecumenical and eternal, and men such as John Ayres helped fuel it – before he died of 'apoplexy' (probably a stroke) across the river in Vauxhall.

Another Bow Street neighbour was a second artistic Dutchmen

who also benefited from being in the middle of things. Marcellus Laroon is best known for his 1687 drawings of the *Cryes of London Drawne after the Life* (some are used to illustrate this book). There had been illustrated publications of the street sellers of London before, but the figures had been arrayed in a grid upon a single page. Laroon invested each subject with their own page. Looking at them, it is impossible not to believe that they were not, as advertised, 'drawne after the life'.

There were fewer shops in the late seventeenth century and London's poorer classes typically bought their wares from markets or from wandering street salesmen, who were a staple figure of London's streets for centuries; their cry, more a rhythmic cadence than specific words, repeated loudly to attract custom from neighbouring streets.[34] In Laroon's illustrations, we can see the faces and figures of real London street sellers who wandered through or near Bow Street in the 1680s. What conversations did Laroon have with his subjects, one wonders, and what did he pay them to let him draw them? What became of them, once they were too old or too weak to sell strawberries or 'fair cherryes'?

Only one subject is drawn twice, an acrobat whom he describes as 'the famous Dutch Woman'. Perhaps she was his favourite and, presumably, they chatted in their native Dutch. The concentration on her pretty gamine face is palpable as she walks the tightrope or skims through the air above an undrawn London street. Here is one true face of Restoration London.

Such was the book's success that it was immediately expanded from forty to seventy-four illustrations. It remained in print until 1821 and a host of subsequent books on the 'Cries of London' over the next 200 years very much followed in its path. One of London's most long-lived literary forms was drawn and shaped in Bow Street.

Nor was Bow Street merely a place to live or watch passing street sellers. It was a place to gossip and *the* place to talk literature in Restoration London. At some stage in the 1660s, one William Urwin established a coffee house on the corner of Bow Street and Russell Street.[35] By 1671 it was called Will's and it was the favourite of John Dryden, poet, playwright, literary man about town and, from 1668, Poet Laureate.

When Samuel Pepys visited it on the evening of 3 February 1664, he recorded:

> I stopped at the great coffee-house there, where I never was before; where Dryden the poet (I knew at Cambridge), and all the wits of the town, and Harris the player . . . it will be good coming thither, for there, I perceive is very witty and pleasant discourse.

Seventeenth- and eighteenth-century coffee houses are now principally remembered as the origins of the London Stock Exchange and Lloyd's insurance market. (The former grew out of Jonathan's Coffee House on Change Alley and the latter eponymously out of Lloyd's Coffee House on Tower Street.) However, coffee houses were not simply embryo financial institutions. They pervaded the street culture of London, and other towns and cities, from the 1660s until the late eighteenth century: a mix of club, pub, office, telephone, newspaper and social media. So powerfully and erroneously do we think of the past as being entirely class-bound and stratified that it is hard to realise how open to talent and enthusiasm London was in its period of greatest energy and wealth creation.

Coffee houses were an important way in which new men met those already established to discuss commerce or culture, law or literature. Unlike clubs, which became more pervasive during the late eighteenth century, they were normally open to anyone who could pay a penny for admission and his cup of coffee. Unlike modern pubs, conversation could be general and open to all. There was no need for an introduction to the great man who might be presiding. Unlike social media, intercourse was bound by some conventions of etiquette and good manners (though arguments could and did lead to lethal duels – putting the dilemma of being 'cancelled' into some perspective).[36]

As Tom Brown (a real-life eighteenth-century writer, not the fictional nineteenth-century schoolboy) put it, the coffee house was 'the place where several knights-errant come to seat themselves at the same table without knowing one another, and yet talk familiarly together as if they had been of many years' acquaintance'. Some coffee houses were referred to as penny universities, because so much conversation and learning was to be had within for the price of a coffee.

Each had their own character and clientele, and some were smarter than others. At one coffee house you might be more likely to discuss mathematics and astronomy, at another to meet fellow clergymen; while at others you might find pimps, prostitutes or market traders.[37] But they genuinely welcomed anyone who could pay for their penny coffee (in practice all but the most impoverished). The elite was open, and one of the most prestigious of London's coffee houses was Will's in Bow Street, where Dryden held court.

At Will's, Pepys used to drop in to meet his friends, and it was there that Dryden was sought out by the young Alexander Pope, anxious to meet his hero – a meeting subsequently fantasised in a Victorian historical painting by Eyre Crowe. It does not seem to have gone well. Pope recalled Dryden as 'a plump man with a down look and not very conversible'.

At Will's, critics rehearsed their encomiums – or their stings. The pamphleteer and satirist, Jonathan Swift, wrote:

> Be sure at Will's the following day
> Lie snug, and hear what critics say;
> And if you find the general vogue
> Pronounces you a stupid rogue,
> Damns all your thoughts as low and little;
> Sit still, and swallow down your spittle.

Jonathan Swift did not like Will's. He complained that 'the worst conversation he ever heard in his life was at Will's Coffee-house, where the wits (as they were called) used formerly to assemble . . . and entertained one another with their trifling composures, in so important an air as if they had been the noblest efforts of human nature, or that the fate of kingdoms depended on them.'

He need not have worried; fashion is fleeting. Will's lost its cachet after Dryden's death in 1701 and the literary journal the *Tatler* recalled eight years later that 'you used to see songs, epigrams, and satires in the hands of every man you met; you have now only a pack of cards.' By 1743, Will's coffee house was known as Chapman's and fashion was forgotten. Later drinking establishments in the street were less salubrious as Covent Garden became more disreputable; when the dissolute diarist William Hickey referred to doing 'the old Bow Street rounds' when he was 'brim full of wine', he was feting Venus as well as Bacchus.

Into this busy street in 1749 moved the father of the English novel, Henry Fielding. He was not attracted by its literary reputation, but obliged to move by his appointment to his second job as London's magistrate on the death of his predecessor, the libidinous Sir Thomas de Veil.[38] We first met de Veil in the chapter on Leicester Square. In 1740, he left the square, where he had twice been attacked, and moved to a former doctor's house at No. 4 Bow Street, where the modern extension to the Royal Opera House now stands.[39]

Henry Fielding was a writer of genius who, not content with a torrent of essays, political satire and plays, invented the English novel (a 'comic epic poem in prose', as he put it) and ran a second career as a barrister and magistrate to pay the bills. It was not quite as incongruous as it sounds. Writing paid badly, he had studied law academically at Leiden University in the Netherlands and practically for several of his publications.

Law enforcement in eighteenth-century London was struggling to keep up with the growing city. It depended on a network of parish constables and night watchmen (or 'Charlies'), who were salaried but often part-time, and it was subsidised by a system of generous state bounties (£100 for the conviction of a highwayman). These rewards had encouraged the growth of private thief-takers, many of whom were corrupt and several of whom became crime lords, not only taking payments from criminals to avoid prosecution but acting as 'fences' between thief and victim.

The most notorious had been Jonathan Wild, who had secured the prosecution of Jack Sheppard after he would not pay him off, and whose noxious deeds were recounted by Henry Fielding in his second novel, *The Life and Death of Jonathan Wild, the Great*.

In 1750, Henry Fielding was joined as assistant by his half-brother John, and their fraternal combination of energetic public advocacy and private efficiency was irresistible. Working from 4 Bow Street in four short years together, followed by John Fielding's twenty-six years alone (Henry died in 1754 and John took his place), the Fielding brothers proceeded to pave the way for the practice of modern English policing.

They committed three acts of genius. The first was to *combine* the two existing systems of law enforcement: in 1749 Henry Fielding organised eight, already salaried, parish constables as thief-takers, making use of the system of government bounties to pay for their extra efforts. It was payment on results. This was enough to get cracking, but not enough to keep going. In 1753, 'Mr Fielding's People', as they were originally known, went on strike.

The subsequent second act of genius was to persuade the government to subsidise the team of constables so that they could operate more confidently. The government approved a budget of £200 in late 1753 to support the team. This permitted their nature to change from part-time parish constables with a job on the side, to full-time, state-supported thief-takers. They were paid a guinea each per week and the Fielding brothers referred to them as runners to distinguish them from the corrupt thief-takers. The 'Bow Street Runners' were born.

The third act of genius was to realise that this work needed to be publicised if the public were to report crimes and provide evidence. Henry initially justified and promoted his work in a series of pamphlets. Subsequently the brothers launched the privately printed *Public Advertiser*, in which publicly funded advertisements were placed to report crime and stolen goods. Policing was born with a major conflict of interest at its heart.

After Henry's early death at the age of forty-seven, John Fielding worked alone. He managed his team efficiently and well, adding a team on horseback to patrol the roads out of London, moulding the first English police force in all but name. He persuaded the government to triple his budget from £200 to £600 and transformed 4 Bow Street from a private house to an office in which to report crime and a quasi-court in which to hear evidence. Throughout, he kept the activities of his growing team of runners and clerks in the public eye in the *Public Advertiser* and more broadly through press fascination and reporting.

His approach to punishment was emphatically liberal. He was reluctant to send children to prison, once writing of two boy thieves, 'It is certain that sending such boys into prison is much more likely to corrupt than reform their morals.' The importance of his work was understood both high and low. He was knighted in 1761 and known affectionately throughout London as 'the blind beak' of Bow Street.

For, throughout these thirty years of effort and energy, of leadership and vision, John Fielding was completely blind. In its myopic ignorance, modern political debate often imagines that all that is good is modern and all that is past is bad. But the opposite is often true. In 500 years, only one other blind man has had scope for a comparable influence on British law enforcement: David Blunkett was Home Secretary from 2001 to 2004, but it is hard to argue that his four years survives comparison with the legacy of the blind beak's thirty.

Yet so fickle are the paths of fame that John Fielding is now entirely forgotten. No statue stands to him and none but the specialist has heard of him. His one biographer, R. Leslie-Melville in 1934, concluded that 'no one has played a greater part than he in moulding London to the form we now know.' This is exaggeration, but it is hard to point to many who had so benign and so great an influence. Little Bow Street has a lot to answer for.

Walking down modern Bow Street is not unpleasant. Some of the historic 'finely grained' house pattern survives, particularly at Nos. 35–39, where three pubs and taverns compete for custom, including the site of the former Will's Coffee House, now the

Marquess of Anglesey pub. Many of the taller, late Victorian buildings have made the street rather alley-like in its proportions, though not disastrously so. Worse, two crudely smooth, over-sized and under-detailed buildings have been hammered into the street, disrupting its rhythm and rendering sections of it dull and threatening; the worst culprit, as so often, is a public commission. The arrogant £200 million extension to the Royal Opera House works well within, but treats Bow Street without with machine-cut contempt.

The street is a husk of what it was. The brothels and the police are gone, the homes are vanished. The profusion of offices has robbed Bow Street of its heterodox vitality and it is hard not to sigh for the cries of London, with which it once pulsated. Old London was smaller and more intense than New London. Its *Monopoly* streets were more densely lived than could now be comprehended. It was a model that traffic modernism broke in the long twentieth century, but which may be coming back. If it does, Bow Street will be the better for it.

Chapter 10

MAYFAIR

The ordering of georgian Growth

*I passed an amazing Scene of new Foundations, not
of Houses only, but as I might say of new Cities. New
Towns, new Squares, and fine Buildings, the like of
which no City, no Town, nay, no Place in the World can
shew; nor is it possible to judge where or when, they will
make an end or stop of Building.*
Daniel Defoe, *Applebee's Weekly Journal*, 1725

L ondon's most expensive neighbourhoods march west with
the names of Cheshire villages: Eaton, Belgrave, Eccleston,
Chester, rather than the ancient field names such as More
Gardens, Broadmore and Little Horseleyes, which they could so
readily carry. They would never have done so had not London's
Great Plague of 1665 numbered amongst its estimated 100,000
victims, an aspirant property developer, Alexander Davies, who
died in early July, aged only twenty-nine.

His premature death mattered because he had inherited the
Manor of Ebury, covering most of modern Mayfair, Belgravia
and Pimlico, and his plans to develop them were barely begun
when he died, precariously poised with debt taken on to create

streets and their infrastructure, but with no payments coming in to offset them. His estate was rich in promise and bankrupt in practice. To make matters worse, he was intestate, his wife was only twenty-one and his daughter, Mary, only six months old.

In the resolution of that dilemma, the development pattern that Thomas Wriothesley and Henry Jermyn had pioneered in Bloomsbury and St James's would be perfected, and Mayfair, Belgravia and Pimlico would be created. This story has been told as the success of the Grosvenor dynasty, who married Mary, advancing from Cheshire baronets to Dukes of Westminster as they rose from mere county prosperity to princely opulence as Europe's richest ducal dynasty. But Mayfair was a suburb of social advancement for more than one family.

The story of its creation is also the chronicle of the surveyors, lawyers, builders, bricklayers, plasterers and joiners who designed, built and speculated in Mayfair's streets, going bust or making their own fortunes according to chance. It is also a demonstration of the importance of laws and regulation in understanding the streets that can, and cannot, be built.

For the Manor of Ebury had been lying to the west of London for centuries, owned successively by Norman knights, Westminster Abbey, Henry VIII, and an array of lawyers and speculators. But what turned low-lying farmland into a crock of gold was the transformation in the approach that king and Parliament took to London's physical growth, from banning it to regulating and ordering it to standards of Palladian rectitude. Freed from the medieval instability that demanded city walls and from the state-imposed green belt that echoed them, London was ready to fight its way to being the richest city in Christendom.

And Mayfair was the spear-point.

The London of Elizabeth I and James I, of Globe and Gunpowder Plot, of Civil War, Cromwell and Commonwealth, may have had little in common with the modern city. However, like today's capital, it had a green belt. Elizabethan and Jacobean London was not allowed to grow.

From 1580 until 1661, City of London authorities attempted not just to regulate *what* was built but also *where* it was built. Under pressure from London's Mayor and Alderman, four successive monarchs and the Parliamentary Commonwealth all attempted to prevent building beyond the city limits. At least three Acts of Parliament, nine Royal Proclamations and innumerable Orders in Star Chamber and letters to and from the Privy Council attempted to ban the construction of new building within one, two, three or five miles of the City Gates and of Westminster (details changed over time), other than on existing foundations.

From 1608, no new building or rebuilding was possible without a licence, under pain of imprisonment and demolition. As Simon Jenkins put it, 'modern planning regulations seem puny by comparison.' Under Cromwell, any new home built within ten miles of London required four acres of land with it.

These attempts to prevent the city's growth were not fully effective, but it was not for the want of trying. The Courts of Alderman and of the Star Chamber were active in prosecuting illegal building and many new structures were certainly pulled down. In 1615, a commission was established to monitor new buildings and prevent construction within the prescribed zone. Over time, the ban seems to have evolved into a modestly more controlled system, where government demanded returns of new houses to be submitted and where some building was permitted under licence and on payment of a fine. But you needed to know the right people and to have the cash up front.

The 4th Earl of Bedford and William Newton were able to

build Covent Garden and Lincoln's Inn Fields respectively, but it was a complex and expensive process. In the fields around London, the state had nationalised a landowner's right to build. Nothing substantial was legal without case-by-case permission.

Motivations for this Elizabethan green belt were complex. They included the City authorities' desire to maintain control, but also a dislike of immigrants to the city, a desire for 'the preservacon of the healthe of the Cittie', and a dislike of 'the desire of Profitte' of 'covertous Buylders'. If these motivations seem very familiar in the modern debate about housing, so do some of the consequences. Fearful that new buildings might be pulled down, development seems to have been of lower quality.

The main study of the growth of Stuart London and its regulations concluded:

> The various restrictions on building tended to produce the very evils they were presumably intended to prevent or cure. Only the cheapest houses were erected as there was a risk of their being pulled down for a breach of the building rules, and these were put as far as possible out of the way . . . Another result was cheap additions with big cellars underneath.

Big cellars in London due to high prices and regulation – history does not repeat, but it can rhyme. One of London's great seventeenth-century developers, Nicholas Barbon (whom we first met building near the Strand), also concluded that building restrictions had encouraged emigration to the New World. Perhaps America owes some of its origins to the Elizabethan and early Stuart green belt?

After the 1666 Great Fire of London, there was a sea change. The authorities abandoned their attempt to constrain growth and focused instead on quality control. Regulation rather than prohibition became the order of the day. The crucial step was the 1667 Rebuilding of London Act. This remarkable piece of legislation brought together, systematised and improved on at least 400 years of edicts, City regulation and common law. It did not control the *right* to build. However, it did constrain *what* could be built. It dictated not only the material (brick and tiles), but also set the height and types of buildings based on the width and nature of the road.

The Act also determined the development of facade design and decoration by setting only four types of building that could be built and where they could be built: 'fronting by-streets and lanes . . . fronting streets and lanes of note and the Thames . . . fronting high and principal streets . . . [and for] persons of extra-ordinary quality, not fronting either of the three former ways.' Storey heights, wall width and number of storeys were all set,[40] and surveyors were appointed to ensure that the rules were followed. Crucially, the Act contained no prohibition on building beyond London.

A few further attempts were made to constrain building beyond the City boundaries (for example in 1671, 1677 and 1709), but they could not win parliamentary support. The desire for exemptions and support for the quality of the extended city being built was too strong.

The 1667 Act set the direction of building regulations for the next 250 years. It only applied to the City of London. However, a further series of London Building Acts extended that to Westminster (in 1707 and 1709) and then to the entire, now rapidly growing city (in 1774). These Acts also enhanced protection against fire with increasingly strict rules against exposed timbers in box sashes, and introduced rules on bow windows, shop windows and doorways.

In turn, a series of builders and developers published standard plans for houses that were compliant with legislation. To look at them now is to look at London, and they are very easily dated as they adapted to evolving legislation. From 1774, windows were obliged to have recessed reveals and, still today, it is easy to date houses built before and after this legislation. Most houses in London for nearly 200 years were built to fairly standard patterns taken straight from books.[41] The Georgian city looks like it does not simply due to 'fashion', but because statute said what it could look like.

London landowners and their agents were keen to take advantage of the legislation by laying out patterns of blocks, streets and squares, which did not only meet but went beyond the statutory minimums. Without deep debt and credit markets, rather than develop homes themselves, landowners leased out homes to smaller builders and developers. They typically insisted on similar facade and materials via covenants and contracts, which also directly invoked the Building Acts.

Foremost among those developing London in the wake of these acts were skilled stewards, surveyors, builders and architects such as Richard and Robert Andrews, John Simmonds, Edward Shepherd, Thomas Barlow and Colen Campbell. These men developed, designed and built Mayfair for Sir Richard Grosvenor as London's largest, richest and most important new suburb, instantly fashionable in the 1720s, colour-coded purple in the *Monopoly* board of the 1930s, and still exclusively expensive 300 years after construction.

Poor Mary Davies, the heir to Andrew Davies's encumbered estate, was not vouchsafed happiness by her vast potential wealth. Her mother promptly married again and together with her new husband tried to shake off the shroud of unpaid creditors following her first husband's disastrously unfinished development. She could not come close to paying them off. The solution was to sell her daughter, or to put it more decorously, arrange an appropriately advantageous marriage in exchange for a cash payment.

The obvious 'deal' was with Lord Berkeley, who had made his name, but not his fortune, fighting for the king in the Civil War, who owned neighbouring land (where Berkeley Square now stands) and whose son, Charles, was only three years older than Mary. A surviving colour-coded map shows the logic. The deal was done: Mary's hand in return for £5,000 cash and a jointure of land worth £3,000 a year settled upon Charles at marriage.

Unfortunately, it all went wrong. Lord Berkeley paid over some of the money (promptly used to pay off creditors), but could not raise the rest – and young Charles then died. The deal collapsed and Lord Berkeley asked for his money back, which Mary's mother could no more pay than she could fly to the moon.

The answer was clear. She had to sell her daughter, still only twelve, again. This time Mary's betrothed was rather older and the price marginally cheaper, but the deal stuck. Sir Thomas Grosvenor was twenty-one and a modest Cheshire landowner with ambition. The cost was £6,500 to pay off Lord Berkeley, two years' allowance of £500 until Mary was fourteen, and an annuity for the governess. However, Mary's story was not finished. Having fathered an heir, her husband died young and she converted to Catholicism (not a wise move in early eighteenth-century England), began to show signs of mental instability, and travelled to the Continent with her poorly chosen Catholic chaplain and companion, Father Fenwick.

In Paris, she was fraudulently obliged to marry Fenwick's brother (she denied it and fled back to England) and a complex and expensive series of court cases proceeded to do their best to impoverish the estate. Only after 1717 was the estate sufficiently unencumbered for serious development to begin, under the guidance of her son, Sir Richard Grosvenor, who was the ultimate beneficiary of the three untimely deaths of Alexander Davies, Charles Berkeley and his own father.

Had the dice of premature mortality rolled differently, the development of west London might have followed a different pattern as either middle-class speculation or as the Berkeley Estate.

But Richard Grosvenor's timing was good and it was worth the wait. The 1707 and 1709 Building Acts had enhanced the reputation of new streets over old, and the wealthy and the prosperous were keen to move out of the crowded ancient city for the larger homes and cleaner lines of the West End. Fashion was moving west. Meanwhile the government was stable after the Peace of Utrecht and the Jacobite rebellion's destruction; investors were optimistic and credit for mortgages was readily available in the City. Demand, supply and a confident and liquid market all combined.

The estate's surveyor, Thomas Barlow, and the estate's agent, Richard Andrews, rose to the opportunity. Barlow drew up a master plan (illustrated in 1723) for Mayfair's 'hundred acres', as the area was generally known at the time. It was as close as London's town planning has ever got to the clean symmetry of an American grid pattern: straight lines, clear blocks, and at its heart the princely dimensions of Grosvenor Square with eight acres of garden and 680 and 530 feet between the buildings. So large was it that one of London's first balloon flights was launched from the square in 1784 – sporting the blue and buff colours of the Whigs put there by the Duchess of Devonshire.

Grosvenor Square's scale was enhanced by setting the

Was it ever this Venetian even on a sunny day? 'Entrance to the River Fleet', Samuel Scott, 1750.

The Holbein Gate: one of the sites of London until it was demolished in 1759. Henry VIII married Anne Boleyn there and it was one of his favourite rooms as he got old, fat and immobile.

Right: 'The Squire of Alsatia'
by Marcellus Laroon, 1687.
One of the 'Cryes of London'.
Was this beau in London's most
notorious district perpetrator
or victim?

Below: A late seventeenth-century
street acrobat: 'The Famous
Dutch Woman'. The real face
and figure of one of London's
unrecorded millions. What
happened to her?

THE SQUIRE OF ALSATIA.

The Famous Dutch Woman

The famous Dutch Woman
La fameuse Hollandoise

Left: Angel, Islington: London's 'airport hotel' for over 200 years. The frontage, courtyard and rooms of the Angel in 1818 – probably first built against London's Jacobean green belt regulations in 1638.

Door going into the Chapel.

Door leading out of the Chapel.

First door between the Chapel & the leads

George Cruikshank

Second door in the same passage.

Below: Jack Sheppard the infamous prison breaker was executed at the end of Oxford Street before a crowd said to number 200,000. He lived long in the popular memory. These engravings of his escapes were drawn by George Cruikshank over a century after his death.

The water wheel on London Bridge. Putting sewage into London's water supply from 1582.

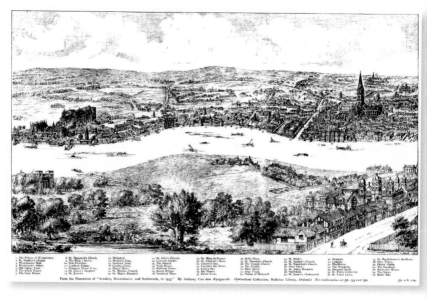

A London Thames bank scene, with the ancient road west (just south of the current Pall Mall) visible in the upper left. It runs past the former lepers' hospital of St James's. From Anton van den Wyngaerde's survey of 1543.

Above: Northumberland House prior to its demolition following the Metropolitan Board of Work's purchase in 1874. The Percy Lion can be seen above the gatehouse. After nearly 300 years, the main entrance is now below the level of the pavement. The shadow of Nelson's column could, at times, be seen against the building. New meets old.

Left: Stephen Geary's King's Cross monument to George IV. Quickly forgotten in all but name. The neighbourhood used to be known as Battle Bridge but no more.

Right: Robert Adam's plans for one of inner London's vanishingly few large modern classical buildings.

Left: A rope, a lamppost, and very little traffic made for a children's game in the post-war East End. Note the bomb-damaged house behind.

Right: The Coventry Street Corner House was an institution: a junior chef explains the 'black bottom' dance to Lyons Nippies in the rest room. Their uniform included starched caps and pearl buttons.

Left: Battersea Power Station burning coal in 1934 before the second half (Battersea B) was added in the 1950s.

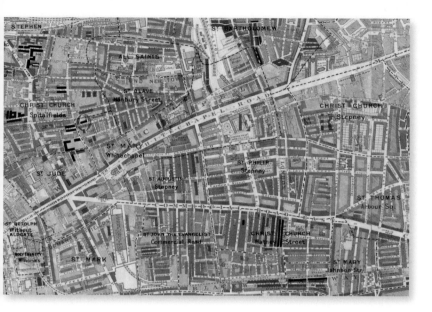

Late Victorian Whitechapel as shown by Charles Booth's poverty map.
The red along Whitechapel Road signifies 'middle class'.

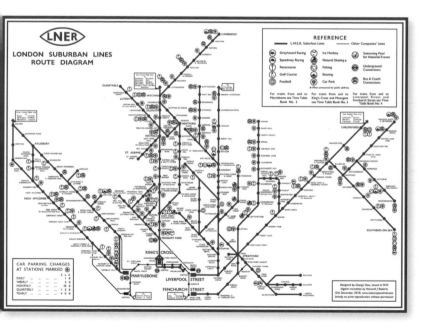

1939 map of the LNER network showing the four Monopoly stations. Did
Victor Watson and Marjory Phillips select their stations from a similar map?

Above and right: Two realities for Fitzroy Square just south of Euston Road. As planned by Traffic in Towns and, thankfully, as it still is.

A new vision for Euston Road with trams, trees and Doric Propylaeum, by Francis Terry and Create Streets

Photo credits on final page of book.

houses in the square thirty feet back from the frontages of the streets leading into it, so that the square 'opened up' as you entered. For the first time, a square was conceived of as a uniform, palatial whole. Appropriately for so grand a space in so ambitious and rich a development, the architect and author of the imperially conceived *Vitruvius Britannicus*, Colen Campbell, was employed to design the whole of the square's east side as one architectural entity.

But it was not to be. Although the plan was grand, and the pace of initial development was incredibly impressive (with many leases signed between 1720 and 1730), the Grosvenors did not have the capital required to develop Mayfair themselves. Like nearly every other landowner, they followed the model evolved by Thomas Wriothesley and Henry Jermyn in Bloomsbury and St James's, leasing out plots or sections of streets to developers and craftsmen to develop themselves, initially at peppercorn ground rents to help make building pay. In this way, risk was transferred and shared and development at scale and pace made possible.

However, the consequence was that Barlow and Andrews were not as architecturally ambitious as Barlow's plan merited or Campbell wished. Grosvenor Square was not as unified as initially hoped – although experienced developing builders such as John Simmonds and Edward Shepherd did the best they could in the circumstances, following the 1709 building act that gave all homes comparable principles and proportions.[42] The estate also invested heavily in the square's garden (at least sixteen separate gardeners and landscape architects presented bills for its creation) and in the gilded statue of King George I at its heart. At any rate, the overall quality was good enough; though it was slow to lease at first, within a few years the square was staunchly aristocratic, as intended.

The family gave the lead by living in the square themselves – if not living above the shop, certainly living in it. (How many CEOs of modern development firms live in their own developments?) Of the fifty-one first ratepaying residents, there were sixteen peers, six children of peers, four baronets, four knights and five titled widows; other residents included a bishop and a retired general. Only Henry Jermyn's St James's Square, which was much smaller and closer to the palace, was comparable.

Eleven of the ratepaying heads of households were women. Being a rich widow was to be powerful and emancipated, liberated from the legal leadership of a husband, and able once more to own property and to represent herself in court.[43] Where the aristocracy gathered, fashion and fortune wished to follow. One lady in David Garrick's play, *The Clandestine Marriage*, longed to escape the 'dull districts' of the city to be 'transported to the dear regions of Grosvenor Square'.

Beyond Grosvenor Square, most of Mayfair within the 'one hundred acres' was built within fifty years, with the main surges of development happening in the 1720s and 1740s. The least popular section was the one that approached Oxford Street, tainted as we have seen earlier by its proximity to the riots and ribaldry of hanging days at the Tyburn Tree. Exclusive dwelling could not be too close to the London mob at play.

Arguably the true heroes of the development management were the generations of talented agents and surveyors who planned and managed Mayfair's growth, and the builders, joiners and speculators who took the real risks in developing it. Many of these men came from very humble backgrounds and grew in wealth and social status alongside the estate. Something of the rising but still uncertain social status of the estate's agents and surveyors is caught in the relationship between Mr Darcy (landowner) and Mr Wickham (the son of his father's estate manager) in Jane Austen's 1813 novel *Pride and Prejudice*. Mr Wickham can pass as a gentleman, but he is still a cad.

The genius of the Grosvenors was in avoiding amoral cads and continually picking the right men, indeed the right families, for the job. Edward Shepherd started life as a plasterer and became both a brilliant architect and a commercially successful developer: designing and taking the risk on houses in Brook Street, Grosvenor Square and North Audley Street. The Barlow family started as bricklayers in Mayfair, worked for at least three generations on the estate, and ended as baronets serving the Indian empire.

Even more notably, the professional partnership that the estate's agent, Richard Andrews, started in 1722 to serve the Grosvenors can be traced through direct commercial descent and many changes of name straight to the modern firm of Boodle Hatfield LLP, who still work for the Grosvenor Estate. Many others were less lucky. By 1738, at least sixteen of the roughly thirty builders taking plots around the square were insolvent or worse. Development is a dangerous business: land ownership rather less so.

Something of Mayfair's scale and scope has consistently appealed to a New World sensibility. Appropriately for a neighbourhood that was as close as London has ever got to American town planning, Mayfair has strong American links. The first American ambassador to the Court of St James, and second American president, John Adams, lived at No. 9 Grosvenor Square. Dwight Eisenhower set up his London headquarters during the Second World War a few doors down at No. 20.

One Grosvenor Square was briefly used as the American Embassy post war, before the US government bought the bomb-damaged Nos. 24–32 on a 999-year lease for £1 million (several Dukes of Westminster refused to sell the freehold, despite the direct request of President John F. Kennedy). Round the corner in Grosvenor Street, the American army and the forerunner of the CIA (the Office of Strategic Services or OSS) also had their wartime headquarters.

Tales of aristocratic or arriviste excess have been a constant theme of Mayfair from 1720 until today.[44] Nothing exceeds like excess.

When the NHS vacated the St George's Hospital site, just across Hyde Park Corner from Mayfair in 1980, the Duke of Westminster promptly took up an option to buy the building for £6,000 (its nineteenth-century value), as his records told him he might and as the public sector had forgotten.[45] When it comes to land and London, the best way to be rich is to buy land, to plan for the long not the short term, and to manage cash flows over three hundred years not thirty; also to keep good records. The fearsome fate of poor Mary Davies and the vehemence with which her mother defended Mary's inheritance may not have brought any happiness to either woman, but it has harvested untold billions for their descendants. The long view pays, the future is mutable and history, like it or not, is not bunk.

Chapter 11

MARLBOROUGH STREET

Pantheon lost

The most elegant structure in Europe, if not on the globe . . . No person of taste in architecture, or music who remembers the Pantheon, its exhibitions, its numerous, splendid, and elegant assemblies, can hear it mentioned without a sigh.

Charles Burney, 1819, on London's Pantheon, between Oxford Street and Great Marlborough Street

The scale is wrong, the symmetry is wrong. The proximity to a classical façade put up by the same firm at the same time is wrong, and the goings-on of a store behind such a façade (and below those twisted Tudor chimneys) are wrongest of all.

Nikolaus Pevsner on the design of Liberty & Co in 1924, on the corner of Great Marlborough Street

Historians should be wary of heydays. Few ages are golden if you are poor or feckless. Nevertheless, much of the long eighteenth century (from Restoration to Regency) was a good time to enjoy London. The city was less crowded and cleaner than previously; less filthy and polluted than it would become. The plague had vanished after 1665 and cholera had not yet appeared. Drinking water was getting dirtier, but it had not yet plumbed the foetid depths of the industrial city.

London was the perfect size: still small enough to get around, to know everyone you needed to know, and to escape readily to rural tavern or villa. But now big enough to have larger homes, more space, more public squares. The upper strata of power and wealth were increasingly open to talent, gumption and energy. Theatre and coffee house, pleasure garden and spectacle were not exclusive; everyman was welcome who paid their penny or could afford the pit. New palaces for pleasure and spectacle were opening all the time. But their noon was often brief and their future uncertain.

No building illustrates this more clearly than the Pantheon, which sat between Tyburn Road (Oxford Street) and Great Marlborough Street (it was incorrectly named on the *Monopoly* board). The product of a very young architect and builder and in large part the brainchild of two female entrepreneurs, for a while the Pantheon was London's most famous building, but its demise was rapid. In Georgian London, chance did come knocking, but fire and changing fashion could just as frequently chase it away again.

Great Marlborough Street demonstrates, perhaps more clearly than any other *Monopoly* street, the consequence for town centre streets when fashion and homes move out and commerce and industry rush in. Old money leaves and new money is made. The street declines, men rise, and women play a greater role than is normally vouchsafed them by historians. Unlike Mayfair, Great Marlborough Street has lost its modish sheen, but it has played host to generations of self-made men and women, and given its name (if misspelt) to the world's best-selling cigarette brand. Meanwhile, the Pantheon is forgotten, though its ultimate inter-war destruction has only recently passed out of living memory.

Great Marlborough Street started grandly and with imperial pretension and has been going sideways ever since. Various landlords (mainly Sir Benjamin Maddox but also the Pollet Estate and the Duke of Argyll) and their lessees collaborated on its creation with common building lines and a co-ordinated approach to creating sewers. The method was the normal one of individual craftsmen leasing houses in return for their services over a group of houses, and then selling them to meet costs, raise more capital and, hopefully, make a profit.

Like Mafeking Roads in Edwardian suburbs, the name dates the street immediately. Great Marlborough Street celebrates the Duke of Marlborough's victory over the French at the battle of Blenheim in 1704 – the year the street was begun. A neighbouring side street was initially called Blenheim Street.

The street was very wide for the three-storey height of its initial houses and it must have felt very generous to walk along or live in. The anti-Jacobite Scottish spy James MacKay (who had first given warning of James II's planned invasion in 1692) wrote that it surpassed 'any Thing that is called a Street, in the Magnificence of its Buildings and Gardens, and inhabited all by prime Quality'.

He had a point. Despite Great Marlborough Street's proximity to the dubious charms of Oxford Street, it managed to attract good tenants. Five peers out of a 1714 list of one hundred lived on Great Marlborough Street and of a surviving 1749 list of twenty-one residents, eleven were gentlemen and ten were tradesmen–though the distinction could be a fine one. As fashionable neighbourhoods spread west into Mayfair and beyond, and when it was left on the 'wrong side' of Regent Street, the street became more commercial with architects and musical firms moving in. There is still a music shop at No. 48 in one of the very few partially original buildings to survive.

One notable intervention was the conversion of the Pantheon from theatre and concert hall to shopping arcade in 1834 and its extension to include a back entrance at No. 5–9 Great Marlborough Street. The Pantheon's birth had been golden – and strikingly feminine. In the 1760s, 'several Noblemen and persons of Fashion' had suggested 'that a place of public entertainment was wanted for the Winter Season similar to that of Ranelagh for the Summer'. The Ranelagh Gardens were a spectacularly successful pleasure gardens with a rococo rotunda in the middle, where Chelsea Hospital Gardens now lie.

Two rich ladies of fashion and one landowner took up the cry. The landowner was one Philip Trust who had inherited the plot from his aunt, Elizabeth Turst. The ladies of fashion were Margaretta Ellice (also 'a person of fortune') and Mrs Cornelys, who was a powerful society hostess. The process was fractious, but they managed to persuade sufficient investors to subscribe to the scheme. They employed the very young Wyatt brothers, Samuel and James, as builder and architect respectively, and two other Wyatt brothers were investors and treasurer.

So huge a success was the theatre, with its domed hall and assembly room, that James Wyatt made his name at the age of only twenty-six. The French ambassador, Monsieur de Guisnes, in conversation with Horace Walpole during a visit in 1771, was one of many fans, declaring, *C'est ne qu'à Londres qu'on peut faire tout ça*. After having spent two millennia in the shade of great European capitals, London's great mercantile wealth was starting to outshine them.

But fashion is fickle. The popularity of the masquerades and fetes started to decline. Prices were reduced and profitability fell. It was converted into a theatre and opera hall, burnt down and was rebuilt, but never managed to attract sufficient punters or obtain permission from the Lord Chancellor to operate as a theatre under subsequent management. Throughout, the freehold remained in the Turst family, particularly Salome Trust one of many female landowners whose role is too readily overlooked.

It was Salome who sold the site on to the next generation of young entrepreneurs, who extended the Pantheon to Great Marlborough Street as the Pantheon Bazaar. The investors in the bazaar were two sets of brothers from Dickens's home town of Rochester. Samuel and George Baker were the builders, and Edward and James Day were the gentlemen, who presumably provided some of the finance and the connections and tone that the bazaar required; but the distinction is loose. When we get into the practical detail of the history of our streets, we find that the line between gentleman and trade is infinitely porous.

The new Great Marlborough Street entrance was given a conservatory and aviary, and the whole was covered in papier-mâché ornaments. When it came to selling in Victorian London, more was more. Appropriately for a street in social decline, the architect was Sydney Smirke, the unfashionable brother of Sir Robert Smirke, who designed the British Museum. The investors took a 10 per cent cut of all sales. No doubt they would have charged more if they could have got away with it, but they couldn't.

The bazaar was repurchased after thirty-three years by another generation of men on the make. Walter and Alfred Gilbey were the sons of a Hertfordshire innkeeper who had volunteered for civilian service in the Crimean War and proceeded to make a fortune importing drinks efficiently and in bulk. They had first focused on low tariff South African wine, and then on clarets and sparkling Loire wines when tariffs from France were lowered from twelve to two shillings per dozen bottles in 1861. So successful was the business that they purchased the Château Loudenne in Bordeaux and two whisky distilleries in Scotland, so they could cut out the middleman and maintain value chain efficiency.

In 1867, they bought the Pantheon as headquarters, bottling department, store and shop. Where once government censorship had banned the productive use of the Pantheon as a temple of pleasure, now William Gladstone's free trade policy was facilitating it as a mart of liquor. Gilbeys continued to use the Pantheon for sixty years before selling to Marks & Spencer, who demolished the building. The descendant of the Gilbey empire is now part of the international drinks conglomerate, Diageo.

Drink was only one of Great Marlborough Street's sins. The magistrates' court at No. 21 (which gives the street its orange colour on the *Monopoly* board) witnessed the 9th Marquess of Queensberry's libel trial against Oscar Wilde, and Gladstone's evidence against a blackmailer who had claimed he frequented prostitutes in Leicester Square. Later John Lennon was tried for obscenity there and Mick Jagger for drugs possession.

The street also sold cars and made cigarettes. At least three car companies had their showrooms in the street in the early twentieth century. But it is through a factory for cigarettes that the street has, indirectly, found its greatest, if misspelt, fame. The Whitechapel-born son of a German immigrant, Philip Morris, opened a tobacconist's shop in fashionable Bond Street in 1847. With poetic justice, Philip died young from cancer in 1873 but his widow, Margaret, and brother, Leopold, carried on the business. They opened a factory in Great Marlborough Street in 1881 and used the name Marlborough for lighter cigarettes targeted at women – 'The ladies' favourite'.

Through various partnerships and investments, the company passed into American hands and registered the more phonetically straightforward name Marlboro in the US in 1908, before launching the brand in America as a mild, luxury cigarette in 1923, long after production in Great Marlborough Street had ceased. Again, it targeted the female market with the slogan, 'Beauty tips to keep the paper from your lips,' but sales were sluggish.

Only in the 1950s was it relaunched as a filtered cigarette aimed at the male market, supposedly safer but now 'full flavour'. 'Marlboro County' and a hundred different cowboy-focused advertisements followed with huge success. Since 1972 it has been the world's number one selling cigarette brand.[46] Thus, by an oddly circuitous route, a street built to house English aristocrats and named after the military dukedom of a Wiltshire market town gave its name to a global cigarette brand, which most people assume is named after somewhere in the American Midwest. Sometimes history walks sideways.

Great Marlborough Street has also made brushes and woollen goods (at No. 11), harps and pianos (at Nos. 17–18) and china (at Nos. 175–181). Meanwhile, Great Marlborough Street's buildings have matched her eclectic history as architectural fashion and regulation became less stylistically exigent. In 1875, Arthur Liberty, the 32-year-old, self-propelled son of a Buckinghamshire draper, opened his eponymous fabric and fashion shop on the corner of Great Marlborough Street and Regent Street. Liberty was another of Great Marlborough Street's self-made heroes, who ended his life a knighted, estate-owning country gentleman.

When Regent Street was extended in the early twentieth century as the landowners' leases fell in, the back of the store was rebuilt discordantly from the rest as a Tudor revival building.

The past provided the material as well as the inspiration for the building. Recovered timbers from two former Royal Navy ships, HMS *Howe* and HMS *Hindustan*, provided 24,000 cubic feet of ships' timbers for the superstructure from 3,040 100-year-old New Forest oaks. The Great Marlborough Street frontage is said precisely to match the length and height of HMS *Hindustan*. Such a joyfully, shamelessly derivative building in happy communion with the past as well as the future has proved hugely popular and it is now listed. It has also attracted professional derision through most of the twentieth century, with the high priests of modernism deriding everything about the shop as a morally malign act of 'historicism'. The architectural historian Nikolaus Pevsner, particularly, was coruscating in his criticism.

More popular with some, as it conforms more neatly to one of history's straight lines, is the building opposite: Ideal House, now called Palladium House. Built only a few years after Liberty's in 1928, its lead architect was the master of early North American skyscrapers, Raymond Hood. It has been described as 'a very unusual instance of a London-scaled American tower block design'. And so it is, with all the variegated playfulness of early skyscrapers: black granite and Egyptian champlevé enamelling, but with the repetitive insistence of a Georgian window pattern. Is it Art Deco? Or Moderne?

It hardly matters. Great Marlborough Street is nothing if not eclectic in use and look even today: a heterodox mix of shops, hotels, offices and buildings. Some are nearly 300 years old; some are barely thirty. In lower stretches you can sense, almost, its old stateliness and generosity of breadth, but nothing of its original use or tone.

The Pantheon is very nearly forgotten but not quite. If you look up their branches on the Marks & Spencer website you will find that the branch listed at 169–173 Oxford Street and Great Marlborough Street has a name. It is the Pantheon (in fact you can still see 'The Pantheon' written in green neon lettering on the parapet above the Oxford Street front).[47]

Just as Great Marlborough Street has changed from one of London's most fashionable to one of its most forgotten streets and from a coherent place of homes to a near random mesh of shops and offices, so a theatre for the fashionable became a shopping bazaar, a wine merchant and then a department store. But the plot from which Marks & Spencer is selling sensible clothes today is the plot that the brothers Baker and Day adjudged attractive to the early Victorian shopper desiring reasonable prices with an accessible infusion of the Orient. Our streets evolve and we may forget their past uses, but they still contain us.

Chapter 12

PENTONVILLE ROAD

A bypass for cows

Something of an extraordinary nature will turn up.
Mr Micawber, fictional resident of Pentonville in
Charles Dickens's *David Copperfield*

London's place names, like her streets, tend to come and stay, but of Pentonville, the forgotten suburb, only Pentonville Road remains. Even that is a solecism. For the first century of its existence, Pentonville Road was simply the New Road, the easternmost stretch of London's first bypass, renamed in 1857 by the Metropolitan Board of Works when they took over management from the St Marylebone and Islington Turnpike trusts. But by then Pentonville, like Great Marlborough Street in the previous chapter, was already in a spiral of change from a bypass through the country to a street through the town; from a place in which to live if you could, to one in which to work if you had to, and could not escape from its noise, industry and traffic, as John Betjeman was to do.

He was not the first. Traffic is as old as cities. The Roman poet Juvenal complained that sleep was impossible in ancient Rome for 'the movement of heavy wagons through constricted streets and the oaths of stalled cattle drovers would break the sleep of a deaf man or a lazy walrus . . . most sick men die here from insomnia.'

In London most people walked or rode, but from about 1580 there were an increasing number of carts and coaches. In 1631, householders petitioned the Privy Council against the proliferation of coaches. In 1661, Samuel Pepys got caught in traffic for an hour and a half and in 1666, so bad was the traffic that he gave up and went shopping. Cities create traffic and successful cities create more. Men may fight against it, but more often than not the remedy simply compounds the problem, so-called 'induced traffic'. Modern studies show that traffic can grow by nearly 50 per cent *more* where bypasses are built than where they are not.

For the last 250 years, London's history has been one of successful efforts to create more traffic and fitful attempts to tame it. The first effort began 170 years ago as a casebook exercise of gentlemanly capitalism.

The 1750s was a momentous decade of war and wealth as Britain, France, Spain and Prussia fought for suzerainty and influence across three continents. The so-called Seven Years' War was to alter the European balance of power, to formalise Britain's dominance upon the wide seas, and to set France upon her winding path to revolution. Amid these world-shattering and empire-building events, at some stage a successful international trader, Charles Dingley, had some conversations about traffic.

Travelling into London in the 1750s was no joke. The roads

thronged not only with people and carriages, but with drovers shepherding thousands of animals to fill Londoners' stomachs. Daniel Defoe wrote that 150,000 turkeys were driven to London each year. So were geese, pigs, goats and, above all, cows and sheep. Each year about 74,000 cattle and 570,000 sheep made their way to Smithfield market alone to be slaughtered. When it was first formally established, Smithfield was beside open fields (the clue is in the name). By the time John Rocque was surveying for his great 1746 London map, Smithfield was enclosed by city streets that thronged with animals approaching the twice-weekly market. One is called Cow Cross Street to this day.

One important approach road from the west was Oxford Street. In between the crowds on hanging days, animals coming to Smithfield were normally driven past Tyburn, yet further reducing its attraction as a place to live. Put simply, London was becoming too hard to get into or to leave if you had schedules to make, or produce to transport. It was time to do something about it, reasoned Charles Dingley. But how?

One of Dingley's first conversations was probably with his brother Robert, who was an architect and could advise on the technicalities; in the eighteenth century, architects' expertise ranged far wider than now and there were no highway engineers. Other conversations were with Hammond Crosse, a brewer, Richard Whishaw, a Lincoln's Inn lawyer, and George Errington and William Godfrey, who both owned land in Middlesex and Essex. All were well-connected gentlemen in the mixed world of trade, land, wealth and enterprise that made for eighteenth-century, polite mercantile society. All stood to benefit, as owners, businessmen or investors from a better road into London that could charge tolls for the privilege of its use.

They therefore hatched a plan to build London's first bypass.

To achieve this, they started by hiring one William Godfrey as a 'parliamentary agent' (like a present-day lobbyist) to represent them and they petitioned for private legislation to build a 'New Road'. This was normal parliamentary practice, as most eighteenth-century legislation was private not official, promoting public works, permitting divorce or settling estates. A flourishing and well-paid service sector of advisors and agents existed to help petitions on their way.

The 'New Road' proposed to MPs in 1756 was to start at the (rural) junction of the Harrow and Edgware Roads and then to head east to the equally rural Battle Bridge (now King's Cross) before joining the Angel Inn at Islington, from which the existing St John Street could then enter the city directly to Smithfield.[48] This would permit people and the twice weekly flood of animals approaching London from the west to bypass the city's streets for three further miles and prevent them needing to walk, eat and (critically) excrete their way through Oxford Street, Broad St Giles and High Holborn.

In his evidence to the parliamentary committee in February 1756, Dingley predicted confidently that the road would be 'one of the most profitable undertakings he ever knew' (and he knew about making money – having made his fortune alongside his brother trading with Russia and Persia). He offered to subscribe £1,000 personally to pay for tollhouses.

Some complained. The Duke of Bedford worried about dust blowing onto his land and the Islington turnpike trustees were worried about loss of revenue to existing streets. But parliamentary and public opinion was supportive. Roads made people richer and this one would ease the hooves of commerce. The *Gentleman's Magazine* argued that 'streets and roads are to inland trade what seas are to foreign' and new roads were a 'kind of new mine that increases the wealth of the community'.

In May 1756 the Act was passed, commissioners were appointed and a surveyor, Mr Marsh, paid five guineas to plan the road. By modern standards, progress was spectacularly fast, and it was entirely built during the 1756 summer. By 13 September, carts were passing over the Pentonville Road stretch of the New Road and by 17 September over the whole road.

One reason for the speed of bypass construction of which the modern world can only dream was that the road itself was not physically ambitious. Construction was mainly removing hedges and banks, levelling the surface and digging ditches. Fences, gates and tollhouses were then erected, mainly using recycled ships' timbers, in which there was a ready secondary market. The road was not paved, so that it could be used by drovers and their livestock. However, potholes and wagon marks were filled with gravel and ballast and, in practice, much of the surface was soon gravelled.

The Act required that compensation be paid to landowners and leaseholders for 40 feet worth of road and 10 feet worth of ditches and fencing. Another clause forbade building within 50 feet of the road. This would keep the road dry and spacious and prevent dust from troubling nearby residents. It may not have been a modern dual carriageway, but the principles were the same: keep the road wide and straight for traffic and keep the troublesome people and obfuscating houses away from the road. Road first; surroundings second. It is a design approach used by highway engineers to this day.

For the first time since the Romans, London was building a road not a street; and London had her first bypass, built not for cars but for cows.

The New Road's eastern stretch ran through the lands of Henry Penton, from whose family it was to derive its Victorian name, and to whom the commissioners had paid compensation. The estate's history mirrored that of many others: initially church land, it had ended up in the hands of successful Jacobean politicians (the Wood family, who lost their money) and was thence bought for £8,930 in 1710 by Henry Penton's grandfather.

The Penton family came from wool. Every century has its sector of wild riches: oil in the twentieth century, digital in the early twenty-first. In late medieval England it was wool. For a thousand years, exports of wool from the cloudy, rainy and fertile island of Britain (good for grass and sheep) were a mainstay of the economy, explaining high levels of foreign coinage in Anglo-Saxon Lundenwic and subsidising the creation of wool churches and market crosses from the Cotswolds to East Anglia. It was also to fund the development of London's lost suburb – Pentonville, which was to grow up around and transform forever London's first bypass.

In 1756, Henry Penton clearly had no conception that the building of the New Road would transform his estate's potential value. He argued with 'very great objections' against an alternative route that would have passed more completely through his land, creating more street frontage for him to exploit. Instead, he supported and achieved a route through the south of his land, thus minimising his estate's ultimate economic gain.

He was thinking 'smaller picture'. London was still far away and a more immediate benefit was to increase the agricultural value of his land. All those passing animals needed to eat and what better income than to rent out the grazing rights by the night? His land was also dug for gravel and clay to make London bricks and tiles. When next you look at an eighteenth-century London stock brick, it may well have started its life in a Pentonville 'brickfield'.

Indeed, it was one of the 'brickfield farmers', William Lloyd, who probably first understood the economic consequences of the New Road for the surrounding fields. In 1764 he signed a contract with Henry Penton's son (also called Henry) to build five houses on the New Road's southern side. Although nothing was built for five years, this began the creation of Pentonville, the suburb, and the transformation of the rural New Road into an urban street. The model followed was the one perfected by the Grosvenors: the estate laid out streets and craftsmen leased developing plots. The estate was served over generations by the same families and the Watsons worked as surveyors in Pentonville from at least the 1780s until 1912.

By the 1820s, most of the suburb was built; good quality, three- or four-storey houses on the New Road, with two- or three-storey houses on the adjoining streets. Most of the houses on the main road obeyed the New Road Act and were set 50 feet back in a series of grandly entitled rows. Even though most of the original houses have vanished, this set back still gives the street a generous tone today. The turnpike trustees continued to administer the New Road itself, paying off the debt of the investors, until they were replaced by the Metropolitan Board of Works in 1857.

Early residents were gentlemen or nearly gentlemen: surgeons, physicians, engravers, 'a chain-maker, two chronometer-makers, a zinc worker, cabinet-makers, printers, and bookbinders', shopkeepers and tradesmen. The writers Charles Lamb and Thomas Carlyle briefly lodged here and so did John Stuart Mill's father. It was not smart, but it was respectable, running up the hill overlooking the Cities of London and Westminster.

During the nineteenth century, more homes were built to the north and railway lines and stations to the south. The inner-city air filled with smoke and it was impossible for Pentonville to keep its cachet. It was not green and spacious like the expanding suburbs, nor fashionably situated like Mayfair or St James's. Homes were turned into boarding houses and Charles Dickens tellingly lodged the indebted but ever-hopeful Wilkins Micawber in 'lodgings in Pentonville', when he wrote *David Copperfield* in 1849. In the same decade, an academy for 'young gentlemen' in White Lion Street just behind the New Road closed and the premises were taken over as a reformatory for prostitutes.

If not fashionably placed, Pentonville Road (as it was rechristened by the Metropolitan Board of Works) was well situated for commuters or for national distribution. In 1829 the coachbuilder, George Shillibeer, adapted a long, horse-drawn coach he had designed in Paris as London's first omnibus (or, briefly, 'Shillibus'), which ran down the street and thence to the city. From 1855, when Smithfield cattle market was moved to Islington, Pentonville Road no longer had to accommodate thousands of animals, but it was up the hill from the new King's Cross and St Pancras stations. From the 1860s, manufacturing workshops were increasingly built on to back gardens and, forgetting the 50 feet rule, shops on to front ones.[49]

Like Great Marlborough Street, Pentonville Road was industrialising.

Cocoa, musical instruments, furniture, jewellery and artificial flowers: all were manufactured on Pentonville Road to be distributed round London or further. As public transport improved, particularly the introduction of trams in the 1900s, even the factory workers and craftsmen could afford to live further out. The demand for homes declined and one shopkeeper, Henry Vincent, complained in 1908 that 'the Electric trams have took the trade from the shop'. The once-proud suburb was thoroughly impoverished. In 1911, neighbouring Cumming

Street, 'once the pride of Finsbury' was as 'more like a fair than an English street . . . All day long men women and children sit and lay outside the house. At night there is generally a street organ until past eleven o'clock, while boys, girls and drunken men and women dance and sing as loud as they can.'

Increasingly, two or three homes were acquired and a new factory or warehouse created. With their Crittall windows and plain brick pilasters, several of these survive, including at No. 91, where Pentonville Road's very first homes had been built.

The best remembered of Pentonville's many workshops today is that of G. Betjemann & Sons, manufacturers of trolleys, patent locks, ornamental dressing cases, and the type of gadgetry and cabinetwork beloved to the Victorians. Founded by a Dutch immigrant in 1820, the firm moved to 34–44 Pentonville Road in 1859 and flourished, patenting 'the Alexandra Palace patent lock', 'the Betjemann device for hansom cabs' and, best known, the 'Tantalus on which the family fortune had been made', which was a lockable drinks cabinet capable of remaining on display whilst firmly locked against the pilfering of 'servants and younger sons getting at the whisky'.

In the years before and during the First World War, the fourth generation of the family, the future poet laureate John Betjeman, used to visit with his father 'in early-morning pipe-smoke on the tram'.[50] He recalled in his 1960s blank verse autobiography, *Summoned by Bells*:

> When you rang
> The front-bell a watchful packer pulled
> A polished lever twenty yards away,
> And this released the catch into a world
> Of shining showrooms full of secret drawers
> And Maharajah's dressing cases.

Although 'the works' were a cornucopia of Victoriana that the older poet would have loved, to Betjeman's lifelong guilt, the young Betjeman did not fall in love with his family tradition:

> 'Well now my boy, I want your solemn word
> To carry on the firm when I am gone:
> Fourth generation, John – they'll look to you
> They're artist-craftsmen to their fingertips . . .
> Go on creating beauty.'
> What is beauty?
> Here, where I write, the green Atlantic bursts
> In cannonades of white along Pentire
> There's beauty here . . .
> But none to me in polished wood and stone

When John Betjeman's father died, he closed the business in 1945 – a ripe metaphor for Pentonville's twentieth-century history.[51] As the neighbourhood's challenges mounted, the Pentons tried to be good landlords. They became increasingly philanthropic, rebuilding community halls and working with the council to improve homes as leases fell in. However, due to subleasing, the family's control over properties was often weak.

After the war, the Penton Estate limped on for a few years, but the neighbourhood's decline and the fashion for publicly owned housing were overwhelming. In 1951, the estate was put up for auction. Much of it ended up in the hands of the local council and during the 1950s and 1960s, the surrounding streets were comprehensively replanned as a series of modernist estates. The late-Georgian grid of blocks and terraced houses that was Pentonville was swept away in a fit of well-intentioned, twentieth-century slum clearance and de-urbanisation.

The replacing housing estates were also given new names:

Priory Green and Weston Rise. Pentonville the suburb was forgotten and its name lingers on only in the road and a prison opened in 1842 some miles to the north.

Pentonville Road also had problems: its businesses increasingly failed as the challenges (commercial and regulatory) to manufacturing within the city continued to rise. Local government made matters worse. First Finsbury council, then Islington its successor, tried to prevent industrial expansion immediately after the war and then to restrict the very sensible substitution of offices for failing manufacturing firms. It is rarely wise to try to micro-manage street use from city hall, a problem that has been repeated as councils attempt to control declining modern high streets, rather than letting them evolve.

Pentonville Road started life as a rural bypass with pasture for feeding sheep, but bypasses create new traffic and are defined by them. By turns industrial and commercial, Pentonville Road now has a growing number of homes again. Though most are fairly grim, some warehouses have been elegantly repurposed and Penton Rise has new student blocks. Had the council permitted readier 'change of use' (as planners put it) from industrial to commercial in the 1960s and 1970s, the street would have been in better condition when London at last ended its long twentieth-century decline and ceased to shrink in the 1980s.

Streets change and wise councils let them. The alternative is worse.

ELECTRIC COMPANY

He shewes that 't is the seacoale smoake
That allways London doth Inviron,
Which doth our Lungs and Spiritts choake,
Our hanging spoyle, and rust our Iron.
Lett none att Fumifuge be scoffing
Who heard att Church our Sundaye's Coughing.
Ballad of Gresham College, 1633.

As Lords temporal, Lords spiritual and commoners gathered in London for Parliament in the week after Whit Sunday 1306, they were greeted by a new and unfamiliar acrid smell for many of them. It was burning coal, increasingly being transported by ship from Newcastle, landed at Seacoal and Newcastle Wharfs on the river Fleet (still recalled in Old Seacoal Lane and Newcastle Close), and burned by blacksmiths, artisans, and even domestically across the capital.

Coal burned longer, hotter and slower than mere wood; who would not want to use that? It also stank. Revolted, the Lords temporal, Lords spiritual and commoners passed a ban on burning coal while Parliament was in session. Had anyone paid any attention to this customary official attempt to ban novelty, then the history of London, Britain and indeed the world might be completely different. But no one did.

It is not too fanciful to say that Londoners' ready access to sea coal, together with the nation's propensity to use it, helped propel not only the city but the entire country from a provincial backwater to the centre of the world's economy. Of course, in doing so, they also ushered in the 'Anthropocene', the current geological age in which human activity has become the dominant influence on climate and the environment for better or, almost certainly, for worse. How London has needed and made heat and light over the centuries really matters.

A filthy trinity of good and bad luck explains why London started using coal en masse before any other global city. Firstly, it was running out of wood to burn. The high value and ready exportability of wool encouraged widespread deforestation of an already small and (by late medieval standards) highly populated island. Secondly, there was coal available within the British Isles. Thirdly, and arguably most important of all, the coal was accessible by river and sea, thus rendering economically viable a dense commodity that would otherwise have been far too heavy to transport in bulk. Not for nothing was coal normally called sea coal for hundreds of years.

One might add a final factor: official attempts to ban innovation and enterprise, common in many countries and many centuries, were consistently and culturally ineffective in England.

These factors 'tipped over' in the 1570s. Growing concerns about deforestation and the rising price of wood led to dozens of Elizabethan commissions into the decay and spoilation of England's forests and to increasingly severe penalties. In Essex, those caught 'hedge stealing' were to 'be whipped till they bleed well'. The wood shortage bit most deeply in London, the largest city and with the widest expanse of deforested land about it. As wood prices rose, and as the climatic Little Ice Age created longer and colder winters well into the eighteenth century, the relative curves of demand and supply crossed and the use of domestic coal surged strongly in the 1570s.

Astonishingly by 1600, coal was probably the capital's main source of fuel. It was a trend that was not to be reversed for over 350 years and was to allow cold and rainy London to be Europe's largest city by 1750.

Making possible this total transformation in London's primary source of fuel, and in turn being promoted by the ongoing change, was the development of the efficient and cost-effective brick chimney, with narrower flues to encourage the proper draw of air. In 1500 such chimneys were rare, but by 1650 they were nearly ubiquitous. In 1577, the clergyman chronicler William Harrison wrote that there were 'old men yet dwelling' who had noted 'the multitude of chimneys late erected . . . within their sound remembrance'. Sometimes change comes slowly, at other times in a rapid jumble. The brick chimney was a technological change of internet proportions.

Coal was not without consequences, however. As early as 1578, it was said that Elizabeth I was 'greatly grieved and annoyed with the taste and smoke of sea-coales'. And throughout the seventeenth century, the problem worsened. In 1661, the diarist John Evelyn penned a diatribe against coal and its multiple pollutions, *Fumifugium*.[52] He blamed coal, correctly, for pollution and illness. Coal smoke, he wrote, left 'a sooty crust of fur' upon all, 'corroding the very iron bars and hardest stones with those piercing and acrimonious spirits which accompany its sulphur'.

London's coal fires did not just blacken streets; they destroyed their vegetation as well. Late medieval London was densely studded with gardens and orchards. No more. Evelyn complained that coal smoke killed bees and flowers and suffered only a 'few wretched fruits to survive', which had a 'bitter and ungrateful' flavour. The elm tree was chosen for Georgian London streets because it alone 'endures the coal smoke very well'. And a few *rus in urbe* sheep left in Cavendish Square were removed due to the inelegance of their 'sooty fleeces'.

Londoners kept using coal, of course, because it was cheaper and more efficient. It has been estimated that a poor family in London spent about 10 per cent of its income on coal. To enjoy the same heat from firewood would have cost two to five times as much.

Ironically, the powerful, heat-giving coal made London streets and squares darker. This mattered, because the London authorities seemed particularly reluctant to try and light them. London was very underlit by modern standards and was probably Europe's worst lit capital city.

Amsterdam and Paris both had oil street lamps by the late seventeenth century: 2,400 in Amsterdam, 2,736 in Paris. London instead, by laws or proclamations of 1416, 1661, 1668, 1690 and 1716, merely required householders to erect lamps themselves. The frequent repetition implies ongoing non-compliance, however, and the rules did not effectively stipulate what type of lamps. Again, this mattered because most pre-electric lamps bordered on the functionally useless in the face of the Vulcan-like darkness of a smoggy winter's night. A good candle provides only one hundredth of the power of a single 100-watt light bulb.

In 1685, one Edward Hemming was granted a monopoly to organise oil lights outside every tenth house on the main thoroughfares. Then in 1736, London's local parishes took control of the supervision of street lighting; however, things did not improve much. Londoners remained fearful of going out at night, due to the risk of being 'blinded, knocked down, cut or stabbed'. Many employed the moving torches of linkmen or linkboys, but this was not risk free either.

John Gay warned against their employment to light your way home:

> Though thou art tempted by the linkman's call,
> Yet trust him not along the lonely wall:
> In the midway, he'll quench the flattering brand,
> And share the booty with the pilfering hand.

So dark was the nocturnal London street that in May (not midwinter) 1763, James Boswell was able to pick up a 'strong, jolly young damsel', conduct her to Westminster Bridge, put on a condom ('in armour complete' as he put it), and then 'engage her upon this noble edifice. The whim of doing it there with the Thames rolling below us amused me much.' A city in which it is possible to engage a prostitute publicly on one of the only two central London bridges at the time, is more river Styx than river Thames.

Again, coal was to provide the answer to London streets' Stygian darkness. But in doing so, yet again it would make the long-term challenge of pollution far worse. An impoverished Scottish peer, the 8th Earl of Dundonald, who invented a patented method of making coal tar, first produced flammable coal gas. He lit his own house in 1790, but did not exploit his invention.[53] A few years later a Scottish inventor, William Murdoch, made a similar discovery whilst he was working in Cornwall, and went on to light a cotton mill in Manchester.[54] In 1807, an extrovert Moravian refugee, Frederick Winsor, laid lead pipes along the north side of one of our *Monopoly* streets, Pall Mall, and lit it with Winsor's Patent Gas, thus illuminating Carlton House to honour the king's birthday. It was a publicity stunt worthy of Richard Branson and with similar intent.

Winsor founded the Gas Light and Coke Company (the oldest company from which British Gas plc is directly descended) and went on to light Westminster Bridge, the Drury Lane Theatre and the St James's Park pagoda – which caught fire. Gas was made at Cannon Row in Westminster and then at Shoreditch, Spitalfields and Finsbury. The largest factory opened near Regent's Canal.

Each ton of coal was transformed into 10,000 cubic feet of gas, 10 gallons of tar, 12 gallons of ammonia water and 13 hundredweight of coke. By the mid-1820s, 70,000 domestic and street lamps were being supplied. Gas lamps were meagre by modern standards – about 25 watts, and laying gas piping was disruptive and could be dangerous; explosions were quite common initially. Nevertheless, London streets were dark no more. By 1880, the year the gas fire was introduced, London's streets had a million street lamps and were consuming 6.5 million tons of coal a year.

London's gas lamps needed to be turned on individually and this, in turn, created the Victorian street rhythm of the nightly lamplighter.

Of course, all this coal-created heat and light also increased pollution. Already, by 1810, over 200 years of coal fires had left the 'fronts of houses all blackened by the smoke of the coal'. During the nineteenth century and into the 1960s, London's voracious appetite for power caused fogs and pollution on a scale that would have left John Evelyn aghast – and coughing. Victorian and Edwardian London was the age of smog, of 'pea-soupers', of 'the London peculiar'. And it was in London's streets that the smog most lingered, like 'fluid ink' as Thomas Carlyle put it, changing the very nature and experience of London, sequestrating each street from its neighbour.

Peter Ackroyd called London's fog 'the greatest character in nineteenth-century fiction'. It is certainly impossible to imagine the London of Sherlock Holmes or Dr Jekyll and Mr Hyde without it, though the filth of coal-polluted London streets flowed into twentieth-century literature as well. T.S. Eliot imagined:

> . . . the yellow smoke that slides along the street,
> Rubbing its back upon the window-panes.

Pollution kills. In 1873 there were an estimated 700 extra deaths due to pollution, nineteen of them of pedestrians, unable to see in front of them, walking into the Thames or the docks. One possible solution was the new miracle of electricity. This was the answer that Victor Watson and Marjory Phillips would have known on their 1935 day trip to London. This was safer (no risk of explosions) and much more luminous, but it still relied on burning coal for generation. Early electricity generators were almost neighbourly. The first, at 57 Holborn Viaduct, illuminated the Old Bailey and the General Post Office. Other power stations followed in the Strand, at Kensington Court, Kensington High Street and in another *Monopoly* street, Bond Street.

By 1914, London had seventy power stations, all still polluting London's air. During the twentieth century, electricity generation was concentrated along the Thames, where the same economic logic that had first brought sea coal from Newcastle to London dictated that it could be unloaded most cost-effectively. Barking, Southwark and Battersea were the main power plants. Battersea particularly has proved consistently popular with the public, one of the world's largest brick buildings, whose industrial cathedral style is none the less striking for having become a cliché.

Giles Gilbert Scott is normally cited as the architect, but in fact he was brought into the project quite late and partly to appease sceptical public opinion. Much of the work was done by the largely forgotten Leonard Pearce, chief engineer of the London Power Company. Battersea Power Station was built in two halves and for twenty years had only two chimneys. If Victor Watson and Marjory Phillips saw an electricity-generating power station on their trip, it is this demi-Battersea that they would probably have seen.

As with the water supply, keeping London warm and lit caused huge problems as the city grew. The coal-created 'crust of fur' that John Evelyn complained about in 1661 was to thicken for 400 years: coal fires, coal gas, coal electricity generators. In the 1950s, thousands were still dying from asphyxiation and bronchial asthma. My father remembers visiting London on a 1950s day trip from Cambridge and coming back with his collar black with filth. The Victorians started winning the battle against water-borne pollutants in the 1860s, but they never beat coal.

Only with the 1956 Clean Air Act did London's air start improving; and only in the 1980s was coal-fired electricity production finally removed from metropolitan London, ending a scourge that can be said to have begun under Good Queen Bess in the 1570s, or arguably under Edward I in the fourteenth century. The black crust is still being cleansed from some buildings, including the bright red bricks and shining terracotta that Victorian architects often used so they would remain visible under the shroud of a London fog.

However, the climatic dangers of heat and of flooding, created by over 400 years of fossil fuel consumption, still remain – with London and the world.

Chapter 13

REGENT STREET

Paradise in plaster

The sinuous line of Regent Street was . . . the developers'
line of maximum profit.
J. Mordaunt Crook

The history of London is the history of leases sold and leases reverting, of freeholders with insufficient ready money, and of developing leaseholders taking the real risk and trying to make a pile. London has never had an Emperor Augustus, a Pope Sixtus V, or a Baron Haussmann with a comprehensive blueprint to beautify the city. No one has tried to mirror Rome or Paris. But by a happy coincidence one of London's important leases reverted to the Crown at precisely the moment when royal patronage, vision, business acumen and sheer courage were perfectly positioned to seize the opportunity.

The creation of Regent Street and Regent's Park is often described as London's only example of 'town planning'. This is unfair. If the creation of new neighbourhoods such as St James's or Mayfair was not comprehensive 'town planning', then nothing is. What was unique about the creation of the Regent's Park

Estate was that it was simultaneously the planning of a new neighbourhood *and* the insertion of a major new street (Regent Street) through the existing town.

Many such streets were to follow (including another *Monopoly* street – Northumberland Avenue), but none were so curvaceously picturesque, or so self-consciously conceived to lead to a new proto-suburban neighbourhood. Regent Street was a road to the suburbs. However, despite its princely name and ambitions, it is impossible to understand Regent Street's creation without seeing it as the victory of the common and commercial man, of the architect builder using cheap stucco, not pricey stone.

For, without a heady dose of upward mobility and entrepreneurial flair mixed into royal patronage, the street would certainly never have existed, and without middle-class shopping, it would never have flourished and been reborn when only a century old.

Regent Street is about money, enterprise and reinvention first: princes second.

An Englishman, a Welshman and two Scotsmen created Regent Street. First up, the Englishman: in 1766, the self-taught English architect and writer John Gwynn wrote an angry book of forgotten genius, *London and Westminster Improved*, which anticipated and predicted many Victorian interventions from Waterloo Bridge to Trafalgar Square.[55] He was particularly exercised about the maze of streets and alleys to the north-west of Piccadilly.

Gwynn, who was a 'lively, rattling fellow' and a friend of Dr Johnson, suggested that 'a street is opened from the top of the Hay-Market of the same width and continued to Oxford Road' and thence to the 'New Road' bypass running from the Edgware Road to the Angel Inn. The proposed route was a little to the east of the route that Regent Street now takes.

Few paid any immediate attention, but our first Scotsman, John Fordyce, the Scottish-born Surveyor General of Woods, Forests, Parks and Chases (the precursor of the Crown Estate), may have read his book. In any case, he hatched a very similar plan. In 1794, Fordyce leased out the royal grounds of the 500-acre Marylebone Park for farming for a mere seventeen years. It was a short lease, because Fordyce could see that, liberated from the constraints of the Stuart green belt, London was heading north. Fordyce therefore commissioned a survey of the estate and, over four reports, planned a street similar to the one proposed by Gwynn. The Crown's future tenants needed to be able to get into town if they were to pay good rents.

Our Welshman, John Nash, enters the story shortly before Marylebone Park reverted to the Crown in 1811 – and what an entry. Of humble birth, the son of a Welsh millwright (a skilled factory worker), brought up in Lambeth and apprenticed at fourteen to the architect Sir Robert Taylor, Nash's speed and talent seemed destined to raise him far above his station. But he got his timing wrong and went bust in 1783. Worse, he married foolishly; his wife was a spendthrift jilt who fell pregnant to another man and ran up unpayable debts.

Nash fled to his native Wales and restarted. Within several years, and working with the landscape designer Humphry Repton, he was the premier designer of manor houses to the Welsh gentry. Returning to London, he designed a conservatory for the Prince of Wales and then remarried the much younger Mary Anne Bradley who was rumoured to be the Prince Regent's mistress; though whether he was 'making an honest woman' of her or was subsequently cuckolded by the prince is unclear.

Either way, Nash was appointed as Architect to the Surveyor General of Woods, Forests, Parks and Chases, and then Deputy Surveyor General 'by direct command of the Prince Regent'. He had a royal patron and from being a failed developer and provincial designer, he was suddenly the most important architect in the country, by some distance. He re-conceived the development of the Marylebone Park Estate as a series of idiosyncratic villas in a picturesque park, with a replanned New Street, soon named Regent Street, separating Mayfair from Soho.

This meant the street was longer: it led from the prince's residence at Carlton House (where those first gas lights had been lit in 1807) up to a new circus with Piccadilly, curved around a quadrant, absorbed Swallow Street, formed another circus with Oxford Street, and then headed north before forming a stucco crescent facing into the new Regent's Park. 'Every length of architecture would be terminated by a façade of beautiful architecture,' he wrote.

The reshaped Regent Street maximised the potential for profitable shops and homes and formed, as Nash put it, 'a complete separation between the streets and squares occupied by the Nobility and Gentry, and the narrower streets and meaner houses occupied by mechanics and the trading part of the community.' Sometimes streets divide as well as unite. Regent Street may have been the dream of a working-class Welsh architect, but it was princely stuff, and underneath it even had an important new sewer channelling filth to the Thames.

The problem, of course, was how to pay for it all. The Prince Regent got the New Street Act through parliament in 1813 permitting the compulsory purchase of the required land, but he had nothing like enough ready capital.

Enter our second Scotsman and one of London's most successful property developers, James Burton. Unlike Nash, who was a working-class man performing a professional role, James Burton, né Haliburton, was a gentleman who had gone into commerce. So shocked were his Scottish gentry relatives that James changed his name to Burton, to spare them the disgrace. They would have done better to stick by him. Burton was a developer of genius, a risk taker and a spendthrift, who nevertheless managed to keep ahead of his creditors. He began his first development, aged twenty-one, across the river in Lambeth and had built over 600 homes, mainly in Bloomsbury, before he was forty.

The governors of the Foundling Hospital, whom he advised, regarded him as a man of outstanding qualities: 'Without such a man, possessed of very considerable talents, unwearied industry and a capital of his own, the extraordinary success of the improvements of the Foundling Estate could not have taken place.'

Then, as now, money bought status. Burton ended his days not only rich but socially lauded, founder of the Athenaeum Club, and able to count both Princess Victoria and her mother, the Duchess of Kent, amongst his friends. He also developed 191 of the houses of Regent Street and thus paid for and built more of the street than anyone else. The Regent may have named it, but Burton paid for it.

However, even Burton would not finance everything. In order to tempt developers, Nash had abandoned his plan for a continuous facade and designed a series of symmetrical groupings that could alter to meet the preferences of individual developers. This approach did not work, however, for the sinuous Quadrant that curved into Piccadilly. This was the hardest portion to build and finance, as its curving form required both aesthetic continuity and continuous physical construction, instead of plot-by-plot development at the speed that individual developers could manage.

James Burton was already over-committed and would not take the risk. So instead, John Nash turned developer and put together a consortium of tradesmen who were willing to invest in the speculation in lieu of cash payment. Unfettered by others, Nash gave the Quadrant a Continental feel, with a colonnade of slim iron pillars shielding shoppers from the London rain. The whole financial edifice could have collapsed at any moment, but it didn't and somehow Regent Street was completed.

By 1820, London had one of the finest and most picturesque new streets in Europe.[56] Built on a commercial budget, stucco did not only remove the need for stone, it also permitted cheaper, non-facing bricks. It thus became possible to travel elegantly from St James's Park by Whitehall and Westminster right up to Regent's Park with its surrounding villas and terraces. Contemporaries had conflicting views; they were shocked by the profligacy and pomposity of it all. (Despite private investment, the scheme's overall cost to the public purse rose from Nash's first forecast of £385,000 to £1,533,000 – which appeared in line with George IV's debauched and profligate lifestyle.

Nash died in 1835, widely criticised for the amount of money spent on this and other schemes.[57] However, contemporaries also felt that Regent Street was worthy of London and her imperial achievements. It was Regent Street that the architectural writer, James Elmes, most had in mind when he called London 'the Rome of Modern History'. Meanwhile the 'thousands of poor' previously living in the 'filthy labyrinthine environs' and 'dirty courts' of Swallow Street and displaced by 'Nash's housebreakers' were largely forgotten.

Victorian Regent Street flourished by day and night. Above all, drapery stores moved there, encouraged by large, plate glass windows and modern gas lighting. Swan and Edgar (in 1820), Dickins and Jones (in the 1830s), Liberty's (in the 1870s) and Jaeger (in the 1890s). Photographers' studios, exploiting another new technology, flocked there in the 1860s – as did 'fancy dog sellers' for 'young ladies' in the same decade.

Some shoppers were grand. When Queen Victoria's family visited Swan and Edgar, the owner William Edgar (who had started life running a stall in St James's Market beneath which he slept at night) was always asked to assist the royal family personally. But most shoppers were middle class. Where better for the modestly genteel to come shopping and ogle the merchandise? Nineteenth-century memoires abound with recollections of therapeutic visits to the delights of Regent Street. Molly Hughes wrote of her childhood trips to town in the 1870s that 'my delight was to walk down Regent Street and gaze in the shop-windows, pointing out all the things I would like to have.'

By night, Victorian Regent Street had a seamier character and served a very different market. The largely demolished Swallow Street had been a centre for prostitution but, as Victorian London's historian Jerry White put it, the new development 'had not removed prostitution from the old line of Swallow Street, just provided a more gilded playground for its display'. Regent Street, and more especially Nash's cast-iron colonnade, became the best place to find high-class prostitutes. Henry Mayhew referred to a 'house of assignation' in Regent Street.

The colonnade was removed in 1848 as a 'haven' for streetwalkers and their 'lounger' clients, but the rich demand and expensive supply remained. The eccentric Victorian diarist and civil servant, Arthur Munby, who recounted his meetings with working-class women, met the prostitute Sarah Tanner in Regent Street in 1854 'in glorious apparel'. She made so much money from her trade that a few years later she was able to purchase and run a coffee house near Waterloo.

During the First World War, the *Weekly Dispatch* noted that 'a young officer from Scotland was accosted sixteen times in the course of walking from his hotel near Regent Street to Piccadilly Tube.' Fashionable cafés such as the Café Royale, very much a

French import in contrast to the English pub or tavern, attracted generations of nocturnal custom to their 'lounging' before other assignations were attempted.[58]

Sometimes the Regent Street of day and night mingled. One respectable dressmaker, Miss Case, was unfairly arrested for soliciting in Regent Street in 1887, but other Regent Street shop girls were less innocent. The gynaecologist, Dr William Acton, wrote of those whom he termed 'dollymops', who prostituted themselves with customers met behind the shop counter for pleasure or extra income. One, Annie King, rechristened herself Mabel Gray and became one of the most famous, and photographed, women in London. She missed 'by an eyelash' marrying into the upper classes. One American journalist recalled, surely ironically, that 'in every shop window the features of Mabel Gray are flaunted at one along with the portraits of . . . the Queen, the Princess of Wales, and other virtuous and good women.'

Regent Street was born when the Marylebone Park lease fell in and it was transformed when its own leases did likewise. Most of the street had been sold on 99-year leases and by the turn of the twentieth century, the renamed Commissioners of Woods, Forests and Land Revenues were seeking to reinvest. Regent Street was out of fashion and out of favour; dismissed as 'sham' stucco by John Ruskin, many of Nash's buildings, it was claimed, had been 'shoddily' built.[59] Shopkeepers were finding that they needed larger shops and windows, and their increasingly middle-class clients were inclined to look more and purchase less. One complained of too many 'ladies who want things in quite the most up-to-date style at a very moderate outlay'.

In 1904, therefore, the Commissioners of Woods, Forests and Land Revenues engaged the architect Norman Shaw, the principal creator of the 'Queen Anne Revival' style, to redesign the Quadrant. However, his plans, in the manner of a fifteenth-century Florentine palazzo, were highly unpopular with the shopkeepers, who objected to the height, the general disruption and the obscuring of the windows by rusticated basement pillars. The managing director of Regent Street's most 'establishment' drapery store, Swan and Edgar, declared, 'I would almost say that rather than have such a building . . . we would remove or shut up shop.' Nourished by the contemporary cult of ugliness, Nimbyism may be more prominent in twenty-first-century Britain, but it is not new.

Despite the protests, the Crown, as Simon Jenkins put it, was 'eager to rid itself of Nash's masterpiece'. A trio of architectural heavies, all schooled in the baroque beaux arts of late nineteenth-century Europe, were brought in to fit the plans to the needs of the shopkeepers. Hundreds of metres of terraces between Waterloo Place and Langham Place were demolished and, delayed by the First World War, a new Regent Street emerged to the designs of Reginald Blomfield, Aston Webb and Ernest Newton: in stone not stucco, seven storeys not four or five, and rather heavier than before in tone and timbre; an imperial heavy brigade not a Regency recce, though not without character.

Meanwhile architectural writers were getting distinctly nervous as they began to rediscover John Nash's merits. In 1910, his original plans for Regent Street and Regent's Park were exhibited at a public exhibition and found to be rather good. The popular topographer, Edwin Beresford Chancellor, wrote in 1927 (the same year that George V rode in state down the new Regent Street to open it):

There will always be an argument as to whether this is an improvement or not . . . are the angels, one wonders, in favour of the immense structures that tower up towards their abode . . . or would they rather have retained the gracious curve which Nash gave to his street? . . . In the new Regent Street, we have many wonderful and some amazing buildings . . . But there are some who regret the passing of the old street whose homogeneity is irretrievably lost and whose quiet distinction has been replaced by something very large and very expensive; but just a little ostentatious and, as some think, not a little vulgar.

Regent Street was the first nineteenth-century street to punch heartlessly through a slum, though far from the last. It was English development on a European scale – not once but twice within a century. For sparing All Souls' Church, some sewers and Lower Regent Street, the Regent Street of John Nash and James Burton is totally destroyed. What we see now is the Edwardian vision of the 'city beautiful', maybe better, certainly bigger than the original, and made of imperial stone not Regency stucco.

In 1927, it was not yet time for full-throated resistance to the demolition of London's historic streets. The new buildings were good and they were still centred around streets. But many of those who expressed concern about the fate of Regent Street in the 1920s went on to argue against the destruction of Carlton House Terrace and the Adelphi in the 1930s, and thence to the creation of the Georgian Group in 1937 and a rapidly growing desire to preserve the remaining streets of Georgian England.

Nash's Regent Street may have been an imperfect exercise in picturesque town planning. It might have been short-lived: some buildings lasted less than a century. But its creation was heroic and it did not die in vain.

Chapter 14
NORTHUMBERLAND AVENUE
How the Victorians managed traffic

A double row of carts and wagons, the generality drawn by horses as large as elephants, each row striving in a different direction, and not infrequently brought to a standstill. Oh, the cracking of the whips, the shouts and oaths of the carters, and the grating of wheels upon the enormous stones that formed the pavement.
George Barrow, *Lavengo*, 1851

At some point in the 1840s, London became the most populous city in the world. Despite nearly 200 years of physical growth since the Stuart 'green belt' was unfastened in 1667, it was bursting at the seams. The Georgian houses of Spitalfields or Stepney were sublet by the room, so that homes designed for one household might house eight. The medieval streets of the City or the Strand were struggling to convey the thousands of hackney carriages and commuters disgorged from the train stations and the omnibuses. The sewers were overwhelmed with the hundreds of thousands of new water closets and the millions of people using them.

London's governance and infrastructure had not kept pace with its growth. Over 300 local government bodies, over 250 Acts of Parliament, an impenetrable multitude of parish vestries, paving boards and tollgate trusts were endlessly able to wallow in inertia and to pass the buck amongst themselves.

Encouraged by the campaigning social reformer, Edwin Chadwick, and obliged by cholera and typhus epidemics, in 1855 Parliament finally merged the parish boards into fifteen 'district boards', obliged direct election of parish boards and created the Metropolitan Board of Works, which was given responsibility for sewers and infrastructure throughout the capital. Was London's infrastructure finally going to catch up with the city's size and needs?

Unfortunately, the cost of Regent Street cast a long shadow. John Nash's plans for the street had been conceived with three aims: 'Utility to the Public', 'Beauty of Metropolis' and 'Practicability'. These were not a bad public works variant of Vitruvius's architectural principles of *firmitas*, *utilitas* and *venustas*, or 'strength', 'utility' and 'beauty'. However, as we have seen, once George IV died, John Nash lost his protector, was dismissed from his job and severely, and rather unfairly, criticised by a parliamentary committee for 'inexcusable irregularity and great negligence'.

The Duke of Wellington personally blocked the baronetcy that the king had requested for him and his ongoing work, for example on Buckingham Palace, was suspended. Most ominously for the future, the Select Committee on Metropolis Improvements reported in 1838 that 'embellishment' should henceforth be 'regarded as a matter of subordinate importance'. Victorian Britain did not like spending the taxpayers' money. It only did so reluctantly and when compelled by events.

One priority for urban improvement was clearly the sewers. Another was traffic. For the most quintessential phenomenon of Victorian London, though forgotten today, was the equine traffic jam. The thousands of horse-drawn hackney cabs, barouches, dogcarts, landaus, hansom cabs, clarences, tilburies, omnibuses and heaven knows how many other types of coach may not have emitted noxious fumes; but their horses did excrete. And the longer they stood stationary, as wheels jammed against wheels, the worse the smell and the higher the piles into which passing pedestrians might inadvertently step.

A third priority was what we would now call 'urban regeneration', but which at the time expressed itself as a fear about the moral, political and sanitary consequences of the girdle of dangerously overcrowded neighbourhoods that surrounded the Cities of London and Westminster. Even before the creation of the Metropolitan Board of Works, the Select Committee on Metropolis Improvements had reported to Parliament in 1838:

> There are some districts in this vast city through which no great thoroughfares pass, and which being wholly occupied by a dense population, composed of the lowest class of labourers, entirely secluded from the observation and influence of wealthier and better educated neighbours, exhibit a state of moral and physical degradation deeply to be deplored . . . The moral condition of these poorer occupants must necessarily be improved by immediate communications with a more respectable inhabitancy; and the introduction at the same time of improved habits and a freer circulation of air, will tend materially to extirpate those prevalent diseases which are now not only so destructive among themselves, but so dangerous to the neighbourhood around them.

An editorial in *The Times* approved: 'As we cut through our woods and roads through our forests, so it should be our policy to divide these thick jungles of crime and misery.' Thus began the Victorian programme of driving new streets through dense slums to 'aerate' them, improve traffic, underpin them with sewers and encourage social mingling. But whereas Nash had used Regent Street as a shoreline to hem in the slums, the ambition now was to destroy them with streets. New Oxford Street, Shaftesbury Avenue and Charing Cross Road were driven through the 'rookeries' of St Giles; Victoria Street sliced through the slums of 'Devil's Acre' between Westminster and Victoria Station; and Commercial Street erased some of the courts, yards and cesspits of Spitalfields and Whitechapel.

At first the street creation was led by the Commissioners of Woods, Forests and Land Revenues (who, appropriately, were overseen by one of John Nash's protégé's, James Pennethorne).[60] They were rechristened the Commissioners of Works and Public Buildings and then replaced in 1855 by the Metropolitan Board of Works, whose main programme was the brilliantly executed and conceived Embankment project.

Other new streets were more mixed in their consequences. New Oxford Street was a rational new connection, but economics required a narrower street than James Pennethorne imagined and the neighbourhood was not transformed. No new homes were provided for the poor souls who were displaced and they could not, as had been hoped, move to the growing suburbs, even if they could afford to, due to the casual nature of their work in the service economy. The poorest needed constantly to be on site and available for work.

The overcrowding became even worse. In 1841, the neighbourhood had just under five people living in it per room. By 1847, *after* New Oxford Street was completed, this had increased to eight per room. Charles Dickens was unimpressed: 'Thus, we make our New Oxford Streets, and our other new streets, never heeding, never asking, where the wretches whom we clear out, crowd.'

The Times agreed: 'The dock and wharf labourer, the porter and costermonger cannot remove. You may pull down their wretched homes; they must find others, and make their new dwellings more crowded and wretched than their old ones. The tailor, shoemaker and other workmen are in much the same position. It is mockery to speak of the suburbs to them.'

Undeterred, and buoyed by its undoubted success on the Embankment, in June 1874 the Metropolitan Board of Works purchased the land on which they were to create one of central London's newest streets: Northumberland Avenue. However, this time, instead of pulling down multiple homes of the very poorest, they were minded to demolish only one home, though of the very richest.

Few aristocrats can have been as delighted by the death of Elizabeth I and the accession of James I in 1603 as was Henry Howard. He had consistently failed to win the Queen's favour, bedevilled by rumours of his Catholicism and correspondence with Mary, Queen of Scots. His attempts at flattery were crude and did not impress. Quite simply, the Queen did not like him. Howard spent at least one spell in Fleet Prison and was reduced to travelling in Europe to keep out of trouble.

James I, it transpired, was more readily flattered. Whilst James was still waiting for his aunt to die, Henry Howard showered the Scottish king with letters proffering supportive advice and was rewarded, within little more than a year of James's succession, with a plethora of creations and elevations:

as Privy Counsellor, Garter-recipient, High Steward of Oxford, Chancellor of Cambridge, Lord Privy Seal, Baron Marnhull and 1st Earl of Northumberland. After sixty years of fruitless advent, all of Howard's Christmases had come at once.

Such sudden wealth and influence deserved a London base and within a couple of years of James's accession, Howard was buying plots, cottages and gardens from the Cooke, Reade, Brett and Apsley families in Charing Cross, where Whitehall and the Strand meet. On this land he built Northumberland House, the last and one of the greatest of the Strand palaces, which his heir and their descendants (latterly the Dukes of Northumberland) were to use as their London home for nearly 300 years and uniquely for the palaces of the Strand, survived into the age of the photograph.

Northumberland House was a cross between a medieval hall, an Oxbridge college and a Renaissance palace; built of brick with stone dressings, surrounded by four flanking towers, with a great hall and separate apartments arranged around a central courtyard. Behind, a fashionably formal parterre garden stretched down nearly to the river; in front, an elaborately incorrect four-storey gatehouse muddled ornate pilasters, eight niches, and an elongated oriel window in a pattern that captured some of the form and none of the proportional spirit of classical design.

Above, in the way that can still be seen at Hardwick Hall in Derbyshire, stone letters in an 'openwork' parapet spelt out a motto or initials. They did not survive to be painted or photographed, but we know they were there because at the Queen's funeral in 1619, one letter fell off and killed one William Appleyard. His burial register at St Martin-in-the-Fields records the cause of death through a falling letter 'S': presumably a unique entry in all the country's parish records.

Over 250 years, fashion and society moved consistently west to St James's and Mayfair. The Strand and Whitehall were no longer places to live, but places to work. However, the Dukes of Northumberland continued to cherish, use and invest in their London palace. The garden was replanned, periodic fire damage was made good, an 11-foot-long lion (the family symbol) was placed above the gatehouse, and new garden wings with a monumental Picture Gallery were added. Above all, the fashionable architects of the day were commissioned to reimagine and reinvent the interior. One of Robert Adam's most celebrated commissions was the Glass Drawing Room in Northumberland House, one of the redecorated state rooms.

The last of the Strand's great palaces, and the closest to Whitehall, was also the last to be demolished. By 1850 no others survived. Left to his own devices, Algernon Percy, the 6th Duke of Northumberland would probably have continued to use his ancestors' home. However, the Metropolitan Board of Works had other plans, and this brings us back to the traffic.

For over a century, it had been difficult to get to the wharfs on the river from Charing Cross. An updated 1720 edition of John Stow's classic *Survey of the Cities of London and Westminster* described the main route, Hartshorn Lane, as 'a Place much clogged and pestered with Carts repairing to the Wharfs; and therefore not well inhabited.' The creation of the Embankment to the south and Trafalgar Square to the north-west only exacerbated the problem. When a fire damaged the building, the duke sold the house for half a million pounds (about £47 million in 2021 money) and, not without some criticism, the Board of Works promptly pulled it all down.

Not everything was lost. Some of the internal fittings were repositioned in other Percy residences, the entrance lion was re-erected at Syon House in west London, and one archway has ended up at a health centre at Bromley-by-Bow in east London.

It now seems inconceivable that such a historic treasure, so rich with physical value and with historical connotations, could be so readily destroyed. But no one cared less for heritage than the Victorians; the future they could create was too efficient and elegant to bother looking back. Hauntingly, in the last photos taken of Northumberland House, the shadow of Nelson's column can be seen falling across its Renaissance facade.

What to put in Northumberland House's place? One common misunderstanding of London's planning history is that it was unregulated. It was not. All new Victorian streets had to follow the 1844 Metropolitan Building Act, which had replaced and extended the 1774 London Building Act's geographic reach. The Metropolitan Board of Works, which was creating Northumberland Avenue, had to be particularly stringent, as it was also their job to administer the Act.

One of the Act's stipulations was that no new streets should be less than 40 feet wide and that buildings adjacent to them should be no higher than the width of the street. In such a central location, the Board wanted to build high and to recoup their investment. They had in mind a street of six- and seven-storey hotels and offices, making use of the new technology of metal-framed buildings. This in turn required a wide street, which is what they laid out. The street itself, as a thoroughfare, was opened speedily in 1876, with this legal potential for 'building high' embedded in its width.

In booming, late imperial London, the buildings quickly followed. The confident headquarters of the Royal Colonial Society or for Thomas Edison's London operations; the Grand, the Metropole and the Victoria hotels, with hundreds of bedrooms, huge kitchens, and elaborate function rooms for commercial and club dinners. All were big and burlesque in their style. Supposedly, the oriel window and arched entrance to the Victoria Hotel was in conscious (though much larger) imitation of Northumberland House.

Osbert Lancaster described better than anyone the 'terrifying proportions and elephantine decoration' of late Victorian and Edwardian baroque that predominates in Northumberland Avenue:

> Beneath circular windows the size of the round pond, vast swags of Brobdingnagian fruit sprawled across the facade, threatening all beneath with instant annihilation should their security have been overestimated by the architect. In attitudes of acute discomfort, nymphs and tribal deities of excessive female physique and alarming size balanced precariously on broken pediments, threatening the passer-by with a shower of stone fruit from the cavernous interiors of their inevitable cornucopia.

Northumberland Avenue rapidly found its niche. Its reputation for hotels was so firmly and so fast established that Arthur Conan Doyle boarded several of Sherlock Holmes' hotel-resident clients here – including Sir Henry Baskerville at the fictional Northumberland Hotel in *The Hound of the Baskervilles*. Edward VII entertained guests at the Hotel Metropole and clubs and societies queued to host their dinners or their balls there. One of the great Victorian hoteliers, Frederick Gordon, made much of his fortune in Northumberland Avenue.

The twentieth century was less kind. The new 1930s hotels of Park Lane were able to out-compete them on scale and access to a park view, and several buildings were blitzed in the war (though, thankfully, with more damage internally than externally).

More grievously, the rising British state, expanding through war, empire and socialism, overflowed its Whitehall home during the First World War and proceeded to use much of the street for offices and government accommodation for most of the twentieth century. MI9 the body founded to help allied prisoners' escape and evasion behind enemy lines, worked for its first year from a reportedly 'vast' room 424 in the Hotel Metropole (MI9's historian talked of the room's 'wide open spaces') before moving to Sussex.

Mid-twentieth century Northumberland Avenue was a dismal place. Its lavishly late Victorian corbels and pediments were smeared with coal and had degraded from hotels for prosperous Americans to unloved and internally butchered government offices. The historian Lionel Esher contrasted his 1951 visit to the Festival of Britain on the South Bank with 'the gloomy chasm of Northumberland Avenue'.

However, over the last quarter-century the street has been transformed: pavements have been widened and facades cleaned, offices have turned back into hotels, and London plane trees have grown. Like so many *Monopoly* streets, Northumberland Avenue has turned full circle. The faint stylistic echoes of Northumberland House no longer seem quite ridiculous.

What began as a shoddy act of civil despoilation under an inefficient chair of a public body, created a cliché of a street for passing trade or for military officials jammed into hotel rooms, and was unloved and under-cared for during seventy years, has recently blossomed as an avenue whose height and width, cleaned stone facades and beaux-arts excess, ironically recalls Paris more than it does London. For a street that was built on the cheap, that's not bad.

Materials, decoration, paving, street trees and street furniture really matter. This is why the nineteenth-century rebuilding of Vienna or of Paris is loved globally, but why the twentieth-century rebuilding of London has proved so pathetically temporary. If you love a street, or a city, it will love you back.

Chapter 15

VINE STREET

Lost streets

Where is Vine Street?
The author's son, 2021

It is a good question. Where and what is Vine Street? And why did Victor Watson choose a short alley tucked into the triangle between Piccadilly and curvaceous Regent Street? It used to be three times in length. London has lost surprisingly few streets in its long history, but Vine Street is (very nearly) one of them.

Why do streets and public spaces disappear, and which types of streets tend to meet the urban chopping board – and what matters most: who owns the surrounding buildings, who uses them, or the geography of where streets go?

Vine Street's ownership has been consistent for half a millennium, but it only properly existed as a street that went somewhere for 130 years. Seized from monastic ownership by Henry VIII, it is still owned by the Crown and was part of the land leased by Charles II to Henry Jermyn, his mother's

207

confidant and the developer of St James's. Vine Street's creation, alongside Swallow Street and Glasshouse Street, was very much a commercial afterthought in Jermyn's development of fashionable St James's: squashed into the unmodish north-east of the lands he leased from the Crown, furthest away from the delights of court and St James's Park.

It was a dark, narrow L-shaped street, turning the corner from running north-south to east-west. It was not a place for the rich to live but for their needs to be serviced; for their marquetry to be made or their servants' beer to be brewed: a carpenter's yard and a brewery were amongst the early tenants. The street's name is probably inspired by a tavern (late seventeenth-century England was too cold for grapes) and a neighbouring street, Air Street, is named after a brewer; a little later, two sculptors lived on Vine Street. Prostitutes were amongst the street's residents, including at least one who focused on, or at any rate accepted, more 'specialised' requirements.[61]

John Nash's creation of Regent Street sliced Vine Street in two. The northern half was then entirely lost in Regent Street's Edwardian enlargement, when two blocks were combined into one. Vine Street's rump, little more than a short alley running east-west, was a place for trade, service and social genuflection: it was the back door to hotels and concert halls, a local courthouse and a police station. For forty-seven years, Vine Street was the back entrance to London's best-selling concert hall, the extravagantly decorated St James's Hall.

However, the police station was Victor Watson's excuse for choosing the street, alongside orange Bow Street and the misnamed Marlborough Street, which both had magistrates' courts. Even Vine Street's court closed in 1940, five years after Victor Watson's fleeting street-scouting 1935 London visit. Nowadays, though many recognise the name from *Monopoly*, no one knows where

Vine Street is. The buildings are higher and the lane darker than ever before. Late-night drunks and revellers emerging from West End pubs pee in it; but few, if any, know its name.

Vine Street was diminished because a larger new street bisected it and an extended block ate two-thirds of what remained. Its local role in helping turn the corner from Swallow Street to Warwick Street was less important than a new requirement to get from the stuccoed villas of Regent's Park to the joys of court or clubland, in Westminster or St James's. Newer beat older; longer trumped shorter.

Surprisingly few London streets have fallen victim to road-making, though several *Monopoly* streets or their near neighbours have been among the assassins. There have been two great surges of street destruction. The first was the parallel programme of nineteenth-century railway creation and metropolitan 'improvements', which began with Regent Street, continued with Northumberland Street, and ended with the last and largest, the 28-acre, £3.6 billion (in 2021 prices) Kingsway and Aldwych improvement scheme.[62]

Its most poignant victim is Wych Street, which used to run between St Clement Danes on the Strand and Drury Lane. Certainly medieval, probably Anglo-Saxon, in origin, Wych Street was a tumbledown amalgam of gable-ended, overhanging, timber-framed, elaborately fenestrated, pre-fire taverns, book-sellers, homes and offices, pepper-potted with Georgian insertions and smeared everywhere with the soot and stains of a thousand years. Sunless and dreary in the late Victorian smog, it was a street to run from or sink into.

The master prison breaker Jack Sheppard had been apprenticed on Wych Street and met there the prostitute Elizabeth Lyon, whose gratification was to help drive him to crime and, ultimately, to the gallows. Criminals conspired in the Wych Street taverns, most notoriously the Black Lion and the White Lion.

Neighbouring Holywell Street was little better. Named for the revered and bucolic springs that had once provided the City of London's generous water supply, Holywell Street was, in addition to being poor and dirty, the centre of London's pornographic book trade. An 1846 letter to *The Times* complained of the streets' windows that 'display books and pictures of the most disgusting and obscene character, and which are alike loathsome to the eye and offensive to the morals of any person of well-regulated mind'. All attempts to stamp out the trade failed: the most notorious pornographer, William Dugdale, was arrested at least five times, but two of his brothers and one of his sons nevertheless joined him in the business.

In 1900, overhung and ungovernable, both streets must have seemed, and temporally were, centuries away from the gleaming Portland stone and Edwardian baroque of the newly fashionable Strand. Why *not* drive a new route to the north through them and clean out the moral and physical degradation?

Just before they were erased (alongside Vere Street, Stanhope Street, Blackmoor Street and a half-dozen others), Londoners began to see behind the filth. Photographers scoured both streets before they were demolished. Their photographs reveal not just the streets' antiquity, but also their joyfully Victorian exuberance: the Shakespeare Head tavern had a splendid cut-glass ornamental lantern, for example.

The *Pall Mall Gazette* recorded wistfully, as the streets were being torn down:

There still remains some picturesque old patchwork buildings . . . [with] varied and uncertain angles of tottering timbers and the promiscuous arrangement of windows which protrude and overhang the little shops . . . Staircases lead to dingy shops with hilly floors and blackened beams running at all angles, drooping and groaning under the mingled weight of years and heavy tread.

If they still survived, they would all be Grade I listed, 'jewels' as Jerry White put it, that would have been 'treasured almost beyond compare'. But changing sentiment was too late. One-hundred-foot-wide Kingsway, the crescent of the anachronistically misnamed Aldwych and the twentieth-century secular temples of Bush House, Australia House and the Indian High Commission now stand where they led.

Vine Street, Wych Street and Holywell Street did make urban connections, but most London streets that have disappeared were not in fact streets, but mean courts or back alleys. They did not go from somewhere to somewhere else, but were squeezed within blocks or behind existing streets; urban cul-de-sacs stealing the land that had once been a garden or orchard in pre-modern London, but which was transformed by Georgian or Victorian landlord into cheap lodgings, warehouse or factory. There was more money in squeezing in paupers or storing beer than in failing to grow smog-stained apples.

The Kingsway scheme and neighbouring improvements destroyed far more courts and alleys than they did streets. On the unfashionable side of the Strand, where aristocratic palaces had *not* stepped down to the river, could be found Drury Court, Denman Yard, Windsor Court, Angel Court, Helmet Court, Craven Yard, Clare Court, White Horse Yard, Granby Place, Feathers Court, Clare Court and George Yard. They were mean, insanitary and insalubrious. Clare Market was described in 1903 as 'one of those filthy, dilapidated rookeries that clung desperately to a sordid existence amid a changing environment'. It had a reputation for prize fighters.

All were destroyed to be replaced with Edwardian hotels or offices in rollicking baroque or ornamented Venetian Gothic. Some inhabitants moved sideways into remaining central London slums. Most were able to escape to the rapidly growing, working-class, east London commuter suburbs accessed via cheap trains: Leyton, Walthamstow, West Ham, East Ham and Barking Town. Outer London's population trebled to two million between 1871 and 1901.

The second great surge of street destruction was the post-war wave of road widening, office development and estate creation, which ran from the 1950s to the late 1970s and which was instigated, though not necessitated, by the Blitz. Some post-war estates were squeezed into goods marshalling yards or into the no-man's-land between railway and historic street network. Other post-war offices and estates were created on bomb-damaged, but rarely bomb-destroyed, historic streets. Redevelopment was a conscious and not ineluctable choice. As always, it was the streets of the poor or the streets that led nowhere which were most at risk.

One of the saddest losses was the destruction of the three- to four-storey Carlton Mews. Designed by John Nash to stable the horses of the aristocratic and plutocratic in Carlton House Terrace, it was a uniquely 'high density' stables with carriages on the ground floor, horses on the first, and humans on the one or two storeys above. By the mid-twentieth century, as with so many mews built for horses, it was inhabited by humans and clearly delightful, as surviving photographs and descriptions attest: 'In addition to its own attractive qualities, the Mews had the charm of surprise: a passer-by could turn off Cockspur Street, through a narrow entry, and there was the double height mews complete with its tree'd court.'

The owners, the Crown Estate Commissioners, had no time for such sentimental tosh. It was listed, but the Crown did not (at the time) require planning permission and they demolished the lot. With what the doyenne of 'Lost London', Hermione Hobhouse, termed a 'philistine touch of irony', the replacement for this exquisite corner of British architectural history was an institution dedicated to the diffusion of British culture and learning overseas, the British Council. John Betjeman or Osbert Lancaster did not need to make it up.

Most inner London streets have lasted centuries. Those that have not were destroyed or cut about for many reasons: improving journey times, making money, aerating the slums or building clean flats for the respectably poor. To end at the beginning: which types of streets tend to meet the urban chopping board? Streets that do not go anywhere, that house the poor or their businesses, and have one large public or institutional landowner are the most likely to be comprehensively 'replanned'. Streets that survive tend to have a beginning and an end, to be complicated to redevelop with many owners and, more normally than not, to house or help the prosperous and well connected.

There are fewer poor nimbys than rich ones, certainly fewer effective ones, and the policemen, prostitutes, pornographers, servants and brewers of Vine Street, Wych Street and Holywell Street were not amongst their number.

Chapter 16
PARK LANE
Rotten road

An example of this absurdity evidently appears in that heap
of buildings lately erected from Oxford Road to Hyde Park
Corner whose back fronts are seen from the Park.
John Gwynn, *London and Westminster Improved*, 1766

More defiant, spurning frown and foe,
With slackened rein swift Skittles rules the Row.
Though frowning matrons champing steeds restrain,
She flaunts propriety with flapping mane.
Alfred Austin, *The Season: A Satire*, 1861

Had you been riding down Park Lane in the early summer
of 1861 or 1862, where the traffic now thunders, you might
have seen crossing your path, followed by grooms and by titled
admirers, a dashing and very young equestrienne riding side-
saddle, exquisitely dressed, nodding to the passing gentlemen, by
turns holding her hands behind her back or artfully leaning over
to listen to the compliments of a walking admirer.

This was Catherine Walters, known as 'Skittles', on her ride

215

into Hyde Park. She had arrived in London, aged sixteen or seventeen, in 1856 from her native Liverpool, where her father had been an Irish customs officer. She initially worked as a high-class prostitute, probably in the Haymarket, but such was her charm, wit and intelligence that her clients kept falling for her. Within five years she was the darling of the London scene and the future Duke of Devonshire was uncontrollably and generously in love with her.

Skittles was, by some distance, Victorian England's greatest *grande horizontale*, the equal of Nell Gwyn and very possibly one of the most skilful and successful courtesans who has ever lived. Park Lane, then at its apogee and where bucolic charm met urban fashion, was her parade ground.

Park Lane is a street of contrasts. The great themes of its history are mud, highway planning and the aristocratic love of a park view. Created backwards by accident, it was the epitome of fashion for a hundred years before falling victim to the most destructive act of road widening in London's history. No *Monopoly* street has had so varied a history, from *rus* to *urbs*. No *Monopoly* street manifests so starkly the shift from a city of horses to a city of cars, nor has risen so high or fallen so low. From rural lane to pinnacle of fashion, from *le beau monde* to a polluted traffic sewer, from unmanaged mud to an over-planned dual carriageway, Park Lane has seen it all.

Like all streets, Park Lane exists because it was the easiest way to get from A to B. In this case it was the rural route north to the village of Tyburn and the hanging tree; carriages heading north and crowds flocking from Westminster to enjoy the hangings came this way. For centuries it was known as Tyburn Lane, but its nature started to change entirely when Henry VIII seized the manor of Hyde and transformed it into a deer park. To keep the animals in and the people out, Charles II enclosed the royal park with a brick wall. Rather than being a purely rural lane through the countryside, Tyburn Lane thus became a more monotonous lane along an estate wall, rather as you might see today at Blenheim or at Woburn.

But if the Hyde Estate to the west was to be preserved for princely pleasures, the owner of the Ebury Estate, Sir Richard Grosvenor, had a different vision for the east. As his agents started to build out the hundred acres of Mayfair, their master plan initially turned its back on the deer park. After all, what was the interest in staring at a brick wall, and Tyburn Lane itself was busy, muddy and pockmarked. Nearly all the first streets and squares to be built in Mayfair faced inwardly or to the south-east. Only one terrace, King's Row, faced on to the street and this was set back behind freshly planted trees.

When Dunraven Street was built in the 1750s, it turned its back on the park and its face to the new street. Tyburn Lane was a busy public place best avoided. The new Dunraven Street by contrast could be controlled by the estate: gates and beadles permitted access only to residents, visitors or respectably dressed tradesmen. Rents were high at the eastern end of Grosvenor Square nearer London, but *further* from the park.

The estate's main interest in Hyde Park was utilitarian; it was a source of water. A Chelsea Water Works Company was incorporated under an Act of 1722 and obtained a royal warrant to build a reservoir at Hyde Park's eastern edge.[63] The water itself came via a network of canals and basins linking to the Grosvenor estate's Pimlico land, whence it was pumped to the higher land in Hyde Park.

Nevertheless, the increased traffic going up and down the lane was overwhelming the Middlesex mud. In 1741, the Kensington

Turnpike Trust (one of the first of a series of Turnpike Trusts that were to manage the main thoroughfares out of London for over a century) took over the street's management. Parliament legislated for them, because 'by reason of many heavy Carriages, frequently passing through the same, [Tyburn Lane had] become very ruinous, and many Parts thereof are, in the Winter and wet Seasons, so bad, that the same are dangerous to Passengers.' The Trust paved the road's southern end, but merely repaired with ballast from the estate's building operations the northern part running past the Grosvenor Estate.

More consequential than the changes in the street's management from the 1740s were the wider improvements overseen by the architect Decimus Burton and the road builder James McAdam during the 1820s. The high brick wall was replaced with elegant railings, the entrance gate was better aligned to the street pattern, and the road surface was improved using the revolutionary new 'macadam method' pioneered by James McAdam's father – a cambered surface of gravel placed above large stones, representing the single greatest improvement to road construction since the Romans.

To the south, Decimus Burton designed a fashionably Roman Ionic entrance to the park at Hyde Park Corner. No longer a muddy road by a long wall, but an elegant street between park and mansions, Tyburn Lane was reborn as Park Lane. Dozens of houses were remodelled to face the park, with new verandas or balconies fitted looking to the west – and the park views paid. Old Dudley House leased for £6,510 in 1789. By 1826 it was worth £24,000. In 1845, one Mayfair house was advertised as 'one of the most recherché in London, enjoying the Varied Scenery of the Park, the distant Hills of Surrey, and the salubrious Air therefrom, while at the same time it is placed in the Centre of Fashion.'

One of the timeless rules of property prices is that people want to be in the middle of things, but they will pay even more to be in the middle of things with a nice garden or easy access to greenery. During the nineteenth century, as London filled with people and smog, this value only increased and Park Lane fitted the bill. Its social trajectory was ever upwards, though always tinged with the taint of rather more fashion than sense. Park Lane was London home to the ancient but profligate Crawley family in William Makepeace Thackeray's *Vanity Fair* and the voguish 'Park Lane shoulder knot aristocracy' are contrasted to those living in the socially fading Bloomsbury.[64]

By 1871, the largest homes in Mayfair with the most servants were on or next to Park Lane. The average house on Grosvenor Square, that Mayfair epitome of late Georgian fashion, had just under eleven servants. The Earl and Countess of Dudley on Park Lane had twenty-eight domestic servants, two coachmen and seven stable 'helpers'. Their neighbours included the ballast of old money, though living in newly erected mansions such as Grosvenor House or Dorchester House, as well as the pinnacles of new money: banking Rothschilds and art-dealing Duveens, whose fortune was based on the simple observation that 'Europe has a great deal of art, and America has a great deal of money.'

Just as Samuel Pepys had walked fashionably in St James's Park in the seventeenth century, so Victorian society, demi-monde or fully respectable, began to patronise Hyde Park. Anyone riding or in a carriage and of smart appearance was permitted entry via the elegant, newly created gates set within the 1820s railings. (Thus it can correctly be said that prostitutes were permitted access to the park, but only if they could ride.) Everyone who was anyone or who wished to be anyone came to be seen.

The Frenchman Francis Wey, who visited London in 1849,

recalled, 'It is a unique experience, in the very heart of a large city, to embrace at a glance, pompous equipages with powdered attendants and magnificent horses and rustic herds of cows, sheep and goats with elegant women trailing silks and laces among them.' One carriage drive (East Carriage Drive) ran parallel to Park Lane. But Hyde Park's most fashionable riding route was Rotten Row, which ran west from the junction of Park Lane with Hyde Park Corner at ninety degrees from Park Lane. However, fashionable riders or their children could be seen throughout the park at different times of day.

Another French visitor, Hippolyte Taine, recalled:

On fine summer evenings all the youth, beauty, celebrity and wealth of London may be seen on horseback on Rotten Row. [The Duke of Wellington] with his horse walking at a slow pace . . . everyone takes off his hat; and the Duke smiles to the right and to the left . . . All of a sudden a couple come forward at a quick pace. There is room for them and their horses in the midst of Rotten Row, however full it may be, for everyone is eager to make way for them: it is the Queen and her husband, without martial and splendour, without a single naked sword in sight.

This was the world that Park Lane's villas overlooked and, as London grew, their relative remoteness from the City or Whitehall was less problematic. After all, they were only up Constitution Hill from the new royal residence at Buckingham Palace. It is hardly surprising that this is where Catherine Walters or 'Skittles' chose to live. Not only could she show off her superb horsemanship every day in the park. She was also, not to put too fine a point on it, close to her clientele.

Contemporary biographers, who may have been exaggerating,

PARK LANE

recorded that Skittles befriended the owner of a livery stable, who lent her the best horse and carriages and paid for riding habits so close-fitting that she wore nothing underneath them when she crossed Park Lane to go riding in the park. She certainly shopped for riding habits at the Savile Row tailors, Henry Poole & Co. They have over forty pages relating to her orders in their ledgers: 'riding habits ordered in black beaver lined in silk with velvet collars, light blue silk double sewn, bound and braided, blue diagonal Angola lined with silk and grey velvet with silk velvet collar facings and cuffs.'

The effect was clearly electric. One witness, calling her Anonyma, recalled:

> Expectation is raised to its highest pitch: a handsome woman drives rapidly by in a carriage drawn by thoroughbred ponies of surpassing shape and action; the driver is attired in the pork pie hat and the Poole paletot introduced by Anonyma; but alas!, she caused no effect at all, for she is not Anonyma; she is only the Duchess of A–, the Marchioness of B–, the Countess of C–, or some other of Anonyma's many imitators. The crowd, disappointed, reseat themselves, and wait. Another pony carriage succeeds – and another – with the same depressing result.

> At last their patience is rewarded. Anonyma and her ponies appear, and they are satisfied. She threads her way dexterously, with an unconscious air, through the throng, commented upon by the hundreds who admire and the hundreds who envy her. She pulls up her ponies to speak to an acquaintance, and her carriage is instantly surrounded by a multitude; she turns and drives back again towards Apsley House, and then away into the unknown world, nobody knows whither.

221

Who paid for this equestrian finery? Her lovers, clients, friends and financial supporters (it is impossible now to define precise relationships) included the heir to the Duke of Devonshire and the Prince of Wales (the future King Edward VII). Skittles had a rare ability to remain on friendly terms with her former 'friends'. King Edward VII supposedly settled an annuity on her, so grateful was he for the return of his letters. The Duke of Devonshire bought her a Mayfair home and settled £2,000 on her annually, a sum that was continued after his death in 1908. Her last recorded 'grand passion' was in 1879, when she was forty and her lover, Gerald de Saumarez, was nineteen. She lived on at 15 South Street, round the corner from Park Lane, into her eighties, only dying in 1920.

Like Skittles, Park Lane's modish pleasures and charm survived into the twentieth century, but increasingly not as a place to live but a place to be seen. Though it is true that the stylish amalgam of minor royalty, self-publicity and new money that was Lord Louis and Lady Edwina Mountbatten moved *into* Park Lane in the 1920s. They created London's first express lift-accessed penthouse (stylishly simple moderne and nautically themed) in Brook House. However, Edwina had inherited Brook House from her German-born banking grandfather, Ernest Cassel, and, after Louis Mountbatten had created a replica of his Royal Navy cabin complete with cork wall lining and a brass handrail, they sold the house in 1931, complaining that 'socialist' taxes obliged the divestment.

Others made the same decision. With agricultural incomes falling and servants' wages, income tax and death duties all rising, fewer aristocratic families could afford to keep palatial Park Lane homes merely for the London season. Dorchester House, Brook House, Grosvenor House and Camelford House were all demolished in the 1920s or 1930s, one of London's greatest architectural losses. The rich moved into apartments or smaller houses on side streets and huge new hotels were thrown up. Being higher and heavier, they could cope better with the noise and nuisance from the growing and increasingly vehicular traffic.

'Each man kills the thing he loves.' Success certainly did for Park Lane. Noise from buses had first been complained about in 1905, but there had been less noisy, equestrian traffic jams for decades. As early as 1851 a short section of Park Lane had been widened to ease the traffic and more followed in 1866. When demonstrators in favour of the Second Reform Bill destroyed some of the boundary railings, they were not replaced.

But it was no good. As twentieth-century London transformed from a city of horses to a city of cars, Park Lane was getting noisier and nastier and jamming up. It epitomised better than any street the widespread phenomenon whereby main streets, historically sought after and valuable due to their scale and prestige (look at the colouring of London's main streets on the Charles Booth maps), became less attractive in the age of motor traffic. A 1956 Metropolitan Police report estimated that 91,000 vehicles were passing Hyde Park Corner every twelve hours.

One answer, as the Dutch and Danish did and the Parisians are now doing, would have been to ask how to manage the need for so much traffic in central London. Might people 'get through' with less collateral pollution and vehicular clutter? But asking that question was not 'the spirit of age'. In Britain, highways' design was increasingly a simple matter of permitting cars to drive as fast as possible with no thought as to the consequences. For the cars to progress, however, Hyde Park needed to shrink and Park Lane needed to grow.

East Carriage Drive, an existing bridleway inside Hyde Park, was appropriated and turned into the northbound carriageway. The house beside the Duke of Wellington's residence at Apsley House was destroyed and Apsley House turned into a traffic island. Twenty acres of park were lost and ninety-five trees were felled. Park Lane became part of the fearsomely titled London Inner Ring Road. It was London's largest road widening programme for sixty years.

For Park Lane, as a place, the results were predictably disastrous. It was murdered by the dual carriageway. What had once been one of London's most pleasant streets entirely lost its remaining bucolic character. The international rich still come to Park Lane, but fleetingly. Hollywood actors used to stay there. In 1980, Peter Sellers had the heart attack which killed him at the Dorchester hotel at 53 Park Lane. Roman Abramovich did the deal that bought Chelsea Football Club at the same hotel. But few stay long. Who would?

Not everything has changed. Park Lane remains a boundary. As parliamentary forces once enclosed London there with 'bulworkes presently raised in the fields' to fortify the city against royal invasion, and as Park Lane once marked the edge of central London for the 1846 Royal Commission on Metropolitan Railway termini, so today it forms the western boundary of the London congestion zone. But Park Lane is no longer a place, let alone a fashionable street. Several generations of London-resident *Monopoly* players have grown up wondering why Park Lane is worth so much? There may be big hotels, but what a non-event of a street. The cachet is lost.

However, there may be signs of hope. In 2008, the then Mayor of London, Boris Johnson, considered building a tunnel underneath the road so that it could be liberated again. The plans came to nothing, but fines were introduced for idling coaches fouling up the air. In 2020, new bus and bike lanes were introduced on Park Lane, under cover of the global Covid pandemic. Will these changes be permanent or temporary? At the time of writing, it is not yet clear.

There is a growing consensus, certainly among the young on the left and right, that large private cars are not a very sensible way to get about in the town and city centres. The future, equally fast and far healthier, is micro-mobility: bikes, motorbikes, scooters and electric rickshaws, with cars and vans restricted to specific routes, certain users (the disabled) or particular times of day. It is a transformation that Amsterdam, Copenhagen and Paris have already begun. If London were to emulate them, then Park Lane could surely be one of the first streets to re-blossom, to rediscover its role, and to become once again not a drain for speeding cars, but a gateway to the park.

London, and Londoners, would be thankful.

Chapter 17

THE ANGEL, ISLINGTON

'The widest-known hostelry in the world'

Ermine Street, with its successors the Old North Road and the Great North Road, is still to me the one great historic highway in which the whole history of an English through-way from prehistoric trackway to modern motorway can be read, linking as it does the capital of England with the capital of Scotland.
Sir William Addison, *The Old Roads of England*

The link between travelling and drinking is as old as man. For most of time, journeys between towns and cities have been expensive, risky and slow, and therefore inns were brief interludes of comfort, rest and safety. No single element of national culture has been as constant through the vicissitudes of English history as the inn with its roaring fire, good ale, roast beef and (doubtless mock) Tudor panelling.

English inns were first built by monasteries as pilgrims'

hostelries. The Tabard in Southwark, where Chaucer's pilgrims dined, belonged to Hyde Abbey and served the road to Canterbury. The New Inn in Gloucester was built by the monk John Twyning and served pilgrims to the shrine of Edward II. The English good fortune was that the dissolution of the monasteries, and the resulting sale of monastic taverns to their lay tenants, coincided with a period of rapidly improving domestic comfort.

Liberated from a rather fitful monastic mortification of the flesh, exposed to 'market forces' and ultimately funded by the roaring wool trade, Elizabethan taverns underwent a service revolution in their comfort and a supply revolution in their frequency. This was celebrated in fiction by Shakespeare's archetypal Falstaff, whose boisterous love of the Boar's Head Inn, and its landlady, Mistress Quickly, has echoed down the ages.

It was celebrated in reality by the Jacobean traveller Fynes Moryson, who observed: 'The World affords not such Innes as England hath.' He knew what he was talking about, as he had journeyed through eleven other countries from Scotland in the north-west via Poland to Turkey in the south-east. By the late sixteenth century there may have been over 15,000 English alehouses, taverns and inns.

For many hundreds of years, as you journeyed cautiously and possibly protected by armed patrol into the rural north, up the hill of St John's Street from Aldersgate or Smithfield, the first tavern that you came to was the Angel, formerly the Sheepcote. On a clear day you could turn round and see the steeples, chimneys and curling smoke of London, with the New River reservoir in front and the densely wooded rising slopes of Denmark, Forest, Gypsy and Herne hills beyond, now part of inner south London, but then miles beyond it.

Why Victor Watson incongruously named one place on the *Monopoly* board after a tavern and not a street is a little unclear.

The Waddington company history recounts that he had tea there with his secretary Marjory Phillips at the end of a taxi ride around London and they chose it rather than looking further. It may have been on the way back to King's Cross and their train back to Leeds. He was probably unaware of how significantly the construction of the New Road bypass had affected the Angel, but Watson certainly achieved some light blue continuity with Euston Road and Pentonville Road to its west.

It is fortunate that he did, for the story of the Angel tells us not of the streets *within* the Cities of London or Westminster but of the roads that radiated *out* from them, of the coaches and trams that ran along them, and of the taverns that kept people safe as they did. How did people get to and from the centre and how were they adequately fed and watered as they journeyed? Bad roads and good taverns was the answer. The Angel Inn in the hilltop Middlesex village of Islington was the first country tavern as you headed up the muddy and dangerous Great North Road, less the end of London than the start of the rest of England.

England's medieval roads were obviously rough, slow and dangerous by any modern benchmark. Documentary references to their state are sparse, but the snippets are not encouraging. In 1357, the Fosse Way was blocked with trenches, piles and trees; in 1386 the high road from Egham to Staines was obstructed by two 'wells', 12 feet wide and 8 feet deep; and in 1399, so impassable were the roads with the wet weather that Parliament was delayed.

Yet they cannot have been *so* inadequate for the comparably small amount of traffic that used them. Chaucer's *The Canterbury Tales* makes no complaint, or even mention, of the state of the road from London to Canterbury. We know that heavy goods did regularly use the roads: stone for the building of Vale Royal Abbey was transported by road, with the carters making two round trips of six miles every day, even in winter.

Kings were able to move around the country surprisingly fast and with metronomic consistency come rain or shine. King John had only one month of his reign with no move and that was when he was besieging Rochester Castle and Edward I averaged nine moves a month. John Leland, travelling around 1540, rarely complained of the roads.

However, by 1586 when William Harrison was travelling, he complained that the state of the roads had deteriorated sharply over the past twenty years. This was partly due to more traffic with a growing economy, but also due to the dissolution of the monasteries. Monks had effected much of what little medieval road maintenance was done, as surviving royal writs demonstrate. As with the care of the sick and the maintenance of the poor, the destruction of the monkish support net begged the question: what was to be done?

At first, government tried to push the maintenance of the queen's highways upon the parishes. The Highways Act of 1555 noted 'highways being now noisome and very tedious to travel in and dangerous to all passengers and carriages'. The Act provided that two parishioners for every parish should be elected as Waywardens to inspect roads and pavements and report on what they found. Those holding land with an annual value of over £50 or more were required to supply two men with tools for four days (later increased to six) to maintain the roads. Cottagers without land were required to work themselves or provide substitutes.

The system was fine in principle, but only worked fitfully well in practice. William Harrison commented, 'The rich do so cancel their portions and the poor so loiter in their labours that of all the six scarcely two good days' work are performed.'

From 1663 therefore, the maintenance of the roads started to be privatised, with a series of Turnpike Acts creating trusts who were permitted, indeed obliged, to raise toll gates, to levy tolls, and to use the proceeds properly to maintain the roads. By the early nineteenth century, over 1,000 turnpike trusts managed over 18,000 miles, about one fifth of the kingdom's roads, typically the larger and longer ones. The rest remained the responsibility of the parishes through which they passed; most trusts managed lengths of about 20 miles.

Trusts were normally established for eleven, subsequently twenty-one years, with the intent that the improved road would be handed back to the parish. In practice this rarely happened; the need for highway maintenance does not recede. Success was not immediate and was never ubiquitous.

Nevertheless, the state of the king's roads was hugely improved by process, financial incentive and the innovation this promoted. John McAdam's revolutionary insights into road construction (the 'macadam' method of gently cambering layers of small stones) was prompted by his appointment first as a trustee of the Ayrshire Turnpike and then as surveyor to the Bristol Turnpike Trust. He went on to run a Georgian 'megacorp', employing 300 sub-surveyors advising and overseeing improvements to roads the length and breadth of the country.

England's history is one of inspired amateurs. By 1784, the state of the roads was so improved that a theatre proprietor in Bath, John Palmer, was able to revolutionise the English transport system when he conceived the idea of sending the mail by fast coach. Within a few years, passengers were accompanying the mail, eighty coaches were leaving London every night, and travellers could get from London to York in four days – as long as forty horses were available along the route! The 1775 Annual Register estimated that there were 400 coaches on the road and 17,000 four-wheeled carriages. The 'head inn' of a typical market town probably required fifty to sixty horses to be 'on call' in their yard at any one time.

Faster roads, more passengers and far more horses needed more wayside inns. After the roll out of the turnpike and before the invention of the train, the eighteenth century and early nineteenth century were the golden age of the coaching inn. As Hogarth's *Beer Street* print or the archetypal ruddy-cheeked, well-bellied, beer-swilling John Bull demonstrated, small beer and a warm tavern became a national cliché, a contented reflection of an increasingly prosperous and mercantile nation.

There are more than a hundred inns in Dickens and twenty-two in *The Pickwick Papers* alone, appropriately for a coaching novel that does not just celebrate the voyages of the Pickwick Club, but whose 'great hokey-cokey of eccentrics', as Simon Callow described it, still catches today 'an essence of what it is to be English'.

Like many other inns, the Angel had formerly been on monastic land, belonging to Clerkenwell Priory down the hill, though whether the priors ran a hostelry there is unknown. They certainly could have done with profit. The Middlesex village of Islington was rich, supplying water, vegetables and entertainment to Londoners down the hill and profiting mightily from both passing travellers and animals, and visiting Londoners spending a restful day away from the city.

By 1740, a coach from London might cost as little as 6d. A late sixteenth-century map already shows six flag-like signs on one side of the street alone: inns or taverns catering to the heavy passing trade – the Peacock, the White Lion, the Black Boy, the Three Hats, the Pied Bull and the Angel. Names were specifically chosen for easy pictorial representation for the illiterate majority. Later, appropriately for such a busy and important road, a turnpike trust was created and toll gates put across the high street.

So great was the traffic, so incessant the demand, that three of Islington High Street's taverns became great coaching inns, forming a continuous frontage of nearly 200 feet: the White Lion, the Peacock and, above all, the Angel, the first tavern you found as you headed north from London on the Great North Road, or your last chance to rest as you approached the metropolis. Here livestock traders and travellers could sleep and avoid arriving in London after dark, tired and vulnerable.

Here, in the village, land was cheaper, there was stabling for horses, pasture for livestock and a broad frontage of bedrooms (twenty-three at least) instead of the confined courtyards of a London tavern. These enormous inns were, as the *Survey of London* put it, 'the airport hotels of their time'.

We do not know the name of the first publican of the Angel, but we know that by the 1630s it was in the hands of one William Riplingham. He fell foul of London's Jacobean green belt, which forbade building within three to five miles of the city limits, and was fined for erecting the galleried courtyard ranges of rooms and stables that were to house travellers for hundreds of years.

The Angel became a well-known landmark, the most accessible and nearest bit of rural England for urban London. William Hogarth used it as the model for his 1757 print of *The stage-coach, or the country inn yard*. Public meetings were held in the assembly rooms and Thomas Paine is reputed, though not proven, to have begun drafting *Rights of Man* there.

London's growth and changing technologies profoundly affected the Angel, but it did not undermine her fame. First came London's first bypass for drovers, up the hill from the west. The

New Road sliced through the sheep pens and stable yard and left the barn-like stables on the south side of the New Road and the tavern on the north. From being a tavern on Islington's busy High Street, the Angel was now a tavern on one of expanding London's busiest junctions, with traffic approaching the City of London from both the north and the west.

As London marched up the hill and property values rose, the Angel rose from the three storeys it had been since at least the 1660s to four storeys in 1819–20 and to six storeys in 1903. Prosperous city streets grow up and the owners of the Angel made use of their more efficient and taller new building by selling off plots to the north. The Angel was a wide rural tavern no more, but a taller and thinner urban public house, where 'London began in earnest', as Charles Dickens put it in *Oliver Twist*.

Railways killed the coaching trade, but it was replaced by trams and Tubes. In 1883, the stable yard was abandoned and adapted for the horses of the London Street Tramways Company. Every horse-bus line had their depots at outer London pubs, paying for another generation of rich decoration at the Angel. In 1901, London's first deep-line Tube train, the City & South London Railway, was extended north from the city to King's Cross and opened a station just across the road from the ancient inn, complete with some of the first electronic lifts on the network.

The Angel itself was transformed from a sedate Regency tavern to a Victorian public house with 'glittering plate glass' and billiard rooms and then to an Edwardian hotel with biscuit-coloured terracotta facing, a green marble staircase and a lavishly baroque brown dome. In 1921, it evolved again from a hotel to a Lyons Café, though within the same Edwardian building. If Marjory Phillips did take tea in the Angel, before persuading Victor Watson of its merits as a stop on the *Monopoly* board, it was in the Lyons incarnation that she took her refreshments.

But through changing clienteles and sizes, the Angel maintained its fame and, normally, its fortune. The great artist of the mail coach, James Pollard, had painted the Angel. Its owners felt able in 1880 and 1901 to refer to it as 'one of the great landmarks of London' and as 'the widest-known hostelry in the world'. More convincingly, the Tube station opposite was not called Islington High Street or Pentonville Road, but merely Angel. From stagecoach to Tube line all in one name.

Not surprisingly, the mid-twentieth century was less kind to the Angel. Lyons shut their café in 1959 and as London pursued the unwinnable aim of trying to fit as many cars as possible into the city centre, the junction became that bête noir of highways officials, a 'traffic bottleneck'. The whole neighbourhood was consequently infected with the GLC's threat of road widening for a generation. When popular revulsion thankfully prevented the destruction of central London to create a 'motorway box', the Angel was listed and then converted into a Co-operative bank with an office above. Sometimes history has a happy ending. The best buildings get reused.

Crossing the road today between Islington High Street and St John Street, it is impossible to imagine the warming comfort of the village of Islington before, or conceive of why one would stop there for the night before the last dangerous descent into London. Yet through everything, from stagecoach to tram to Tube line, from a wide vision of London to a narrow view of an 'A' Road crossroads, the visceral pull of the pub remains deep.

Bolstered no doubt by *Monopoly*, so resilient is the memory of the Angel that in 1998 a new Angel was opened by J.D. Wetherspoon at 3 Islington High Street. It is beside, not within, the Edwardian terracotta fantasy on the corner, but it *is* within the original coaching tavern's wider boundaries. It is a modern urban pub, not the last rural inn before London. There are no stables, no galleried rooms above them and no garden for the drinking of ale. However, the panelling within is wooden, the design of the booths recalls (just) the wainscoting of Tudor taverns, and the framed pictures recount the pub's illustrious antecedents.

Writing shortly after the golden age of the coaching inn, William Makepeace Thackeray, like Shakespeare and Hogarth had before him, used the metaphor of honest beer to contrast the English with the French:

> Dear Lucy, you know what my wish is, –
>   I hate all your Frenchified fuss:
> Your silly entrées and made dishes
>   Were never intended for us.
> No footman in lace and in ruffles
>   Need dangle behind my arm-chair;
> And never mind seeking for truffles,
>   Although they be ever so rare.
>
> But a plain leg of mutton, my Lucy,
>   I pr'ythee get ready at three:
> Have it smoking, and tender, and juicy,
>   And what better meat can here be?
> And when it has feasted the master,
>   'Twill amply suffice for the maid;
> Meanwhile I will smoke my canaster,
>   And tipple my ale in the shade.

Plus ça change, plus c'est la même chose. Thackeray's world is distant and yet still close. No one smokes a canaster, and no good Islington liberal would be rude about the French; but their compatriots in less high-toned neighbourhoods would.[65] And wayside pubs throughout the country still proudly advertise that, like the well-stabled country inns on the Great North Road, they have a beer garden and ample parking. The Angel, Islington may now be a bank. However, John Falstaff surely lives on and is recalled in the undoubted electoral success of a famous former Islington resident, whose charms and foibles he so anticipated: the populist, free-living, ale-tippling, hyper-articulate, ex-prime minister, Boris Johnson.

RAILWAY STATIONS

Everywhere were bridges that led nowhere;
thoroughfares that were wholly impassable; Babel towers
of chimneys, wanting half their height; temporary
wooden houses and enclosures, in the most unlikely
situations; carcases of ragged tenements, and fragments
of unfinished walls and arches.
Charles Dickens, *Dombey and Son*, 1846–8

Victorian railways were big money. In a period when Treasury bonds rarely paid more than 5 per cent and far fewer companies issued shares, railway companies regularly paid dividends of 10 to 12 per cent. The results were predictable and everyone wanted a bit of the action. With regulations on the creation of joint stock companies reduced and bourgeois wealth and savings on the rise, a whole generation of Londoners invested in the creation of the railways. And they succeeded.

In one of the most astonishingly effective, if brutal, chapters in London's history, its entire surface rail network was completed in little more than twenty years. It is a network we still largely rely upon today. Many investors lost their shirt when the 'railway mania' burst, and fraudulent or merely naïve companies failed. However, many more did not and the railways *were* built. The real victims were the streets that were destroyed and their inhabitants, who were paid off and expelled with the violence and the speed, as Charles Dickens put it, of 'a great earthquake'.

Creating London's great termini, (including Victor Watson's selection of Fenchurch Street, King's Cross, Liverpool Street and Marylebone) was a great deed. And a great wrong. The Victorians did nothing by halves.

To those who believe in fate, the repeal of the 1720 Bubble Act in 1825 should be a sure sign of providence. In the same year that the world's first public railway to use steam locomotives (the Stockton and Darlington Railway) was opened, the restriction on more than five separate investors into the formation of new business ventures was finally lifted, more than a century after the South Sea Bubble had burst. When the potential for steam locomotives to move people and goods by land at hitherto unimagined speeds became clear, speculators and investors started planning potential railways everywhere, above all into London.

The problem was that to do so they needed to win control over the most sacrosanct idol of English Common Law – private property. But for the emergent railway capitalism this was no challenge at all. As Simon Jenkins has put it, 'so potent was the railway's parliamentary lobby that Britain's most sacred liberty, private property, was casually swept aside.' Hundreds of parliamentary acts granted new railway companies the right not just to exist and to build their railways, but compulsorily to purchase all the land they needed en route. Only the powerful and the very rich were able to stand in their way, which is why most of London's first railways headed north, east and south, where land was cheaper, landowners more pliant, and most leaseholders were smaller and poorer.

In south London, for instance, much of the land was owned by the dioceses of Winchester, Rochester, London and Canterbury. They were receptive to the railways and they had permitted the construction of many cheap houses whose occupants were less able to oppose demolition. One of the earliest London railways out of the parliamentary lobbying process and into physical construction was therefore the Commercial Railway, later rechristened the London & Blackwall. Pre-Victorian in conception, 'an Act for making a Railway from the Minories to Blackwall' was passed on 28 July 1836 in the reign (just) of William IV.

With a speed unthinkable to modern infrastructure planners, the land was bought and the line built in less than four years. By July 1840, a parade of brick arches marched three and a quarter miles east to West India Docks and the shipbuilding yards at Blackwall, described in 1836 as 'the finest private ship-building establishment in the world and . . . the largest establishment anywhere for repairing merchants' shipping.' A year later, an extension was built into the far east of the historic City, to Fenchurch Street, the first (and for several years the only) such excursion that the City authorities would tolerate.

Appropriately for this harbinger of modern Victorian transport, the name Fenchurch may be derived from *faenum,* the Latin for hay, fodder to the most ancient of human vehicles, the horse.[66] It must have been a quiet station initially. For the first eight years, carriages were pulled on a cable most of the journey and then descended under their own momentum to Fenchurch Street. In a pattern that was to be repeated throughout the century, around 3,000 people were evicted from the run-down courts and alleys of the East End to make way for the London & Blackwall line. The future had a cost.

Everything about the railway boom that created Fenchurch Street was ecumenical. We suffer from a growing number of prejudices against the past, but Victorian England was an open and commercial society. The wall of cash that railway promoters were able to attract came from all walks of life. One contemporary joked that businessmen's 'clerks left them to become railway jobbers. Their domestic servants studied railway journals.'

The orchestrators and managers of such investment munificence were both well-born and low. Fenchurch Street Station's architect, William Tite, was the son of a prosperous City merchant, one of a generation of architects effortlessly able to summon and shape the ghosts of the past to serve the needs of the present. His most famous building, the City of London's Royal Exchange, applied the Pantheon of Rome's military empire to serve the needs of Britain's commercial one.

By contrast, the railway's chief engineer, Robert Stephenson, had been born in a colliery village and his mother and aunt had been domestic servants. But he was also the son of the inventor of the usable steam locomotive and Victorian England's greatest autodidact, George Stephenson, who had only learnt to read when he was eighteen, and was chief surveyor and engineer of the Stockton and Darlington Railway by the time he was forty.

The railway itself was physically constructed by the hard-drinking, short-living, white van man of the nineteenth century, the navvy. Contrary to myth, most navvies were not Irish (at most one in three were and most came from the surrounding countryside). But all were a culture apart, first formed in the canal boom of the late eighteenth century, whence 'navvy' came from the canals' 'navigations'.

Navvies migrated around the country following the railway lines, were paid daily and drank copiously. They lived in shanty town huts (Dickens's 'temporary wooden houses and enclosures'), which sprang up and migrated down the line as the works were completed. Sanitation was poor; disease and drunkenness common. Hardly surprisingly, disputes and even fights with the sedentary population were frequent, though no real bitterness at the memory of the transitory navvy has lingered in popular culture. Perhaps people felt sorry for them.

The first train lines into London were a success – though not in the way that their investors had anticipated. Heading to London's docks and wharfs, like all early railways the London & Blackwall was intended to move freight more than people.[67] Why would anyone wish to travel so far on a daily basis? But it was artisans, managers and sightseers who travelled copiously and in both directions for work and pleasure; exposed to the weather in the 'stand-ups', or seated five abreast in the 'superior' class. Who can blame them? The train was about forty-five minutes quicker than the only alternative: the steam ferry down the river. Within a decade, the line was carrying 3.5 million people a year.

Unsurprisingly everyone wanted in. In 1844, 244 railway bills were placed before Parliament, and 562 in 1845. So many proposals threatened to slice through the city's streets that a Royal Commission on Metropolis Railway Termini was appointed, which reported in 1846. It followed the logic already established.

The homes of the wealthy and the estates of the (sometimes newly) aristocratic landowners were to be unadulterated, but shanty towns and terraced cottages further out might be demolished. Seventeen of the planned nineteen termini were rejected and the concept of one shared terminus, a London Grand Central, was also rejected. A cordon sanitaire was imposed along London's first bypass, the New Road, in the north and from Borough High Street to Vauxhall Bridge in the south, beyond which the railway might not pass.

One of the best capitalised new railway companies (with £5.6 million, approximately £400 million today) was the Great Northern Railway. Unable to move further south, they decided to site their terminus at the historic village of Battle Bridge, close to the Regent's Canal, the New Road heading east to west, and the

Gray's Inn Road heading south. Land was cheaper here. Much of it was already semi-industrialised, used for dust heaps, brick fields and tile kilns. If you look at an early nineteenth-century north London house with its familiar stock brick brown, there is a good chance you are looking at fired clay hewn from the London earth of the Battle Bridge brick fields.

Perhaps most critically, one large landowner was available and ready to sell. St Bartholomew's Hospital owned 40 acres and operated two hospitals here for treating smallpox. In 1847 the railway bought the land, lock, stock and barrel and demolished the lot. The patients were moved to Islington and Highgate Hill. The surrounding streets (North, Suffolk, Edmund and Ashby) were erased and their inhabitants, like 37,000 other Londoners in the decade to come, were forced to find other lodgings. For the terminus was to be enormous, with extensive goods and marshalling yards.

The Great Northern Railway's terminus would probably have been called Battle Bridge Station (a corruption of Broad Ford Bridge after the ford that used to cross the river Fleet here and the previous name of the area) had it not been for the eccentric efforts of a little-known cemetery and pub designer, Stephen Geary.

Geary, like most architects before the mid-twentieth century, had learnt on the job as an apprentice. He had been working as an architect since he was thirteen and made his modest name as the designer of quintessential Victoriana: Highgate and Nunhead Cemeteries and a barrel of gin palaces (starting with the Bell on the nearby *Monopoly* street, Pentonville Road). In 1830 he designed an ambitious memorial to George IV at Battle Bridge, part building, part pedestal, part statue. It seems not to have been much-loved; George IV was little revered and the statue was pulled down in 1842.

The single room below survived a little longer: it served as a mini-museum, a police station and then a beer shop, before being demolished to ease the traffic flow three years later. This unsuccessful, early Victorian memorial architecture inserted onto a suburban village crossroads achieved immortality, however: so prominently was it positioned that within less than a decade, it had changed the neighbourhood's popular name – from Battle Bridge to King's Cross.

For two years the Great Northern Railway ran a temporary station from north of the Regent's Canal. One of the early trains taken by Queen Victoria (to Scotland in 1851) was from this temporary station – roughly from where a branch of Waitrose's wine section now stands.

When the new King's Cross opened the next year, it was simply magnificent and magnificently simple. Its architect, Lewis Cubitt, said that he designed the station to 'depend for its effect on the largeness of some of its features, its fitness for its purpose, and its characteristic expression of that purpose'. He succeeded. King's Cross remains a temple to transport, a heady and happy mixture of Venetian church and Roman baths, now brilliantly cleansed of its twentieth-century accretions and with its bricks gleaming in the sunlight filtered through its glass roof.

The problem with the ring of termini surrounding London was that it created enormous traffic pressures for those travelling between them. This led directly to the creation of London's and the world's first underground railway, to the creation of new streets, and to a change in the rules. A smattering of railway lines were permitted to punch through the boundaries into the city centre. One such station was Liverpool Street on the City boundaries, whose creation followed a now familiar pattern: constructed beside a street recently renamed after Lord Liverpool and on the site of a hospital (this time the Bethlehem Hospital), thousands were displaced to allow its erection.

The City of London's authorities would not permit a building on the scale of King's Cross and instead the platforms were tucked down below ground level and the building was surprisingly modest for its scale. For Liverpool Street, serving growing armies of commuters from the new suburbs of Hackney and Waltham Forest, was large: six platforms wide and ultimately over 100,00 passengers per day.[68]

London's last mainline terminus, Marylebone Station, was far less ambitious, but also told a similar tale of an ancient place repurposed to the needs of modern Victorian transport. Marylebone was a medieval village; however, being near two Roman roads it was probably much older. Its characteristic name derives from the church of St Mary on the banks of the stream or 'bourne' of the Tyburn. The 'le' was added in the seventeenth century to be fashionable and French, and in deference to St Mary le Bow and St Mary le Strand.

The Great Central Railway's Marylebone Station was only completed in 1899. Its creation had been delayed by the wealthy and hard-fighting residents of St John's Wood and the Marylebone Cricket Club, whose homes, streets and grounds were subsequently, and unsurprisingly, relatively unaffected. It helps to be rich.

The consequences of London's railways for London's streets and nature were immense. An estimated 120,000 were evicted from their homes from 1840–1900.[69] The old coaching inns failed, declining into smaller taverns with cheap homes or stabling for hackney carriage nags. Much of the centre's population was hollowed out, tempted by faster journeys and less pollution, and banished by the rebuilding of its ancient streets as dedicated offices in the latest architectural fashions of Victorian modernity: Gothic, Venetian and Italian Renaissance. The ancient City of London's population was 128,000 in 1851, but within twenty years, it was 76,000. London's stations gave commuters to the City, but they took its citizens.

Random, trivial or fleeting human decisions echo down the decades in ways that few could predict. When Victor Watson and his secretary, Marjory Phillips, travelled down from Leeds to London in 1935 to scout out appropriate London *Monopoly* streets, they could have chosen to travel to St Pancras or to King's Cross. Lines from Leeds ran to both termini.

It is a safe bet that they travelled to King's Cross. The route to St Pancras had been operated since the 1923 grouping of Britain's railways by the London Midland Scottish Railway, who also operated St Pancras station. By contrast the line to King's Cross was operated by the London North Eastern Railway (LNER), successor to, amongst others, the Great Northern Railway that built King's Cross, the Great Eastern that operated Liverpool Street, the Great Central Railway that operated Marylebone, and the successor to the London & Blackwall, which had built Fenchurch Street back in 1841.

Had they looked at an LNER map such as the one in the plate section of this book, in use not long after their visit, they would have seen the metropolis of London represented not by the great stations of the south and west but by the four soon-to-be *Monopoly* stations, of Fenchurch Street, King's Cross, Liverpool Street and Marylebone.

And thus, through the geography of Leeds, the commercial strategy of Victorian railway companies, the conservatism of the rich and the powerlessness of the poor, *Monopoly*'s London stations are named after, respectively, the fodder of horses, a failed monument to George IV, a Victorian prime minister, and a rural parish church beside a long-lost London stream.

Chapter 18

PICCADILLY

Raffles, Dracula and Piccadilly Jim

There is no way back into Paradise, which means
Piccadilly and the MCC.
George Orwell, *Raffles and Miss Blandish*, 1944

Piccadilly is not what it used to be. Walking today along its cliffs of Edwardian Portland stone is to be not just in the middle of London, but of the world's wealth; it is to weave between the global super rich and club men in covert coats, between glossy gold Bugattis and matt-black furled umbrellas, past luxuriant hotels, wallet-emptying restaurants, and barred portals to casinos, art galleries and nameless clubs.

But it was not ever thus. Piccadilly as a street is over 450 years old and we have been disputing the origins of its peculiar name since at least 1656. Until London's spectacular and forgotten great Edwardian rebuilding, Piccadilly was narrower, plainer and more plebian. In fact, its success with the masses as the purveyor of popular music and cheap spectacle is long-lasting. Is Piccadilly really posh or only pretending to be? Chain sushi bars and sandwich shops nestle on the street to this day. In its inception, Piccadilly was not even pleasure-seeking at all but workaday, a street less for clubs than for pubs, a street not for pied-à-terre apartments but for *rus in urbe* mansions, and for the shops and makers' yards of those who serviced their inhabitants.

Even though its modern form is surprisingly youthful, over the last 150 years Piccadilly has conquered the world. Writers, wishing rapidly to establish a character's reputation as a toff, be it a duke or gentleman, billeted him in Piccadilly: Raffles, the gentlemen thief, Jack Worthing in *The Importance of Being Earnest*, Lord Marchmain in *Brideshead Revisited*, Lord Peter Wimsey, a drive of Wodehousian comic heroes, even Count Dracula, all had their London home on or round the corner from Piccadilly.

More than any other *Monopoly* street, Piccadilly has inserted itself into worldwide consciousness: Manchester, York, Canada, Singapore and Australia all have Piccadillies. Birmingham has a Piccadilly Arcade and, alone among the *Monopoly* streets, Piccadilly has a Tube line. A Warwickshire pit village founded in 1904 is even called Piccadilly; supposedly one of the colliery owners asked the miners what name they would like and, when they could not choose, he plumped for Piccadilly. The Elephant and Castle, heart of old south London's shopping and music halls, was known as the 'Piccadilly of South London' until blitzed and then denatured by roundabouts and post-war architecture that only a mother could love.

Why is Piccadilly so ubiquitous? It is, ironically, because it is so easy to place. Most street names could be anywhere or could have other meanings. Is Leicester a square or a town? Is Oxford a university, a county town or a street? Is Bow a weapon or a shape? Is Regent a sinuous road or a presumptuous prince? Almost uniquely, Piccadilly is known ecumenically as a London street name, and one resonant with wine, music and song. If you have a street or a station to name, desire the allure of London's prosperity and pleasure-seeking and do not mind being derivative, why not call it Piccadilly?

Piccadilly is London's most successful slang place name. Picadils were stiff collars made by a prosperous early seventeenth-century tailor, Robert Baker. When he bought land and built a fine house in 1611–12 to the north-east of modern Piccadilly Circus, it was rapidly christened Piccadilly Hall, presumably in derision. For Baker was sharp and a social climber; he styled himself 'a gentleman', but was described as 'a man of a covetous dispocion'. His father-in-law, with whom he worked closely and who outlived him, was even worse: a man 'of a verie naughtie disposition', often 'transported with heate of rage and furie'.

Piccadilly Hall probably contravened ancient Lammas grazing rights and was certainly illegal, in contravention of the Elizabethan and Jacobean prohibitions of building near London. For at least ten years, the authorities tried to have the house pulled down or a large fine paid in recompense, with what success is unclear from the records. Probably 'Piccadilly Hall' was a local cause célèbre, rather as we follow celebrity libel cases in the high court today.

At any rate, with remarkable rapidity the name, Piccadilly, was applied not only to the house but to the street and neighbourhood, and not just in popular but in official parlance. The 1627–8 rate book contains 'Pecadilly' as a street heading for the first time. Why did the name 'catch' and spread? I would speculate that it was a combination of familiarity from the drawn-out legal disputes and that people simply liked the name. It is nice to say.[70]

Most of early Piccadilly was nothing special. Some houses

were thatched and inns abounded, with at least three by 1651: the Crown, the Feathers and the Horns. Houses stood back from the street frontage behind small gardens; this was the suburbs, not the city centre. However, within a few years as building near London was re-permitted and following the lead of the parvenu Robert Baker, aristocrats and politicians began to build their mansions along the street's north side.

It was a good place to be, close to the newly fashionable St James's with a good supply of water, but empty enough to build grandly and high enough to look down the hill to the palaces of St James's and Whitehall. Over 100 years, sumptuous mansions grew like weeds all along the north side: Melbourne House, Clarendon House, Burlington House, Berkeley House, Devonshire House, Apsley House – the skyscrapers of their day, though edifying not beshadowing.

But Piccadilly was not solely an aristocratic suburb for a few, it was also an important road west for the many, and this aristocratic and popular 'double nature' runs throughout its history. In between the mansions and on the street's southern side, inns and shops sprang up to serve their rich neighbours or the carriages heading out of town. Writing in 1720, the clergyman John Strype, described 'Pickadilly . . . a large Street and a great Through-fare' as a succession of inns: the White Horse, the Elephant and the King's Arms. Some were popular drinking spots for common soldiers.

The Hercules Pillars had the best name, but the White Horse was the most famous, christened after the House of Hanover's white horse emblem and managed by Abraham Hatchett. It had a waiting room (or 'travellers' room') for those waiting to board their coach, sleeping cubbyholes for the masses (the Travelodge of their day) and a cellar rich in visitors, drink and gossip. Grocers, stables, masons and statue sellers also had their shops, yards and workshops by Piccadilly, relatively far from the dense glamour of St James's town houses, but still proximate to the custom of Piccadilly's mansions.

Nineteenth-century Piccadilly only added to the mix of popular pleasure alongside exclusive wealth and architectural spectacle. St James's Hall became one of London's most successful concert halls, designed by the now largely forgotten Welsh architect and decorator, Owen Jones, who specialised in polychromy and Islamic design.

Its signature performance, in astonishing continuous production from 1862 until 1904, was the 'blackface minstrels' known as the Christy Minstrels. George Bernard Shaw did not like them ('I was inhumanely tormented by a quadrille band . . . [who] set us all flinching shuddering and grimacing hideously'), but the wider public did. The hall was an odd mixture of high culture and low, for it was also home to the Philharmonic Society, all housed in a rich cake of Owen Jones's Florentine, Moorish and Gothic design.

Even more exotic than St James's Hall was the Egyptian Hall, the first building in England to 'catch' the Regency craze for Egyptian design. It too gave the masses what they wanted at a price they could afford. Designed by Peter Frederick Robinson, who went on to create the eponymous wooden tavern at Swiss Cottage, it had Coade stone statues of Isis and Osiris and was paid for by the traveller, promoter and naturalist William Bullock, who had amassed a collection of 32,000 curiosities. Provided with two large exhibition galleries and stuffed with suits of armour, paintings and ethnographic curiosities, the Egyptian Hall could also house special exhibitions, the most famous of which was Napoleon's field carriage, shown shortly after his defeat at Waterloo.

In short, Piccadilly's Egyptian Hall was a runaway popular

success and William Bullock made a killing. It was often called the London Museum, so great was its fame.

However, much of Piccadilly's rich physical history was to be swept away in a few years by the wealth and self-confidence of Edwardian and inter-war England, as Piccadilly transformed in the early twentieth century from a high street of taverns and mansions to a much wider and higher one of hotels and office blocks. The Edwardians retrofitted a boulevard out of a high street and we have completely forgotten.

London in 1900 was undoubtedly 'the richest, largest, most populous city' there had ever been, the sum, as Jerry White has observed, of Paris, Berlin, St Petersburg and Moscow combined, greater than the next twenty-two British cities, 'illimitable' to Ford Madox Ford, 'immense . . . vast . . . endless' to H.G. Wells.

It was still getting taller as well as wider. Between 1900 and 1914 much of central London was rebuilt in Edwardian classical rococo, rich and rollicking, bigger and brassier and in Portland stone, not stock brick or stucco. We do not think of London as an Edwardian city, but much of it is. The inner London we know today, which survived the bombs or the post-war brutalising, is as likely to be 'Wrenaissance' Edwardian as anything else: this was the exuberant, some would say tasteless, classicism of the imperial high noon against which modernist architects turned so savagely.

Finsbury Square, Cheapside, Gracechurch Street, Throgmorton Street, Holborn and the *Monopoly* streets of Fleet Street and Whitehall were all renatured and grown. But no street was as transformed as Piccadilly.

Piccadilly's recreation had multiple sources. The authorities' desire to widen the street and facilitate the smooth passage of

London's burgeoning traffic, the owners' desire to extract more value from their prime properties, and growing aristocratic distaste for living by the noise and bother of Piccadilly's traffic. The broadening pools of international wealth also meant that the mansions and clubs were no longer sufficient to berth the international businessmen, promoters, industrialists and actors who flocked to London's West End. High hotels could billet more of them more elegantly and more profitably.

The first buildings to go were on the site of the White Horse coaching inn and the recently constructed Walsingham House Hotel (in reality, serviced apartments). Appropriately in the same year as the Francophile Edward VII's successful 1903 visit to Paris, and only one year before the signing of the Anglo-French *entente cordiale*, a French architect, Charles Mewès, and his English partner and protégé, Arthur J. Davis, began one of London's most Parisian buildings with its high Mansard roof, its street arcade reminiscent of the Rue de Rivoli, and its simplified classical stone walls. Both architects were graduates of the rigorous Parisian *École des Beaux-Arts*.

The Ritz Hotel has long been regarded as one of London's masterpieces, 'the product of one of those near miraculous convergences of civilised patron and architects and craftsmen of genius working together in complete harmony, both with each other and with the social and architectural fashions of the day.'[71] Classical architecture has always been about subterfuge (few pilasters perform a structural role), but the Ritz helped take the joys of aesthetic deceit to a new level. It used one of London's earliest, large-scale steel frames that, fittingly for a building created to host the world's elite, was based on an American model and built in Germany – an equally ominous testament to declining British technological prowess.[72]

It is hard to summon up today the heady and voguish popularity of the Ritz from about 1910 until the Second World War. In the Ritz, princes and plutocrats, actors and duchesses could meet as equals – as long as they paid. Edward VIII haunted the Ritz, and Charlie Chaplin, originally from Kennington, came to stay when he was in London. Piccadilly was, secretly, for anyone if they could afford it.

Meanwhile the London County Councils had deeper plans. Having first considered widening the north side of Piccadilly in 1898, the County Council made an agreement with the freeholders, the Commissioners of Woods, Forests and Land Revenues (now the Crown Estate), for road widening by stages as rebuilding took place. Clubs and mansions, the Egyptian Hall and St James's Hall were all swept away, and in their place rose high stone offices, hotels and mansion blocks. Greatest of them all and at the other end of the street was Norman Shaw's Piccadilly Hotel, a slightly younger sister to the more famous Ritz.

Part of a scheme for the whole block that was never completed, the Piccadilly Hotel is one of those mysterious buildings that are astonishing as soon as you look at them, but which curiously few people ever stop to notice. A giant three-storey screen of Ionic columns on Piccadilly shields a second-storey dining terrace and permits the hotel behind to rise even higher. It is sumptuous, but it is supremely wasteful of space. And it was very expensive.

Norman Shaw's biographer Reginald Blomfield, also an architect, was impressed:

> How Shaw got away with it, how he persuaded his clients to expend very large sums on the screen, which serves no practical purpose whatever, remains a standing wonder, but Shaw was a magician in dealing with clients and committees. He seems to have had a way with him that no one could withstand, so clear, so pleasant, so convincing.

In truth, Piccadilly is an embarrassment of late classical and neo-Georgian riches, including the former Wolseley Motors, now a restaurant; enormous but delicately detailed New World classicism without and glistening japanned and lacquered columns within. Jewels abound: Lutyens's exquisite former Midland Bank, respectfully and expertly guarding Wren's St James's Church, and the much later 2007 office block by the modern classical architect, Robert Adam, one of only a handful of large classical buildings created in inner London in the last fifty years.

Playful, innovative and complex, a mix of giant and secondary classical orders turn the corner towards Jermyn Street. Robert Adam recalls, 'Alexander Stoddart sculpted the capitals' one order as courage and the other order as clemency. *Audax* is even written on courage. The idea was that it needs great courage to do a building like this. But we need clemency to the buildings around it.'

It was certainly created in the face of official distaste. 'It was made clear to me,' Adam adds, 'that it had to be more modern.' The Government's official design body pressed for a redesign of the top floor, initially conceived as a temple on a hill, with more 'modern' glass such that it led to overheating, whilst the council officer's intent to refuse the building for daring to use some bricks was only circumvented by getting a meeting with the elected planning committee.

Remarkably few objected to the near total transformation of Piccadilly within one generation. The reason, of course, was that, though different, the new buildings were still gracefully joyful with their heavy rustication and Beaux-Arts bounce. Piccadilly was changed. But it was still itself.

The theatre publicist and BBC broadcaster, Walter MacQueen-Pope (known as 'Popie'), who could recall Piccadilly, the 'Magic Mile' as he termed it, before the First World War, considered that 'although they changed Piccadilly . . . they could not destroy it.' Of sentimental temperament, and looking back from old age in the late 1950s, he recalled:

> Despite the changes, Piccadilly still shone and was the centre of the world. You saw wonderful things happen there and events which stayed in one's memory. I remember with joy the sight of a very lovely and gracious lady who seemed able to defeat time riding down Piccadilly in an open carriage on a summer's day in June in what appeared to be a mist of wild roses. Everybody seemed to be wearing one and Piccadilly had developed a pink flush. We all cheered that Lady of the Roses for she was the beloved and beautiful Queen Alexandra . . . Piccadilly seemed the ideal setting for that pretty picture.

As befitted its mingled history, twentieth-century Piccadilly was not really all queens in carriages and Wodehousian ease. Boots the chemist on Piccadilly Circus was a common place to buy (still legal) heroin pills in the 1940s and later other nearby chemists specialised in the illicit under-the-counter sale of illegal drugs.

Until the Street Offences Act 1959 made it 'an offence for a common prostitute to loiter or solicit in a street or public place', nocturnal Piccadilly was thick with a 'continuous procession . . . moving slowly with a curiously characteristic gait, something like a wild animal stalking its prey, something like a parade which desired to be examined and appraised – the Ladies of the Town.' It was a use of Piccadilly perhaps hinted at by Bram Stoker's siting of Dracula's London residence on the street's south side.

Not all the 'Piccadilly daisies' or 'Piccadilly commandos' were for the top end of the market. The lexicographer

Jonathan Green, tells the story of his mother 'driving down Piccadilly sometime in 1956':

> Fascinated by the flocks of young women chatting momentarily to a succession of strangers, she urged my father to stop the car. So he did. My mother . . . stared. One of the young women detached herself from the mob. She approached the car. Was my mother, she asked, requiring *business*? If not, and here she opened her bag, revealing the handle of a cut-throat razor, perhaps she would care for a *stripe*? And failing that, perhaps she would prefer to move on. My father, who knew enough to appreciate that this stripe did not refer to those he had worn during the still recent engagement with Jerry, duly accelerated away.

HOW PICCADILLY CIRCUS GOT ITS LIGHTS

The postcard clichés of London are red double-decker buses, Big Ben, Buckingham Palace and the illuminated advertisements of Piccadilly Circus. If one of the themes of this book is that London's streets and squares have been more regulated than we have typically imagined, then, appropriately, the creation of Piccadilly Circus's advertisements is due to a failure of by-laws and freeholders' leases.

Piccadilly Circus's illuminated signs may now be publicly loved, officially sanctioned and used to advertise royal jubilees. However, for thirty years the London County Council and the buildings' occupants fought a dogged and drawn-out attritional war over the occupants' right to advertise garishly versus the authorities' right to stop them.

The London County Council won the opening skirmish. In about 1890, occupants of the north-east quadrant of Piccadilly Circus attached 'sky signs' to their roofs, thus obtaining highly visible advertisements with no loss of window light. But they were in contravention of the London Building Act 1894, which required that 'no building or structure should be erected beyond the general line of buildings in any street without the Council's consent.' They were all removed by 1899.

However, the London County Council lost nearly all subsequent battles due to a series of High Court decisions that decided that advertisements upon buildings' facades were neither structures nor projections. This meant that when, in 1904, the first illuminated sign was erected (advertising 'Mellin's Food' in front of No. 48 Regent Street's second-floor windows), the authorities were powerless to act. Further signs followed, advertising cigars, Perrier Water, Perrier Water, Bovril and Schweppes.

The County Council and Westminster City Council made various attempts to remove these and subsequent signs, using the London Building Act, by-laws regulating the lights, signs and structures overhanging the public way, and where possible, the 1880s leases granted by the Metropolitan Board of Works, the County Council's predecessor body. Nearly all these efforts failed as long as the signs were not damaging the building or projecting over the pavement.

By the 1920s, the war was lost and both the County and City Council abandoned normally fruitless, and always expensive, attempts to prevent illuminated advertising. Subsequently laws have been tightened, but have not been applied here.

Elsewhere around Piccadilly Circus, the Crown was the ground landlord. Their much older, 1820s leases were able to prevent signs. That is why, to this day, Piccadilly has electronic advertisements on the north-east side but not elsewhere. The still extant leases forbade it, as those granted in the 1880s could not.

Ironically, a generation later in 1959, when the London County Council was promoting destructive and wildly unpopular plans to destroy Piccadilly Circus and build a fast road and a tower (a scheme thrown out due to public revulsion), the only area of general agreement was 'the accepted desire to have illuminated signs in the new Circus'. Today's cursed vulgarity can become tomorrow's beloved tradition.

Raffles, Dracula and Piccadilly Jim never actually lived, dined, shopped or stayed in Piccadilly. But Edward VII, Queen Alexandra, Edward VIII, the future George VI, his wife and Princess Elizabeth all did. The future Queen Elizabeth II was brought up at No. 145 Piccadilly, until her father became king on her uncle's abdication. A befuddled George VI supposedly asked his daughters on hearing the news, 'If anyone comes through on the telephone, who should I say I am?' They left almost immediately for Buckingham Palace round the corner. Four years later, in 1940, 145 Piccadilly was badly damaged in the Blitz and subsequently demolished. It is now the facelessly bland InterContinental Hotel, a rare incursion of pure modernism into Piccadilly.

The street that the young Princess Elizabeth knew, which we all imagine as we read Bram Stoker or P.G. Wodehouse, has very little in common with what went before. Burlington House and Albany (the former Melbourne House converted into bachelor apartments in 1802) still survive, but they stand behind largely twentieth-century street fronts. The upmarket grocers, Fortnum & Mason, is always listed as dating to 1707, but the fine neo-Georgian building in which we now buy Christmas puddings dates from the 1920s. The Piccadilly that the Ritz's suites overlook is physically transformed from the street in which they were first built. But, at the time of writing, the cheapest room available will still cost you £799 per night. You can spend twice that if you wish.

Piccadilly is still itself. The genius of the Edwardian and 1920s 'Wrenaissance' was to change Piccadilly completely and yet keep it the same.

Chapter 19

WHITECHAPEL ROAD

Escaping the 'London Minotaur'

*Second-hand boots and shoes; cutlery; hats and caps;
rat-traps and mouse-traps and birdcages; flowers and
seeds; skittles; and frames for photographs. Cheap-jacks
have their carts beside the pavement; and with strident
voice proclaim the goodness of their wares, which include
in this district bloaters and dried haddocks, as well as
crockery. And one is amazed, seeing how the open-air
fair goes on, why the shops are kept open at all.*
Walter Besant, *All Sorts and Conditions of Men*, 1882

When Victor Watson and Marjory Phillips took their LNER-transported day trip to London in 1935, they did not visit the East End but they knew all about Whitechapel. It had ever been notorious: the dismal stage for disease and depravity, homicide and political unrest that the popular press reported so luridly. The 'filthy cottages' that John Stow was rude about in 1603, the murder of Harriet Lane by Henry Wainwright in 1874, the bloody Jack the Ripper murders of 1888, Lascar sailors, Jewish immigrants, Latvian revolutionaries, the Siege of Sidney Street in 1911, the riots of 1919, the ongoing rumble of socialist agitation by some of the residents and anti-Semitic prejudice against some of the others.

Dropping Whitechapel Road onto the board was a city-full of variety with one throw of the dice: geographic, social, racial and cultural. The Ripper murders, particularly, loomed consistently large in the public imagination. Molly Hughes, growing up in an 1880s, well-to-do west London suburb, thoroughly insulated by prosperity and distance, was nevertheless transfixed by the Ripper's crimes: 'No one can believe now how terrified and unbalanced we all were by his murders,' she wrote. 'One can only dimly imagine what the terror must have been in those acres of narrow streets where the inhabitants knew the murderer to be lurking.'

Even those actively seeking to help, depicted Whitechapel's sin, poverty and sweated labour hyperbolically. The neighbourhood featured prominently in Salvation Army founder William Booth's best-selling 1890 book, *In Darkest England and the Way Out*, whose core theme was the analogy between England's poorest neighbourhoods and the African continent that European nations were at the time colonising. The worst fate in 'darkest England' was Whitechapel. William Booth recounts a conversation with a 'stalwart youth lately discharged from the militia, and unable to get work', who had been reduced to tramping the streets trying to earn pennies for bread and tea:

> Poor lad! Probably he would soon get into thieves' company, and sink into the depths, for there is no other means of living for many like him; it is starve or steal, even for the young. There are gangs of lad thieves in the low Whitechapel lodging-houses, varying in age from thirteen

to fifteen, who live by thieving eatables and other easily obtained goods from shop fronts.

Throughout the book, 'Whitechapel' is a byword for squalid intemperance and gut-emptying poverty: 'the poorest tramp in Whitechapel'; the 'Whitechapel of New York'. Booth's confederate and Victorian super-journalist, W.T. Stead, ran a sensational series of articles in the *Pall Mall Gazette*, 'The Maiden Tribute of Modern Babylon', evoking the Greek myth of the Athenian maiden tribute to the Cretan Minotaur. The articles told a story of child prostitution that is as painfully shocking to read now as it was then, and the procurement of children via London's fetid and immoral East End, the 'London Minotaur'.

Yet, despite the poverty, the hardships and the 'making-do', as we shall see, many twentieth-century memoirs tell a remarkably different story of family, community and 'lovely times'. One resident recalled to an historian, 'When I think of the East End, I think of all the warmth. Within a radius of two or three streets, you had your own little community. Like a village it was.' One chronicler has gone so far as to speak of a 'golden age' for Whitechapel and its neighbouring streets from about 1900 to the 1950s.

So what happened? Was the Victorian horror overdone or were the tight-knit streets and courts of Whitechapel turned from a liability into an asset? How did Whitechapel escape the 'London Minotaur', or was it never entirely its prisoner?

Whitechapel Road, like the Old Kent Road, Oxford Street and the Angel, Islington, profited because it was on the route to London. It early on attracted cottages and inns, paddocks to graze droves of livestock, and abattoirs to slaughter them.

Vintners, brewers, innkeepers, bakers, butchers, clothworkers and mercers all owned shops and taverns in this slice of medieval 'ribbon development', among them Geoffrey Chaucer's parents, John and Alice.

By 1250, St Mary's chapel had been built for the hamlet's residents. Starkly made of white chalk (known as 'clunch') and prominently positioned, the 'white chapel' gave its name first to the road and thence to the neighbourhood. It became a parish from about 1338, the first of sixty-seven urban daughter parishes to be born from the much larger rural parish of Stepney, which initially stretched from the City walls to the river Lea and from Hackney to the river Thames.

Unlike the City or later development to the west, White-chapel's streets, buildings and trades were not governed by the City of London's building regulations, nor by landowner's leasehold stipulations or the later Housing and Building Acts. For many years, further construction in Whitechapel was, formally though ineffectively, banned by the abortive Elizabethan and Jacobean green belt. Consequently, Whitechapel's buildings were mean and poorly constructed (why build well when it might be pulled down?) and the neighbourhood attracted noxious activities, notably metalworking. Gardens and orchards in the long thin 'burgage' plots were increasingly broken up by alleys and yards.

It was busy. In 1417, St Mary's had four priests, indicating a large congregation. However, London's late sixteenth-century chronicler, John Stow, was not impressed by Whitechapel Road. He was the first recorded non-resident, though by no means the last, to be very rude about the street:

Both the sides of the streete be pestered with Cottages
. . . even up to Whitechappel church: and almost halfe a

mile beyond it, into the common field: all which ought
to lye open & free for all men. But this common field, I
say, being sometime the beauty of this City on that part,
is so incroched upon by building of filthy Cottages . . .
that in some places it scarce remaineth a sufficient high
way for the meeting of Carriages and droves of Cattell,
much lesse is there any faire, pleasant or wholsome way
for people to walke on foot: which is no small blemish
to so famous a city, to have so unsavery and unseemly an
entry or passage.[73]

This was a failure of regulation and street management as well
as a function of filthy trades. Stow specifically complained that
the 'proclamations and Acts of Parliament made to the contrary'
were not working. Seventeenth-century hearth tax returns and
maps show that Whitechapel's houses had low monetary values
and were physically small and short. Writing a century later, John
Strype agreed. Whitechapel Road was pleasant with good inns,
but 'pestered', he wrote, by shoddy and illegally built dwellings.
Whitechapel, initially part of the Manor of Stepney, was unlucky
in its landowners; initially the Bishops of London and then a
complex mess of bankrupt and indebted minor aristocrats. Few
stood up for the parish and few invested in it. None were able to
extract more than fleeting incomes, unlike the wiser landowners
of west London.

Nevertheless, Whitechapel Road was (just) part of London
and was worthy of protection. When parliamentary forces
fortified the city with earthen bulwarks in 1643, one of the
twenty-four earthen forts that spanned the banks was at the end
of Whitechapel Road. The fort's remnants, bolstered by ordure,
survived as 'Whitechapel Mount' on the south of Whitechapel
Road for 170 years; and for nearly two centuries, the mount

signified the eastern extremity of London. Whitechapel nurseries were noted for the excellence of their fruits and the air was clean and green enough for the London Hospital (now the Royal London) to move there in 1757.

What turned Whitechapel from a busy if not very prosperous linear town on London's outskirts was the creation of a vastly expanding East End docklands during the nineteenth century. Georgian London's docks were cramped, inaccessible and bedevilled by monopolies, theft and restrictive practices; losses through crime were estimated at half a million pounds per year, an eye-watering £80 billion in today's terms. In 1793, Parliament therefore licensed the City of London to buy land and create new harbours in the east: a phalanx of docks followed in the Isle of Dogs, Poplar and Blackwall. The first enclosed dock was opened in 1802, the last in 1921.

Hundreds of homes were swept away, but tens of thousands were built to serve the new docks, many with earth fired from the soil of Whitechapel Mount, which was removed in 1807–8 as the rising value of land for building justified the effort. During the nineteenth century, the East End became Britain's largest working-class city, out of sight and mind from those living in *Monopoly* London to the far west.

John Rocque's marvellous 1746 London map shows how the western end of Whitechapel Road beyond St Mary's is still a ribbon surrounded by fields and orchards. By the mid-nineteenth century, these were vanished. Every available furrow was turned into cheap streets and terraced housing in a tight patchwork of blocks and plots. Only the nomenclature of Fieldgate Street remains as a final memory of Whitechapel Road's previous role as an entrance to surrounding pasture, as well as to London.

The expanding docks for a booming London created thousands

of jobs, but they were dangerous and low-paid, insecure and life-limitingly dirty. One 'coal-whipper' (whose job was to lift coal out of a ship's hold) told the peerless biographer of Victorian London, Henry Mayhew, 'I have known the coal-dust to be that thick in a ship's hold that I've been unable to see my mate, though he was only two feet from me.' Mayhew called the docks a 'real hell' with labourers 'coughing and spluttering as they stacked the yellow bins of sulphur and lead-coloured copper-ore.'

But they fought for the privilege. Every morning hundreds queued for the possibility of a day or a half day's casual labour in the largely unregulated docks. There was always more supply than demand and those who were sick, weak, old or merely at the back of the crowd did not succeed.

There has never been a worse time to be poor than in the age of the rapidly growing industrial city whose pollution and sanitary requirements outstripped the authority's capacity to manage them. Families lived in tiny, squalid rooms, where glass broke and was not replaced, beds were shared, water was dirty and meagre cesspits overflowed. During the second half of the nineteenth century, Whitechapel became notorious not only for its physical poverty, but for its perceived moral degradation. A rogues' gallery, a thieves' kitchen, where starving, unshod children stole to eat and poverty-stricken girls sold their bodies for pennies; a place of shameful public exhibition, where the mob bawled and laughed at the physically deformed.

In 1884, the 'elephant man', John Merrick, was exhibited by the showman Tom Norman at the back of a glass warehouseas part of a 'penny gaff' (a temporary theatre) at 259 White-chapel Road.[74]

Writing in 1873, the social reformer Henrietta Barnett described how 'the whole parish was covered with a network of courts and alleys' with some of the houses 'hardly six feet apart, the sanitary accommodation being pits in the cellars; in other courts the houses were lower, wooden and dilapidated, a standpipe at the end providing the only water . . . In these homes people lived in whom it was hard to see the likeness of the Divine.'

However, such dehumanising poverty is categorically *not* Whitechapel's whole story. Whitechapel Road and Whitechapel High Street themselves were thriving if rather grimy. They were on the high road to London and the London Hospital provided a steady stream of retail requirements. Henrietta Barnett conceded that the shopkeepers lived agreeably with their families upstairs and, behind Whitechapel Road, 'there were two or three narrow streets lined with fairly decent cottages.' The poverty maps of London's late Victorian cartographer, Charles Booth, show the same pattern. Whitechapel Road is shown as being red, indicating 'Middle class. Well to-do.'

Proximity to London's docks also meant that there were regular inflows of itinerant sailors, not rich but with back wages saved and limited time to spend them; an important source of revenue for theatres, shops, hostels and brothels. Reading the beautifully detailed building-by-building histories collated by the *Survey of London*, it is hard to corroborate their narratives of thriving workshops, community centres and shops, of the constant rebuilding and reinvestment in the street, with the unremittingly squalid poverty of Victorian legend.

Drapers, tailors, milliners, libraries, reading rooms, music teachers, gentlemen's outfitters, second-hand booksellers, bell manufacturers, tea dealers, tobacconists, confectioners, ginger-bread makers, jewellers, pubs and inns beyond numbers, theatres, music halls and a bustling market rich with costermongers' stalls were all here. There was even an East End craze for roller skating in the 1870s. The Victorians were not always as Victorian as we make them.

LONDON'S COSTERMONGERS AND WHITECHAPEL MARKET

Unable to buy in bulk due to lack of funds, the poor have always been the best customer to the street salesman and the discount store, whose cheapness is a function of low volume rather than a good unit price. A family discount pack of 12 (all for the price of 10) is no good if you can only afford to buy one.

Just east of Whitechapel's parish boundary, along an exceptionally wide 300-to-400-yard stretch of road once referred to as Mile End Waste or 'the waste', Victorian Whitechapel had stalls and costermongers' barrows aplenty, selling everything and anything to the local population. Although local leases provided for the paving of footpaths and the planning of elm trees along 'the waste', this did preclude the market, established by ancient custom as a manorial right from the weakly managed Manor of Stepney.

If any single lost livelihood or word symbolises the stark difference between London's streets past and present, of streets walked on and streets driven in, it is surely the tradition, almost the tribe, of the London costermonger – the doughty and patter-rich wandering salesman of fruit or fish or vegetables (the name derives from 'costers' or apples).

Henry Mayhew's seismic 1851 study of *London Labour and the London Poor* was clear that costermongers and street sellers were almost a species apart from sedentary middle-class lives. His description of their short, sometimes violent lives is brightly coloured.

Costermongers liked skittles ('the game is always for beer, but betting goes on') with a fondness for 'sparring' or boxing. Dances were had a plenty: 'twopenny-hops' at which 'decorum is sometimes but not often violated', with favourite dances being the clog-hornpipe, the polka and the pipe-dance, for which tobacco pipes were laid upon the floor. At 'flash dances', girls showed their legs. Costermongers sang lustily in temporary 'penny-gaff' theatres, whose acts veered between short and bastardised versions of Shakespeare to pure music hall.

Their politics were ignorant, but Chartist ('the working man knows best'). Though most co-habited, very few were legally married or had ever been inside a church. None were educated, though they could spontaneously manage the maths for their wares and sales, and less useful information was ignored. One costermonger told Mayhew, 'I can't say where Naples is, but if you was to ask at Euston Square, they will tell you the fare and the time to go it in.'

They had their own language: 'Kennetseeno' was stinking, 'Flatch kanurd' was half-drunk. Their weights for their sales were often 'beaten out flat to look large' and were several ounces short. Children also joined their fathers very young on the streets:

As soon as the boys are old enough to shout well and loudly his father takes him into the streets. Some of these youths are not above seven years of age, and it is calculated that not more than one in a hundred has ever been to school of any kind. The boy walks with the barrow, or guides the donkey, shouting by turns with the father who, when the goods are sold, will as a reward let him ride home on the tray. The lad attends all markets with his father, who teaches him his business and shows him his tricks of trade; 'for,' said a coster, 'a governor in our line leaves the knowledge of all his dodges to his son, just as the rich coves do their kin.'

At the start of the twentieth century, London and Whitechapel's culture of street selling was in rude good health. Henry Mayhew had estimated in the 1850s that London had as many as 40,000 street sellers. The 1901 census revealed 12,000 costermongers, though most judge that the true figure was probably around 30,000. By 1931, there were still more than 19,000 recorded in the census, and many ex-servicemen used their post-Armistice gratuity to set up market stalls. But authority, and technology, was coming for them with grinding efficiency.

Between 1855 and 1904, first the Whitechapel District Board of Works and then Stepney Council tried to suppress and then to regulate Whitechapel Market, initially to permit readier access to Whitechapel station, then to prevent 'nuisance traders'. It was a harbinger of a London-wide trend. In 1867 the Metropolitan Streets Act effectively prohibited street trading but, following stinging criticism, was amended within weeks to exempt traders who nevertheless became subject to police regulation.

For fifty years the police made little use of this power (though individual constables used it to extract bribes), but from 1921, with growing motor traffic, for the first time the police began to suppress street markets and market stalls. From 1927, market stalls were licensed by local authorities, which was good news for the costermongers that survived: no more daily scramble for places, no more bribes to constables to ensure a good location. But it also systematically undermined the sector and began the long decline of the London costermonger, the perennial and wandering long-lived chancer of the London street, now largely extinct in practice and entirely vanquished in spoken English.

Near starvation poverty was present, but it was not ubiquitous. To their credit, however, and contrary to modern myth, not only Victorian reformers but much of Victorian society became obsessed with the appalling conditions of Whitechapel's residents and streets. As one 1890s writer, P.J. Keating, described, 'It is difficult to exaggerate the degree of interest in the East End shown by settlers, philanthropists, religious missionaries, journalists, Salvationists and sociologists.'

Whitechapel is still richly encrusted with the good deeds of Victorian philanthropists. The fine Working Lads Institute, five storeys of ornate good intent, gable-ended and oriel-windowed, now has flats not classrooms and dormitories, but its successor, the Whitechapel Mission, still provides shelter to the homeless down the road. Nearby the Whitechapel Gallery is still *in situ*, as is the first of the university settlements, Toynbee Hall on Commercial Road. New facilities multiplied. In Whitechapel's new public baths, you could have a 'first-class warm bath' for 6d, a second-class warm bath for 2d, and a second-class cold bath for a penny. The second-class warm bath was the most popular choice. Most, not all, could afford modest luxuries.

Public sympathy and charity were matched by critical changes in employment practice, which made life less risky and more tolerable for a growing proportion of Whitechapel's residents. In a series of high-profile strikes, East End match girls (in 1888) and gas workers and dockhands (in 1889) won better working conditions and more certainty of employment. Fewer workers had to compete for employment every day.

Living conditions continued to improve during the twentieth century. Gilda O'Neill, who interviewed many early twentieth-century East End residents, concluded that life was 'hardly easy but despite the hardships, the poverty and the making-do, there was a cockney spirit, a humour and a vibrancy in the community which are still remembered with great fondness by those who lived there. From the turn of the century to the time of the slum clearances of the 1950s and 1960s, there was a golden age recalled and cherished by many people.'

Many of those memories of a densely interlinked community revolved around the child-friendly, little-driven, public realm of the tight East End terraced streets. Combined with the effect of domestic overcrowding (with two families often squeezed into the two-up, two-down terraced homes), neighbourhood life therefore flowed effortlessly down streets, round corners and, with a little more decorum, into private houses. One recalled:

> People didn't shut their front doors because it was usually shared accommodation, so you had to have the front door open. But the front door was also left open because your neighbour would say, 'I'll come round and have a cup of tea with you at four o'clock.' So, you'd leave it open so you wouldn't have to bother to go and open it.

Pride was shown on the street by polishing the front step ('My mum would go *barmy* if you went anywhere near her clean step.'). Newly married daughters rarely moved more than a few streets away from their mothers ('I'd pop in to have a cup of tea, have a chat. Nothing special. But she was always there.'), and skilled amateur midwives would deliver 'every child' in the street. A street's curtains were drawn, the blinds pulled down, and sawdust thrown on the cobbles to muffle the hooves when a neighbour's funeral hearse processed. The reception was held at the local pub on the corner and the street would 'band together' for a wreath or gift. 'You might be crying, but you'd be doing it together.'

One of the most startling facts to the modern reader is how free children were to congregate and play in the little-driven streets and to move about unsupervised. 'We'd hang around in a group, sitting on the kerb, usually by the lamppost,' recalled one. Cricket, football, skipping, swinging round the lampposts, and elaborate games of catch and chase were played in Whitechapel's public streets. Guy Fawkes bonfires might be built up on streets for days before 5 November, as 'there was hardly any traffic down our little side-turning.'

This was the perennial London experience until the 1960s when all of the city could be a playground and a place to move around safely and readily on foot. It is a pattern that researchers have discovered more broadly: the 'range' of children's unaccompanied right to roam has collapsed over three generations from several miles to the domestic home and garden. The motor car has brought the liberty of a Victorian duke to modern families to drive around the country. But it has destroyed children's liberty to move beyond their front door. Children live more lonely lives in consequence.

The Blitz and post-war planning were not kind to Whitechapel. A comparison of the neighbourhood in 1920 and today shows how widely the houses of Whitechapel were replaced by flats in acres of parking. Street after street to the north or south of Whitechapel Road no longer exists, their tightly threaded capillaries of houses and corner shops severed for a more crudely drawn, simpler network of larger buildings and larger spaces: from city as Lego to city as Duplo. Such places tend to be associated with lower levels of social connectedness, higher indexes of multiple deprivation, and lower property values.

Even where the streets do still stand, few of the original buildings survive and, in a pattern rarely seen so comprehensively in London, many of the streets' names have been lost.

Taking just a slice to the south of Whitechapel Road: Green Street, Charlotte Street, New Street, Rutland Street, Suffolk Street, Norfolk Street, New York Street, Frederick Street, Bedford Street, Bedford Square, Baker Street, John Street and John's Place have all been renamed or entirely swept from the map. Middlesex Street was once Hogg Street (for the pigs kept nearby fatting for slaughter) and then Petticoat Lane (for its second-hand clothing market). Names matter and in Whitechapel they have a habit of changing far more than in most of London. It is the fate of the poor to have 'better' names imposed upon them.[75]

Whitechapel's revised street names are associated with evolving populations as well as top-down 'regeneration'. It is a cliché, but nevertheless true, that Whitechapel – cheap, anonymous, by the docks and close to an infinite demand for labour – has been popular with surges of immigrants down the centuries, fleeing oppression, jumping ship or seeking work. Germans and Jews congregated there in the late nineteenth century; anarchist and revolutionary Russians and Poles followed, including (in 1902) Lenin and Trotsky. There were enough

Russian cafés and tea houses for both men to pick up almost no English during their stay. Seamen from Sylhet in Assam then set up lodging houses in Whitechapel in the 1930s.

The neighbourhood's largest, more recent immigrant population has been Bengali, and by two violent twists of Whitechapel's history, the site of Whitechapel's eponymous St Mary's Church now celebrates its Bengali heritage, not its medieval one. St Mary's Victorian incarnation was bombed on 29 December 1940, demolished in 1952 and turned into St Mary's Gardens in 1966. The park was in turn renamed Altab Ali Park in honour of a 25-year-old Bangladeshi-born clothing worker who was murdered as part of an 'almost continuous and unrelenting battery of Asian people and their property' in 1977–8.

Up the street, Whitechapel Road is dominated less by the Royal London Hospital and far more by the immense 1980s East London Mosque. In between at 32–34 Whitechapel Road sits the now vacant Whitechapel Bell Foundry which, until its melancholy closure in 2017, was Britain's oldest manufacturing company: creating bells continually in Whitechapel since either 1567 or 1572 and on its present site since the 1740s. The inability of the authorities to prevent its closure and sale to a property firm to create a boutique hotel prompted a review of national policy, still ongoing at the time of writing.

With forthcoming luxury hotels and with the community's prosperity rapidly growing, will Whitechapel's near future be as Bangladeshi as her recent past? As each previous surge of immigrants has arrived, so each wave has broken and receded or, more accurately, seeped inshore. Each community has prospered and integrated in the huge and open economy that is London, then the hub of an empire, and still Europe's most global trading city.

In 1902, Charles Booth wrote in terms that feel a little

uncomfortable today that 'Dalston and Canonbury are said to be among the first steps upwards of the Whitechapel Jew.' London's Asians have long since started a similar migration. In 2001, the borough of Tower Hamlets renamed the Spitalfields electoral ward as Spitalfields and Banglatown, as 68 per cent of the ward's population was of Bangladeshi origin. By 2011, only 41 per cent of the ward's population was Bangladeshi.

Meanwhile, what of historic Whitechapel, the circuits of narrow streets, alleys and terraced houses that grew so fast to serve the docks and whose residents strode so fearfully through the late Victorian imagination? Little of it survives, savaged by German bombs or developers' 'slum clearances'. The small number of Whitechapel's' 'two-up two-down' houses still standing have had their glass replaced and their roofs fixed, street trees are planted opposite and they are now 'desirable'. Without mice or rats and with washing machines and tumble dryers, they ooze high-status, period charm and are in walking distance to the City.

At the time of writing, a modest terraced house, built in the years following the Battle of Waterloo, is on sale at 12 Walden Street (formerly Suffolk Street) for £1.5 million, a sum that would have made Henrietta Barnett weak at the knees, which would have been enough to commence a major Victorian road building, and is 25,000 times more than the £60 it costs to buy Whitechapel Road in *Monopoly*. At that price, surely, Whitechapel Road has at last escaped the London Minotaur?

Chapter 20
COVENTRY STREET
Sin and teacakes

We had a rag at Monico's. We had a rag at the Troc,
And the one we had at the Berkeley gave the customers
*   quite a shock.*
John Betjeman, *Varsity Student Rag*, 1931

One evening in 1887, a south London-born struggling street-seller and wannabe showman was closing his market stall in Liverpool. He was forty and, despite a definite 'gift of the gab', his life had been a meandering series of failures. He had razzle, but little commercial acumen or staying power. He had not succeeded as an artist, nor completed his training as an optician, and today sales were going badly: a one shilling, 'three in one' contraption that was part-microscope, part-binocular and part-compass was doing little better than his previous forays touting watches or cheap jewellery. He was, as they said then, 'on his uppers'. Fortunately, fate was about to pour riches into his lap.

It appeared in the form of his distant cousin by marriage, who had come all the way from London to find him. Monte Gluckstein was a partner in a successful family firm of tobacconists, Salmon and Gluckstein, who wanted to branch out into catering. He was interested in his cousin for two reasons: he needed a 'front man' who was content to let Monte manage the numbers, and he needed a member of the extended family whose name was less overtly German or Jewish. Joe Lyons, for that was the street seller's name, had a nice ring to it.

The deal was done after a brief discussion and on one single piece of paper. Thus was born J. Lyons & Company, a firm that for most of the twentieth century was the undisputed king of British catering. Lyons's embers can still be found smouldering (Lyons Tea is the second best-selling brand of tea in Ireland and Lyons cakes are still sold in small numbers in cheaper corner shops). But in its heyday, Lyons burnt far more brightly, influencing the public's tastes, serving monarchs and masses alike and coming, very genuinely, to reflect a form of Britishness back to the nation, of the quiet values of a nice cup of tea, a well-priced cake, and somewhere sensible to relax while you consumed them.

One of the streets that was to play a prominent role in Lyons' story was Coventry Street, between Piccadilly and Leicester Square, where Lyons opened first the Trocadero Restaurant in 1896 and then their first Corner House in 1906. But it was to do so in a manner influenced as much by the place as by the corporation. Coventry Street's creation in 1681 had been partly funded by gambling winnings, and for over 300 years it has been a consistent locale for dining and dancing, gambling and gaming, consuming and cavorting.

Lyons's establishment in Coventry Street was far less quietly genteel than it might have wished and while the Lyons brand and company are nearly vanished from the public memory, Coventry Street itself is marching into the future, arguably doing precisely what it has always done since the late seventeenth century – providing a slightly risqué good time. Streets last longer than companies.

Coventry Street's genesis was gambling. The main landowner responsible for the street's creation was Colonel Thomas Panton, whose life is a story of adventure and excess tempered by good luck, fine judgement and, perhaps undeservedly, a happy ending. As a young man, he raised a regiment of horse in the English Civil War – always a 'pulse-quickening' activity as the Edwardian author, Saki, was later to put it. He served in Charles II's horse and foot guards after the Restoration and then became a phenomenally successful gambler, winning in one night so much money that he resolved never to play again.

He bought estates in Herefordshire and London with his winnings, petitioned the new Surveyor General, Sir Christopher Wren, to be allowed to develop 'a fair street of good building' on the latter, received assent, and proceeded to build Oxendon Street, Panton Street, then a little later Coventry Street and Panton Square. Panton's son became the longest-serving general in the British army and his daughter made a fine and aristocratic marriage. When he died, despite being a Roman Catholic, he was somehow buried in Westminster Abbey. Sometimes gambling pays.

Coventry Street owes its name as well as its creation to gambling. On its corner was a former gambling den, Piccadilly Hall, popularly known as Shaver's Hall (there is still a Shavers Place off Coventry Street), into which had moved Henry Coventry – that rarest of early modern phenomena, a politician who did not enrich himself in office.

As it was born, so did it live. For over 300 years, Coventry Street has not been home to many and those that it did house, somehow it turned to the bad. Panton Square, just off Coventry Street, was more a stabling yard than a proper London square and was gradually built up with houses. In one of these in 1762 lived the Moroccan ambassador.

According to a contemporary memoir by John O'Keeffe, 'One of his attendants happened to displease him: he had him brought up to the garret, and there sliced his head off.' London did not condone the murder of servants. An angry mob consequently gathered before the house. 'They broke into it, demolished the furniture, threw everything they could lay their hands on out of the window, and thrashed and beat the grand Moor and his retinue down the Haymarket, and afterwards attacked them wherever they found them.'

If Coventry Street has never really been domestic, it has instead been a place in which to play and sin. Throughout the eighteenth and nineteenth centuries, a succession of tennis courts, casinos, theatres, cafés and 'subscription theatres' (to avoid licensing laws) served as fulcrums for gambling and prostitution. Increasingly ornate, inside and out, the theatres were periodically shut down for infringing one regulation or another and, tellingly, little is recorded of their artistic productions. In 1846, J.T. Smith wrote that 'there is a considerable number of gaming houses in the neighbourhood . . . the bad character of the place is at least two centuries old.'

Most infamous were the Argyll Rooms, which opened in 1851. Their lavish décor (a newly fashionable Italianate front, a first-floor gallery, full-length gilt-framed mirrors and paintings) anticipated the decorative excess of later in the century and amply signified the lascivious behaviour within. Dancing and drinking went on till dawn and, put simply, rich men went there to pick up high-class prostitutes. Henry Mayhew, describing London prostitution in 1862, recorded how a nearby room was more costly to rent 'on account of its proximity to the Argyll Rooms'. London has always had a market in all things.

The Argyll Rooms were shut down in 1878 and reopened as the Trocadero Palace music hall. Aping a Parisian concert hall of the same name (itself named after a French military victory and subsequently demolished), the London Trocadero had limited success before going bust and being bought in 1894, on the quiet, by Monte Gluckstein, the power behind the throne at Lyons & Co.

Since the launch of J. Lyons & Co in 1887, the company had catered for and then produced an ever-greater series of spectacularly profitable shows and exhibitions: the Newcastle 'Mining, Engineering and Industrial Exhibition', the 'Greatest Show on Earth' for the American duo of Barnum and Bailey, and then 'Venice in London' followed by 'Constantinople' at the Olympia Exhibition Hall. The latter two were entirely produced by J. Lyons & Co., complete with replica canals and bazaars and populated with real life gondoliers, bazaar salesmen, and Tartars on horseback transported to England for the purpose. There was nothing the Victorian public liked better than a bit of safely controlled Eastern exoticism, with a good tea and an easy journey home by Tube or hansom cab for supper. Lyons & Co were both selling the tickets and selling the teas. So what to do with all the profits?

The answer was to 'go permanent'. First, they launched a mass-market chain of tea shops, aimed squarely at the growing middle classes and, unlike pubs, designed as places where respectable ladies might drink tea and eat cakes genteelly; there were even women-only enclaves. Prices were reasonable and quality consistent. Tea shops were opened rapidly across London: Piccadilly, Queen Victoria Street, Regent Street, Chancery Lane and Ludgate Circus. Within fifteen years, there were 130 nationwide. With a savvy mix of showmanship and exquisitely expert management, it was Britain's first restaurant chain.

Secondly, Lyons & Co. went upmarket. Monte Gluckstein brought the same ambition and genius for organisation to the Coventry Street Trocadero, the former hang-out of women by the half hour, when he bought it in auction. Rebuilt and reimagined, it burst into the wealth of late Victorian London freshly gilded and newly respectable with columns of Devon marble, glistening chandeliers, an Arthurian frieze in the foyer, and a Louis XIV Salon, a ballroom for 500, dining rooms almost without number, and a Lodge Room for masons. It was electrically lit and served by the latest technology in fast-moving lifts.

The band of the Scots Guards played at the opening ceremony and one of London's leading playwrights wrote the programme. It was the epitome of new wine in old bottles; old-fashioned style but modern technology and management. Fittingly for the liberal entrepôt and capitalist success that was late Victorian London, the family that owned and ran Lyons & Co were Jewish refugees from European pogroms, who only a few years previously had still been living in Whitechapel.

Down the road at numbers 18–19 Coventry Street, a fishmonger opened another 'supermarket' restaurant: Scott's Oyster and Supper Rooms. A riot of late Victorian excess, it had five storeys of bars and restaurants with pantries and sculleries above. All were architecturally surrounded by swags of scallop shells and lush vegetation in Bath stone. It became a staple of twentieth-century café society. Ian Fleming reportedly enjoyed dry martinis there; POWs in the film *The Great Escape* made a rendezvous to meet there after their safe return to England; and James Bond dined there plaintively in Kingsley Amis's 1968 continuation novel, *Colonel Sun*:

Bond had recently heard that the whole north side of the

[Coventry] street was doomed to demolition, and counted every meal taken in those severe but comfortable panelled rooms a tiny victory over the new hateful London of steel and glass matchbox architecture, flyovers and underpasses, and the endless hysterical clamour of pneumatic drills.

Fortunately, Bond's intelligence was wrong. Coventry Street survives as does the former Scott's Oyster Rooms, though the restaurant itself moved to Mayfair, much of the building's architectural excess has been erased, and it now houses a burger bar – part of the street's relentless march downmarket during the long twentieth century.

The main promoters of Coventry Street's popularisation were Lyons & Co. Not content with operating the Trocadero, thirteen years later they opened another 'supermarket' restaurant, the street's third, but this time aimed firmly at the middle market. They called it the Corner House. It followed the logic of the Trocadero and of Scott's, but with less decoration and much cheaper prices. As the *Globe* reported at the time, 'The idea seems to be to cater to that immense class who, although of modest pockets, like things served well.' Now that the Corner Houses have been completely forgotten, were one to be opened today the *Guardian* or the *Telegraph* (depending on the politics of the owner) would doubtless condemn it for its tacky commercialism. Yet this was London in 1909.

After a whirlwind of advertising, the Corner House on Coventry Street opened on 3 January. Directors and the board were there before sunrise and greeted the arriving staff in person. The doors opened at nine and the public flocked inside. They found a cosmopolitan nirvana: Art Deco and white tiles, shops selling chocolate, cheese, cooked meats and fine wines, a shoe-shine and a hair salon. Upstairs, past the marble colonnade and stairs, were restaurants, bars, grills and tea shops. The public loved it and the commercial success was immediate and immense.

Within a few years Lyons had bought the next-door property (on the site of the former Panton Square where the Moroccan ambassador had murdered his servant) and doubled the facilities to over 4,000 places. Sixty thousand meals could be served a day and for a period it was open for 24 hours. There were 400 staff and a network of rest rooms and staff clubs, including fencing and shooting on the roof. It was certainly one of the largest restaurants in the world.

One American visitor was impressed at how well it catered to the mass market: 'I recall . . . being struck with the size and importance of it . . . It catered to an element not reached in quite the same way in America.' The young novelist Ursula Bloom met her fiancé for tea there and danced to its 'thrilling' bands.

From 1924, the waitresses were officially known as Nippies – with connotations of speed and efficiency. Everyone in mid-century Britain knew who Nippies were and where they worked, though the word is now completely forgotten. Lyons claimed that the Nippies' marriage rate was higher than any other class of working girl, an intentional back-handed compliment to the homely efficiency of their own restaurants. Other Corner Houses followed, on *Monopoly* streets such as Oxford Street and the Strand, and still the public came. Like the Lyons tea shops, Lyons Corner Houses were soon national icons.

During the twentieth century, Lyons went from strength to strength. Increasingly its growth came not from the tea shops, Corner Houses, restaurants and hotels that had made its name, but from selling branded bread, tea and cakes direct to the mass market. If we are what we eat, Britain increasingly *was* Lyons, the epitome of respectable middle England.

However, despite the wholesome intentions of the Lyons

brand, somehow the Coventry Street Corner House never quite managed to be as 'mainstream' as implied. The milieu and the variegated appeals of the West End were a little too racy for everyone to be entirely 1930s genteel. The first open secret was that the Corner House was, as one participant recalled, the 'absolute Mecca of the Gay scene' in mid-twentieth-century London. In addition to the attractive ease of the location and the cosmopolitan tone, the sheer busyness of the place and its everyman nature all nurtured its unintended role.

As one historian of gay London explains, it had 'respectable yet affordable' surroundings, in which 'clerks, shop assistants, and workmen gathered alongside civil servants and metropolitan intelligentsia, "painted boys" alongside the discreet queer.' Men met particularly on the first floor. As one recalled, 'There was nothing to say it was different, but the waitresses knew it and wouldn't let a woman sit anywhere near.' In time, Coventry Street Corner House became known as the 'Lilypond', ostensibly referring to the flowers painted on the walls.

In a world in which homosexuality was still illegal, it was a long way from the brand's refined advertisement for tea and cakes, or from royal visits to Lyons factories. (King George V visited a Lyons factory in the 1920s and Elizabeth II in the 1950s.)

The Reverend Harold Davidson also liked the Lyons Corner House on Coventry Street. Every Sunday from 1906 to 1932 (other than an unsuccessful spell as a Royal Navy chaplain during the First World War), he led holy service at the small Norfolk parish church of St John's.[76] However, from 1920 he spent his weeks in London where, Gladstone-like, he approached young girls to save them, in his own estimation, from a life of vice. By his own reckoning, he approached between 150 and 200 girls a year.

His favourite technique was to affect to confuse them with well-known film actresses before persuading them to take a meal with him. One of Davidson's preferred locales, presumably because it was large enough to be anonymous, was the Coventry Street Corner House. One associate recalled drinking tea with Davidson there, when he suddenly called out to a passing Nippy, 'Excuse me, Miss. You must be the sister of Jessie Matthews,' before offering to get her a part in a new play and rushing off.

Davidson was adamant about the nobility of his motives, styling himself 'the prostitutes' padre . . . the proudest title that a true priest can hold' and telling the Bishop of Norwich, 'I can earnestly assure you in the sight of God that my conscience is free from any knowledge of breach of the moral law.' Others were not convinced. He was banned from many tea shops, though never seemingly the Coventry Street Corner House, before being defrocked in a sensational ecclesiastical court trial, mainly on the evidence of the many girls he had approached. He ended his life working in a circus, where he was mauled to death by a lion upon whose partner's tail he had unfortunately trod.

Lyons's decline was slower than the Reverend Davidson's, but no less certain. The Salmon and Gluckstein families kept close control of the company, but it was too close and later generations lacked the business brilliance of Monte Gluckstein. The business was over-extended, debt was inflated by sterling's decline, and there were no presiding marketing or manufacturing geniuses to keep the services relevant or good value for money. The Coventry Street Corner House closed in 1977 and the remnants of the empire were sold, with Allied Breweries buying the largest stake and becoming Allied Lyons, a name they kept until 1994.

Many were distressed by Lyons's collapse. In the 1970s, a decade that exemplified British economic and commercial decline, little typified the national failure more than the collapse of Lyons &

Co. As if to heighten the symbolism, Margaret Thatcher had even started her career working as a chemist for the company.

The loss was cultural as well as commercial and it extended beyond Britain's shores. Susan Goodman, a *New York Times* journalist, recalled, 'To visitors between the wars, a Lyons Corner House was almost as much an institution as Buckingham Palace.' She recounted how customers were writing letters pleading for the restaurants' preservation. One recalled his favourite Nippy in 1928, called Violet. Another 'recalled a sentimental courtship and sanctuary during a raid in the Blitz,' and a third remembered a childhood visit to a Corner House: 'I had a Knickerbocker Glory sundae and no ice cream has ever tasted so good to me since.'

The Coventry Street Lyons Corner Shop has been gone for over forty years. But if you walk past the building it is still there and, absent fire or revolution, it will continue to stand there for the foreseeable future. No architects have been as derided or ignored as the practitioners of early twentieth-century classicism. They don't fit the prevailing, and false, narrative that all architecture was 'progress' towards modernism. Nevertheless, even the powers that be have recognised the cultural importance of Lyons.

The former Corner House is listed by Historic England and the stones and carvings by W.J. Ancell (the first smaller building) and F.J. Mills (the second larger one) are described on the national list in intricate detail with their 'consoles rising', their 'cupolas', and their 'balustraded parapets' – a 'well-preserved example of the Lyons Corner House style'. Nor have the buildings lost their purpose. Their upper storeys may have been stripped and ransacked of their Art Deco finery for modern offices, but their ground floor still serves passing tourists, less elegantly but no less purposefully.

Where Londoners queued eagerly to sample the first Corner

House on the morning of 3 January 1909, you can still queue, if you wish, to sample a Bubba Gump Shrimp, change money, or buy a 'Premier League souvenir'. Just up the road is the Grosvenor Casino. Coventry Street is still for hire to the highest bidder and still in play to those who will take their chances. Streets, not companies, are the true survivors. Even when they are selling the same things.

Chapter 21

EUSTON ROAD
'The street is disgusting'

Noah was an amateur. The Titanic *was built by professionals.*
Anon., variously attributed

My settled opinion, which is quite a dispassionate one, is that the centres of our great cities must be pulled down and rebuilt, and that the wretched existing belts of suburbs must be abolished and carried farther out . . . Wide avenues must be driven through the centres of our towns . . . To save itself, every great city must rebuild its centre.
Le Corbusier, *The City of Tomorrow and its Planning*

During much of the twentieth century, planners and architects declared war on the city and all its constituent parts and places; on the local, the scruffy and the imperfect, on the corner shop and the roadside café, on the quick walk to the pub for a pint of beer, and the neighbourhood that had grown over the years as local chance, climate or materials dictated. All that was past was suspect; the serendipity of the street was out of date. Man was not, in fact, a complex social being seeking purpose and reassurance, needing both harmony and beauty. He was merely a moving part in the machine, which could be zoned, designed, cut and cleaned from on high. Organic growth was dead and the future was not up to everyone to evolve and discover. It must be planned from above.

The Swiss-French architect, Le Corbusier, the prophet of traffic modernism, of man as machine part and of the city as motorways, towers and landing strips, exhorted his acolytes to take courage from Louis XIV or Napoleon: 'Golden moments when the power of the mind dominated the rabble . . . men can be paltry but the thing we call man is great.'

Inspired by the state's ability to wage total war between 1939 and 1945, academically trained architects, engineers and planners dreamt of winning the peace, of demonstrating their scientific superiority to their self-taught or merely apprenticed predecessors. They were admonished not to let the fearful prejudices of the ignorant multitudes stand in their way. One British high priest of traffic modernism, Maxwell Fry, warned that architects should address 'ourselves only to those capable of understanding us, and let the rest go hang'.

So they did. Before the war, Le Corbusier's *Plan Voisin* sought to sweep away the blocks and boulevards of central Paris and replace them with sixty-storey concrete towers and fast roads in open parkland. During the war, the architect and town planner Patrick Abercrombie's 1944 *Greater London Plan* followed the spirit of this very *dirigiste* revolution in planning theory. The men in Westminster, Whitehall and County Hall were mesmerised. Here surely was the future, all neatly printed and bound in one report.

Therefore, for thirty-five years until Londoners revolted

and stopped it, London was replanned from on high. In the process some good was done; new homes *were* built but in most years nearly as many were demolished, rather undermining the success. But a historic crime was committed against the liveability, walkability and humanity of many of London's historic streets and squares.

One of the streets damaged almost past repair and still scarred to this day was Euston Road, the Georgian bypass built to take the sheep to market and renamed by the Victorians (indirectly) after a Suffolk village. Le Corbusier believed in roads, not streets. Roads should be wide and fast, for travelling quickly by car (he hated trams); streets, where people also lived, worked or congregated, should be removed. 'The street is disgusting,' he wrote, 'why therefore do we not destroy it?' Sadly, when it came to Euston Road, his followers very nearly did.

Euston Road began life as a bypass and has been going downhill ever since. It was the central stretch of the New Road bypass (of which the easterly stretch is now the Pentonville Road) created in 1756 to ease the approach to the City for both man and driven beast. The New Road was supported by the landowner to the north, the Duke of Grafton, whose country estate was at Euston in west Suffolk and one of whose subsidiary titles was the Earl of Euston.

As along the whole New Road, a clause in the original act forbade building within 50 feet. The result was that landowners and their leasing developers laid out a series of elegant terraces with long gardens in front of the houses, or long open squares running along the street, such as Endsleigh Gardens and Euston Square. To the north a Huguenot developer, Jacob Leroux, developed streets on behalf of the landowner Charles Cocks, whose ennoblement as Lord Somers gave the new suburb its name, Somers Town.

By the 1820s, the neighbourhood was middle class and quietly fashionable for the respectably impecunious, far enough from town to enjoy gardens and cleaner air, near enough to be accessible to the City. As always in pre-motor car towns, the main street with its larger homes and bigger gardens was higher status than the quieter, smaller back streets; a pattern that has normally now reversed. Perhaps encouraged by Jacob Leroux, the neighbourhood was popular with French refugees, though not exclusively so. The young Mary Shelley (born Mary Godwin), the daughter of an indebted philosopher and a downwardly mobile feminist, grew up in Somers Town before eloping to Italy to marry her poet lover, Percy Bysshe Shelley.

All changed in 1837 when, having considered alternative locations in Camden Town, the Strand and at Tyburn, Robert Stephenson chose Euston Grove as the site for the London station of the new London & Birmingham Railway. It was to be the first London terminus facing north and it was to start a process that was to create a 'railway mile' of three termini and two goods depots to the north of Euston Road. This was to begrime, clutter up and transform a suburb for the discreetly respectable into a dirty and polluted industrial district. By the time a century of coal-fired railway development was over, the traffic modernists had a point. Euston Road *was* disgusting.

It started with a scalpel not a sledgehammer. The first Euston Station, just north of Euston Square, was little more than a shed; there were not even any locomotives to be seen. The gradient of 1 in 70 running into the station was too great for the early engines, so Robert Stephenson operated the first mile with static engines hauling trains up by cable. The fledgling Euston emitted a periodic 'melancholic mysterious moaning', according to one contemporary. It was a trumpet in the engine house sounded by a blast of air being sent along a pneumatic tube: the signal for the cable to start turning.

The railways' financiers, mostly northern manufacturers, wanted more 'architectural embellishment … opening immediately upon what will necessarily become the Grand Avenue for travelling between the Metropolis and the midland and northern parts of the Kingdom.' They commissioned the supremely talented Philip Hardwick, who deserves to be better known, to design worthy 'gateways' in both London and Birmingham. London's took the form of the 'Euston Arch' (actually a 70-feet-high Doric Propylaeum) in a strict Roman revival style. Euston Arch was a metaphorical gateway to the north, behind which you could glimpse Primrose Hill and through which humans and merchandise might travel to the heart of London.

The 'Arch' was unveiled in May 1838, when the station was less than one year old and before its services extended past Bletchley in Buckinghamshire. The seventeen-year-old Louisa Twining used Euston for the first time a few days later on 2 June 1838. She recorded her breathless excitement: 'Went up to the station at Euston Square at eleven. I had no idea of the extent of the arrangements here or of the building. Nothing can be more regularly or beautifully managed.'

Where Euston Square station led, King's Cross, St Pancras and Somers Town Goods Depot followed. The King's Cross goods yards alone took up nearly 60 acres: to the north of Euston Road along Regent's Canal, warehouses, goods sheds, coke ovens, ice stores, train sheds, stables, offices, coal sheds, a huge granary warehouse, nine gasholders and over 100 sidings multiplied in what some called the 'railway lands'. St Pancras was built by the Midland Railway to bring beer and people to the capital, with the goods station opened in 1867, the passenger station in 1868 (with storage for beer beneath), and Sir Gilbert Scott's era-defining Midland Grand Hotel in 1873. Somers Town Goods Depot followed, a second huge goods depot this time under one roof.

Between 1867 and the late 1890s, when boats became bigger and profited from more efficient steam power and new hydraulic cranes, more goods arrived in London by train than by ship. The dirt, the noise, the need for cheap labour and the working man's muscle was all-conquering. The traffic along and into 'railway mile' was thunderous and Euston Road was thick with it, and like all terminal precincts, it was 'terribly cursed with prostitution'. In *The Picture of Dorian Gray*, Oscar Wilde housed the working-class actress Sibyl Vane (Dorian Gray's mistress in the first uncensored version of the story) in 'shabby lodgings' on Euston Road. To the north, Euston Road was the demesne of depot workers; to the south, according to Charles Booth's maps of London poverty, it remained more middle class.

But all were affected when, for over two years from 1860–3, the road was a building site as London's navvies dug London's first underground railway, the Metropolitan, down the street. Its shops and businesses suffered terribly; some even formed the Euston Road Trade Protection Association to lobby for reparations. They only partly succeeded and the chaos was considerable.

The Victorian contemporary historian of the early railways, Frederick Smeeton Williams, described the mess in his best-selling book *Our Iron Roads*:

> A few wooden houses on wheels first made their appearance and planted themselves by the gutter; then came some wagons loaded with timber, and accompanied by sundry gravel-coloured men with picks and shovels . . . The exact operations could be but dimly seen or heard from the street . . . but as paterfamilias, from his household

hard by, could look down on an infinite chaos of timber, shaft holes, ascending and descending chains and iron buckets which brought rubbish from the load to be carted away; or perhaps one morning he found workmen have been kind of shoring up his family abode with huge timbers to make it safer. A wet week comes, and the gravel in his front garden turns to clay; the tradespeople tread it backwards and forwards to and from the street door; he can hardly get out to business or home to supper without slipping, and he strongly objects to a temporary way of wet planks, erected for his use and the use of the passers-by, over a yawning cavern underneath the pavement.

Even when the mess was cleared away, Euston Road remained a place of trade and of passage and, during the twentieth century, of decline. The railways' infrastructure aged and was insufficiently renewed; in parallel, the roads' capacity was transformed by the lorry and motor car. War only made it worse. Bombs fell on Euston Station's Great Hall, on the junction with Tottenham Court Road, and on the goods yard, which was badly bombed four times during the Blitz and then hit again by a V-1 flying bomb. By 1945 Euston Road was badly blitzed. The traffic modernists were right that something needed to be done. But what?

The establishment view was to destroy more. In the 1920s, Le Corbusier had dreamt of demolishing central Paris and replacing it with fast roads and huge towers in sociologically segregated zones. As he put it, 'the technocratic elite, the industrialists, financiers, engineers, and artists would be located in the city centre, while the workers would be removed to the fringes of the city.'

Sir Patrick Abercrombie's *Greater London Plan* aimed to impose this architectural theocracy upon London. Five enormous ringways would encircle the city, linked by dozens of radials (including an engorged Euston Road). The 'drab and dreary' buildings in between would be cleaned away, with half a million people compulsorily removed to new 'satellite towns'. As always, the poor would have the least choice. Forty per cent of the East End population were to be transported. Monuments and a few historic villages, such as Kensington, would be allowed to remain, but everything else would have to go.

The unapologetic ambition of the scheme meant that lack of funds in post-war Britain hampered progress. Dual carriageways were cut through at London Wall and on Upper and Lower Thames Street, but most of London remained only imperfectly encircled.

The programme of destruction was given fresh impetus by one of the unsung villains of post-war history, Ernest Marples, who was Minister of Transport from 1959 to 1964. If Le Corbusier and Abercrombie were the prophets of London's traffic modernism, then Marples was the high priest. He was a dishonest, serially conflicted owner of a civil engineering company, who rose to become Minister of Transport despite the most profound conflict of interests between his motorway-commissioning public policy and his motorway-constructing private interests.

Amongst the roads that his firm, Marples Ridgway, worked on were the London section of the M1, the M56, and the Chiswick and Hammersmith flyovers. Amongst those commissioned or overseen by the ministry on his watch were the M1, the M56, and the Chiswick and Hammersmith flyovers. It is true that Marples sold his shares in the firm of which he held 80 per cent control during his tenure as a minister: he sold them to his wife. Modern conflict of interest controversies do not even come close. Marples was ultimately forced to flee to Monte Carlo due to thirty years of unpaid taxes and died in France.

In 1960, Marples commissioned the transport planner Sir Colin Buchanan to report on how British towns should be redesigned to accommodate rapidly rising car use. The Buchanan Report, subsequently republished by Penguin as *Traffic in Towns*, made the sensible observation that traffic growth within towns could not be sanctioned forever. It nevertheless proposed as the 'least absurd alternative' dedicating the city centre's ground floor to traffic and sequestrating pedestrians to a city-wide first-storey 'deck'.

Emboldened, the new Greater London Council (GLC) embarked on a public relations exercise. Colourful leaflets such as *Motorways for London* and *London's Roads: A Programme for Action* were delivered door to door. They planned three ringways (reduced from Abercrombie's five) to surround the city. An inner 'motorway box' with linking radials (still including Euston Road) should permit fast traffic readily to reach the heart of London. If this was a compromise between man and motor car, it was an unequal one. The Greater London Council's development plan intended to destroy 100,000 homes and to spend nearly £27 billion (in 2021 prices) on Ringways 1, 2 and 3.

For a period, all new city-centre buildings were obliged to incorporate an elevated podium. You can still see them on Castrol House in Marylebone Road, New Zealand House in Pall Mall, and the Economist Building in St James's Street. How they could have been joined without catastrophic urban destruction is impossible to comprehend. The Blitz would have been a mere irritant in comparison.

Given their totalitarian ambitions to remake the city, but their lack of totalitarian powers to seize land uncompensated, how could the Greater London Council create its dream of ringways? The deal done on Euston Road pointed the way: width for height. In over 400 separate purchases, the property developer Joe Levy had been secretly buying up all the properties on Euston Road around Euston Square and the junction with Tottenham Court Road since the 1950s. In what was effectively a 'permission for cash' deal, he permitted the widening of Euston Road on to his land and funded a £2 million underpass. In return, he got the twelve-and-a-half-acre Euston Centre development, a 35-storey tower looming over Regent's Park and a £22 million profit.

Whilst seventeenth-century London had permitted the dome and cross of Wren's St Paul's Cathedral to rise above the roofs, 1960s London extended the same honour to an office block and luxury flats. A sympathetic 1973 review in the *Sunday Times* described the Euston Centre as rising 'above the thundering swoop of traffic' and of being 'a grand accumulation of every aspect of modern development, wide piazzas, concrete walls, straight rows of small shops, tier upon tier of office windows'.

It was not only at Euston Square. The historic Euston Road was being engrossed into a wide dual carriageway lined by high and smooth modernist blocks. The textured rhythm of walking architecture was giving way to blander driving architecture. Further west it was even worse, as the link from the Euston and Marylebone Roads to the M40 and to the dreamed-of Ringway 1 was turned into an elevated motorway, the so-called Westway. The project, which cost nearly £500 million, required the rehousing of 5,000 families for every mile of road built and left a strip of wasteland beneath for which there were no plans. Even the British Road Federation conceded it was 'insensitive' and 'socially unacceptable'.

At the east end of Euston Road, modernity's attack on London was less destructive of Londoners' homes, but even more powerfully symbolic. Euston Station, the first building on Euston Road's 'railway mile', contained three masterpieces: the Great Hall of the station atrium, described by Sir John Betjeman as 'one of London's finest rooms' and that treated all visitors, rich or poor alike, as guests at a luxury hotel; the Shareholder's Meeting Room upstairs, least known to the public but of a sumptuous magnificence; and the Euston Arch, which by the 1960s had been a symbol of London and of the railways for over 120 years even, rather inaccurately, being used to illustrate 'A is for Arch' in children's books.

British Rail was determined to destroy them all. There was at least some semblance of utilitarian justification for demolishing the station itself, as longer platforms were necessary and the old station crossed their most obvious path. However, abolishing the austerely beautiful Euston Arch was an unnecessary act of modernist malice. The Earl of Euston and John Betjeman spearheaded a spirited and passionate campaign to save it. The contractor offered to re-site it nearby for a modest cost, but British Rail, backed by Ernest Marples and Prime Minister Harold Macmillan, was adamant. Euston Arch was the past – and the past needed to be swept away.

Dodgy reconstruction cost figures (£4.3 million in 2021 money) were chucked about and over the winter of 1961–2 the Arch was demolished. Instead of paying for reconstruction, British Rail paid for most of the stones to be transported to the river Lee in east London, where they secretly dumped them in the Prescott Channel, like murderers hiding the evidence of their crime.

Although they have had sixty years to accustom themselves to it, Londoners have not come to love the new Euston Station. Two generations of use still leaves a featureless concrete box as a featureless concrete box. The semi-subterranean platforms are dark and bare, seemingly designed for troglodytes not humans, and the main hall still looks, as Betjeman put it, 'like a mini-version of London Airport which it seems to be trying to imitate', Even a critic attempting to be sympathetic, the railways historian

Christian Wolmar, has conceded that 'this is still an unlovable terminus with not a single feature of architectural merit.'

Euston Station's demise, and the pitiable ugliness of its replacement, has been an effective recruiting sergeant for heritage preservation ever since. Why support change, when it so palpably makes things worse?

If the battle for Euston Station was lost, the battle for London in the late 1960s was still to be fought. The Greater London Council was determined to press ahead with the 'motorway box' for the city. Their problem was that the people did not agree. Engaged and enraged by what they saw, neighbourhoods across London bandied together to fight the motorway plans; by 1970 there were over 100 opposing groups. As the GLC's plan went out to public consultation, it became clear that the reaction to the Westway was only a precursor of what was to come. Simon Jenkins, who was present at some of them, recalled that 'officials attending meetings in affected areas . . . were lucky to escape unharmed.'

In 1973, the Conservatives were defeated in local elections and the incoming Labour regime wisely abandoned the plan. It seemed the street was not dead yet. Le Corbusier's vision of the future, as Osbert Lancaster put it, 'presupposes a barrenness of spirit to which, despite every indication of its ultimate achievement, we have not yet quite attained'. Perhaps we never will.

Meanwhile what of Euston Road? It is still disgusting, a victim of mid-century traffic modernism. As awareness of the dangers of the invisible air pollution created by cars has increased, the profound health problems of fast dual carriageways within the city have become ever starker. In 2015, the 'Urban Partnership for King's Cross, Euston and St Pancras' proposed the 'Wellbeing

Walk', so that pedestrians could avoid Euston Road altogether, so foul was the life-shortening air upon the main road. A street that you need to avoid, in order to move safely about the city, is rather losing its original purpose.

In 1994, the campaigning architectural historian Dan Cruickshank tracked down the remains of the murdered Euston Arch in the Prescott Channel and salvaged one of the stones. Twenty-nine more were raised in 2009 and the Euston Arch Trust was created to campaign for its reconstruction.

In 2016, the social enterprise I founded, Create Streets, worked with the architect Francis Terry to explore recreating Euston Road as a tree-lined boulevard, celebrating what survives from the past (such as St Pancras Town Hall), and creating higher, more beautiful buildings where possible, with a tram line and the Euston Arch serving as a tram stop (the tunnel beneath would need supporting). Plans for the high-speed link to the north, so-called HS2, also propose to sweep away the 1960s station and, possibly, to restore the arch. However, whether HS2's replacement plan will be any better remains moot; nor have plans to improve Euston Road's air quality yet passed go.

The Euston Road was built as a bypass for sheep and has become a sewer for traffic. It has just about survived the twentieth century and it will always need to carry many people between stations and beyond, but whether it can do so humanely in the future remains to be seen. Will Euston Road stop being disgusting? We do not yet know.

Chapter 22

TRAFALGAR SQUARE

Riot and rediscovery

*The sixteenth day of the same month was burnt the kynges
stable at Charyng crosse otherwise called the Mewse, wherein
was burnt many great Horses and great store of haye.*
Edward Hall, *Hall's Chronicle* (1548), describing the
events of 1534

Who is London for? Who decides what it looks like or what stories its streets and statues tell? No *Monopoly* street is as rich with symbolism as Trafalgar Square, centre point for all road signs indicating London from Cornwall to Cumbria. No London square represents simultaneously both imperial prowess and popular protest, and nowhere else in this book has changed as profoundly as the space where Trafalgar Square now stands. It began as a yard for royal falcons, became a stable under Henry VIII and then a bijou private courtyard for the rich and well connected, before being thrown open in the street-creating frenzy of the nineteenth century.

However, central London's newest public square continually surprises. Named after Britain's greatest imperial victory, Admiral Nelson's seismic 1805 defeat of the French and Spanish navies off Cape Trafalgar, the parsimonious Victorian authorities took forty years to complete it and, in the process, created a venue for populist dissent as well as for imperial pageant.

It is also a space where we can, and do, argue about what our city looks like and what stories we cherish. Was Charles I a tyrant or a martyr? Should extensions to national institutions such as the National Gallery 'fit in' or 'stand out', and be of their time or of their place? Should statues of old generals be pulled down or empty plinths commemorate the Battle of Britain, transgender rights – or nothing at all?

Trafalgar Square also tells a deeply interrelated tale of how we *use* our urban space. It was created when the Commissioners of Woods, Forests and Land Revenues decided in 1826 to 'cut through' from Pall Mall to St Martin's Lane and then got ambitious. It descended, like so many London streets, into a swirling cauldron for noxious traffic; a place for tourists to visit, not for Londoners to enjoy. However, it has since been gloriously reborn due to the simple act of mapping where people want to walk and of building a staircase.

No *Monopoly* street demonstrates London's infinite capacity for renaissance better than Trafalgar Square, where four admirals, two kings, two generals and, at the time of writing, a dollop of whipped cream with a fly on top, stare down Whitehall to the Georgian and Victorian gothic towers of Westminster.

It all begins with falcons. At some passing moment in or shortly before 1273, that epitome of English kingship, Edward I, conqueror of the Welsh, hammer of the Scots, known as 'Longshanks' for his stature and long legs, ordered Thomas de Erleham to look after his falcons when they were moulting and could not be used for hunting. The king offered Thomas nine pence a day and instructed him to perform his duties down the road from the palace in the village of Charing (from the Anglo-Saxon *cerr* meaning a turn and referring to the bend there in the river Thames).

In the thirteenth century, the court still primarily spoke Anglo-Norman French and the building in which the falcons were kept became known as the 'Muwes' after the French, *muer* meaning 'to moult'. Falconry was high cost and high status and the Royal Muwes must rapidly have become quite an establishment. The team of falconers 'dwelling' there was numerous enough to require a chaplain and a chapel. It stood where the north side of Trafalgar Square now stands.

In fact, Edward I very much defined Charing for over 500 years; he even changed its name. A few years after the creation of the Royal Mews, in 1291, a recently bereaved Edward erected the most elaborate and heavily gilded of his twelve Eleanor Crosses to his beloved dead wife, Eleanor of Castile, a few yards to the south of the falconry. The original physical cross is gone, but it remains in nomenclature.

Two hundred and fifty years later, Henry VIII, a temperamental conservative addicted to radical change, pulled down the Royal Mews so that its stone, brick, chalk and tiles could be used for his new palace on Whitehall. The Crown began using the site as a stable instead, certainly after and probably before a fire forced their reconstruction in 1534. However, despite the loss of its avian use, the now anglicised name of 'mews' stuck. It has since become the standard name for any court or street of urban stable buildings in the English-speaking world. Though you could never guess it today, the world's first mews really was at Trafalgar Square.

During the seventeenth century, the Royal Mews became a home to people as well as to horses. Court favourites and officials began to lodge there. It is a transition that has subsequently been eerily echoed by all the mews in all the side streets of central London, as technology inserted cars and then spiralling land costs inserted people where once horses lodged. By 1653, when Oliver Cromwell pulled down the Eleanor Cross and then had the Mews cleared for his own use, it contained 'lodgings, rooms and stables' cheek by jowl.

At the junction (now the south of Trafalgar Square) where Eleanor's Cross had stood and where Whitehall, the Strand and St Martin's Lane met, an equestrian statue of Charles I was installed after the monarchy's restoration and a public pillory placed beside it.[77] The bronze Charles stares down Whitehall to the site of the corporeal Charles's execution outside the Banqueting House.

The statue is a particularly fine one. Already fifty years old at its re-erection, the aptly named metalsmith John Rivet had refused to melt it down as ordered by Parliament during the Commonwealth. Instead, he hid it and fraudulently sold brass-handled knives and forks as being formed from the remains. Charles I is the first and by far the oldest of Trafalgar Square's statues and the only physical survivor from the seventeenth century still *in situ*, as the entire neighbourhood around has been transmogrified.

During the eighteenth century, some architects began to plan such a transformation. Surely such a significant congress of roads to the City, to Westminster, and to the new residential suburbs to the west and north required a more significant public space? In 1766 the architect John Gwynn, as well as proposing the idea of Regent Street, also proposed Trafalgar Square (though he called it King's Square), immediately to the west of St Martin-in-the-Fields.

No one at the time paid any attention, but good ideas get disinterred. The 1826 report of the Commissioners of Woods, Forests and Land Revenues recorded:

> As soon as we were put in possession of the Site of the Lower Mews at Charing Cross, we took measures for proceeding to execute that part of the Improvement, which had for its object the continuation of Pall Mall into Saint Martin's Lane, terminating at the Portico of Saint Martin's Church, and forming an open area in front of the King's Mews, and it . . . appeared to us, after mature consideration, that the unequal lengths of the two sides of the open Area, proposed by the original Plan, would be a deformity, peculiarly striking, in the approach from Whitehall; that a much larger space, than was at first designed, ought to be left open, and the West end of the Strand considerably widened.

And thus, in a moment of urban renaissance that was to be echoed nearly 200 years later, was born Trafalgar Square. The Charing Cross Improvements Act was passed immediately. Charles Arbuthnot, the Commissioner of Woods, Forests and Land Revenues, explained to the House of Commons that the new square would 'embellish and adorn the metropolis' and 'create a more convenient communication between the East and West ends of town'. John Nash was commissioned to design it. The tumbledown and gimcrack houses of St Martin's Lane were torn down,[78] and by 1830 the square was a public open space.

By 1835, it was named after Nelson's naval triumph, agreed by the sailor king William IV, a great admirer of Nelson, in conversation with Sir Thomas Hardy – Nelson's captain on HMS *Victory* and in whose arms the hero had died ('Kiss me,

Hardy'). By 1838, a new National Gallery had been built to house a recently purchased collection of pictures, and to recycle the Corinthian columns from the demolished home of the Prince Regent, Carlton House.

Finishing the square itself took another thirty years. John Nash died and the Commissioners of Woods, Forests and Land Revenues focused their efforts elsewhere. Charles Barry was commissioned to complete Nash's scheme, which he improved by creating a terrace to manage the land sloping down to the river and to enhance the modest two-storey facade of the National Gallery. The Nelson Memorial Committee then sabotaged Barry's design by selecting as the winning design for their Nelson memorial a 203-feet column that overwhelmed his proportions for the square. Public disquiet at the sheer height of the thing, as well as the cost, subsequently reduced the height to 169 feet.[79]

The column cost too much. It broke the budget of the Nelson Memorial Committee, whose funds had been seeded by the same Russian-born financier and Lloyds underwriter, John Julius Angerstein, whose collection of paintings had formed the nucleus of the National Gallery's collection. The Commissioners of Woods, Forests and Land Revenues only paid for the bronze reliefs and the lion statues at the column's base slowly and begrudgingly. The last lion, for which Edwin Landseer normally gets the credit but on which the French sculptor Carlo Marochetti provided most of the technical expertise, was not installed until 1867, over sixty years after Nelson's death. Victorian authorities, though effective, could be lingeringly parsimonious.

Trafalgar Square was intended to be a place to celebrate regal splendour and martial successes. During its first thirty years, statues of George IV and of two heroes of British India, Generals Napier and Havelock, were erected, though they ran out of money for William IV.[80] Admirals were added later.

However, it became firmly linked with political dissent. The Chartist rally of 1848 began in Trafalgar Square and the so-called 'Bloody Sunday' riot of 1887 against unemployment and Irish coercion occurred there. The IRA blew up a bomb there in 1885, as did the Suffragettes in 1913 and 1914. The Campaign for Nuclear Disarmament (CND) rallied against 'the bomb' in Trafalgar Square, and the Vietnam, Afghanistan and Iraq wars were all opposed there. Throughout the 1980s, anti-apartheid protesters picketed South Africa House on the square's east side, and in March 1990, the poll tax riot that helped bring down Margaret Thatcher as prime minister, was centred on Trafalgar Square.

DAME MYRA HESS AND TRAFALGAR SQUARE'S WAR WORK

Trafalgar Square was 'shut up' for the duration of the Second World War. Herbert Le Sueur equestrian statue of Charles I was stored in Leighton Buzzard and the National Gallery's collection was cached in a Welsh slate quarry, the building itself expected to be requisitioned for war work. But the concert pianist Myra Hess had a better idea. She proposed to the Director, Kenneth Clark, a series of lunchtime concerts. He loved the idea: 'Of course I was delighted at the thought of the gallery being used again for its true purpose, the enjoyment of beauty, rather than for the filling in of forms or the sticking up of envelopes.'

Within a few weeks an exemption for the ban on public gatherings was granted, the octagonal Room 36 was selected (with the boardroom curtains hung across to create, in Clark's words, 'a vestige of baroque splendour'), chairs were donated, including by Buckingham Palace, and Steinway and Sons lent a piano, prominently branded on the audience's side. It was tested with a few bars of 'Moonlight Sonata', the acoustics declared magnificent and the first concert held on 10 October 1939.

Myra Hess, who gave the first concert alone in case the whole thing was a flop, expected an audience of forty to fifty and was very nervous. She could not have been more wrong. As her nephew recalled:

The Director of the Gallery came rushing in and said, 'We've got a problem,' and Myra thought, oh goodness, what now? He said, 'There are a thousand people on the pavement snaking all the way around the front of the Gallery and around Trafalgar Square.' And they were only supposed to have 200.

The success was due to pent-up demand with no competition, to the price (only one shilling), but also to the unpretentious, informal atmosphere. There was no advance booking and the audience were free to eat their sandwiches and wander in or out as they chose. Performers were paid a standard fee of five guineas, whoever they were. The only exception was Myra Hess. She presented 1,698 concerts and personally played in 150 of them, but was never paid a penny.

The concerts, and Myra Hess herself, appear fourteen minutes into the bold and poetic 1942 wartime documentary, *Listen to Britain*. Amongst the audience were Queen Elizabeth, the late Queen Mother, and remnants of the West End glitterati, but also Wrens on their lunch break, working-class women, and ordinary soldiers and sailors passing through London. The everyman, 'all in it together' nature of the Second World War was of course emphasised, even exaggerated, but it was not a myth. Behind the audience, the empty frames of the national collection can be seen leaning forlornly against the bare walls.

Kenneth Clark wrote of the very first, oversubscribed concert:

> The moment when she [Myra Hess] played the opening bars of Beethoven's Appassionata will always remain for me one of the great experiences of my life. It was an assurance that all our sufferings were not in vain.

Trafalgar Square is a place of symbolic as well as physical dispute. On 16 November 1940, Hamptons, the National Gallery's neighbouring luxury furniture store, whose contracts included the Royal Yacht *Britannia*, the *Queen Mary*, the Dorchester Hotel and the Nizam of Hyderabad, was eviscerated by an incendiary bomb. Ever since, the National Gallery had aspired to expand into the site, but money and materials were rationed in post-war London. Only in the 1980s was sufficient treasure available.

Angerstein's heirs ran an architectural competition and, true to the culture of 'anti-street' modernism, proposed to build a textbook example of 'driving architecture' with a chunky high-tech tower, which might or might not exhilarate at 50 miles per hour and from 200 yards, but fitted only with difficulty into a London square. It had been designed at the wrong scale.

The problem was that the public were getting tired of their streets and squares being performatively misunderstood. Since the Euston 'Arch' debacle, the emotional tide had turned with, as Jerry White put it, a 'growing feeling that the old was worth saving and the new not worth having'. Officially sanctioned plans to destroy the Tate Gallery, to erase Covent Garden, and to sweep away most of Whitehall and replace it with a road tunnel and a series of ziggurats, had been defeated by near universal public disgust and by the eloquent advocacy of both old (John Summerson, John Betjeman and Osbert Lancaster) and young (Simon Jenkins, Ian Nairn and Nicholas Taylor).

Against this backdrop, Prince Charles, the then Prince of Wales, was invited to give a gala speech at Hampton Court Palace to mark the 150th anniversary of the Royal Institute of British Architects in 1984. The prince was thirty-six and had never previously 'given trouble' on matters architectural; only recently he had opened one of the most formlessly ugly and inhumane buildings in Europe, Milton Keynes Central railway station, without demur. But his profound horror at what the twentieth century was doing to its urban and rural environments was deepening.

In an astonishingly bold speech, Prince Charles spoiled the after-dinner backslapping:

What, then, are we doing to our capital city now? What have we done to it since the bombing during the war? What are we shortly to do to one of its most famous areas – Trafalgar Square? Instead of designing an extension to the elegant facade of the National Gallery which complements it and continues the concept of columns and domes, it looks as if we may be presented with a kind of municipal fire station, complete with the sort of tower that contains the siren. I would understand better this type of high-tech approach if you demolished the whole of Trafalgar Square and started again with a single architect responsible for the entire layout, but what is proposed is like a monstrous carbuncle on the face of a much-loved and elegant friend.

The professional uproar was loud and bitter. But the public agreed, as 99 per cent of the 5,000 letters the prince received after a subsequent film examining his views on architecture were supportive, whilst 0.5 per cent expressed qualified support. More recent controlled polling on related questions corroborates this strong support for less 'faceless architecture'. The National Gallery, more concerned with elite than popular opinion, pressed on gamely, but were refused planning permission the same year. The final building was a better detailed though unbalanced post-modernist mash by the American architects, Venturi, Scott Brown.

Might Trafalgar Square's originally intended nature as a place of calm national symbolism reassert itself after such a princely intervention? Not for long. Since 1999, the square's most discussed sculptures have not been its permanent collection of imperial victors, but its rotating exhibition of conceptual shapes on the empty fourth plinth intended for William IV. They include a head crushed between a book and the roots of a tree, an upside-down resin plinth, a model of a 21-storey coloured building, a blue cockerel, a skeletal horse, an elongated thumb, and a splurge of whipped cream with a cherry and a fly on top. All that is playful, inexplicable, strange or grotesque has been there.

One consistent flavour is present in such studied variety: the desire to startle, to be different, and to contrast with the neighbouring august panjandrums. The Turner Prize-winning sculptor, Antony Gormley, whose own 'sculpture' was an invitation to 2,400 selected members of the public to spend one hour on the plinth over the course of one hundred days, described his intent to elevate 'everyday life' in place of the square's 'military, valedictory and male historical statues'. Is modern Trafalgar Square about culture or counter-culture? And which is which?

The programme of temporary statues, even when ridiculed in the popular press, has nevertheless been a popular success. We love to clutch at our pearls. Three successive London mayors, of left and right, have enjoyed the patronage, and attempts to use the plinth more traditionally have all failed. Historic campaigns to commemorate Cecil Rhodes (in 1936), merchant seamen (in 1950), Winston Churchill (in 1964), Lord Mountbatten (in 1979) or Canada's war dead (in 1988) got nowhere. Nor have more recent essays to celebrate Nelson Mandela, Margaret Thatcher or Keith Park – the New Zealander whose meticulous Battle of Britain leadership of Fighter Command's 11 Group helped save Britain from invasion in 1940.[81]

With popular radicalism came popular renaissance. In a brilliant and bold combination of civic leadership, design intelligence, cross-party working and political guts, Greater London's first ever mayor, Ken Livingstone, closed the northern carriageway to cars, rerouted traffic round the south of the square and installed a prominent and elegantly designed new staircase up to Charles Barry's terrace.

Space Syntax, a University College London spinout firm, analysed how people used Trafalgar Square. They followed 300 people. Only two walked through the square and 298 walked around it. Londoners were simply not engaging with the city's geographic centre. Tim Stonor, who was in the design team, recalled:

The light-bulb moment came in a conversation when we realised that the real answer was creating a central staircase. We took the idea to Norman Foster, who was leading the project. He loved it. It was a big, bold move. It only required the demolition of a Grade I listed wall.

With the carriageway liberated, a prominent central staircase permitted visitors to move and congregate effortlessly and with pleasure into and out of the square. The result has been an unqualified success. The square has emerged from four sides of noxious fumes and been rediscovered as one of London's great places for visitors and residents alike.

No one should doubt Trafalgar Square's symbolic value: those road signs do all count from the statue of King Charles I. William Morris's vision of a future socialist Britain, *News from Nowhere*, imagined a revolution precipitated by the 'massacre of Trafalgar Square'; Adolf Hitler planned to re-erect Nelson's Column in Berlin, had Keith Park not done his work so well, and George Orwell renamed it Victory Square in his dystopian novel, *1984*, with Big Brother's statue usurping Nelson.

Trafalgar Square stares down two of London's oldest streets, Whitehall and the Strand, to Westminster and the City. It celebrates imperial victories remote to most of the public, but it also demonstrates the potential for tradition to be created; Trafalgar Square is not that old, a mere 190-year adolescent in London's long history. It demonstrates, better than anywhere, the potential for streets and squares to be rediscovered. Who is London for? It is for Londoners. And they are, happily, less partisan than our masters.

In a pleasing symbiosis of past and present, and of reverence and renewal, the fourth plinth's most popular success has been 'Nelson's Ship in a Bottle', by the British-Nigerian artist Yinka Shonibare. A lovingly detailed, properly built representative model of Nelson's flagship, HMS *Victory*, it sits, as did the craft creations of so many retired Victorian sailors, in a bottle. However, it is a giant one and the sails rather than being authentically white are a joyous blizzard of patterns and colours, so called 'African fabric'. These are popular as clothes in modern Africa, though are in fact Dutch wax-printed cotton, historically manufactured in Manchester, a typical product of colonial trade flows.[82]

What better symbol could there be for London's maritime past and mingled present than a beautifully colourful, traditionally made sailing ship in a bottle which sings, as Shonibare elegantly put it, of 'the many cultures and ethnicities that are still breathing precious wind into the sails of the United Kingdom'.

CONCLUSION

Advance to Go

*To all Londoners, whether by birth or adoption, and to
all engaged in the government of London, I would say:
guard you well your heritage and your charge. For what
Londoner can look upon London and not love it? London!*
Hugh Green, *How London is Governed*, 1931

L ondon is old and her first streets are older. They allow us
to journey not only in space but through time, from the
impossibly remote past into an unknowable future. By mile
of tarmac, though not by intensity of use, most of London's
streets may be less than 150 years old. But, once built, streets
have this habit of sticking around, particularly when they go
somewhere and are not carved into existing blocks as courts or
back alleys. Only the poorest, most put-upon neighbourhoods
lose their streets to the regenerating slum clearance of the well
intentioned. Where we tread, where our ancestors trod, so
generations yet unborn will tread on London's streets.

Profundity and speed of change, but also its limitations, are
made very real by the first, and oldest, of our *Monopoly* streets,
the Old Kent Road. We left the Old Kent Road in the Middle
Ages as pilgrims journeyed along it to Canterbury or Henry V's
archers returned down it from Agincourt. What happened next?

The Kent Road had changed little by the eighteenth century. In 1746, the talented French-born Huguenot, John Rocque, published his beautiful London map and it shows the road very clearly. It is paved, following an Act of Parliament of 1565, and is lined with a single row of generously gardened terraced houses. Then the buildings give way to a landscape of small fields, orchards, hedgerows and market gardens. The Kent Road is dotted with the odd inn, turnpike or farmhouse, but by the time you are barely more than a mile out of London the road is thoroughly rural, with little but fields and fruit trees until you approach the village of Deptford.

Birch twigs were gathered to make brooms. New homes, when they were built, were large and generous. An elegant crescent, the Paragon, was created for those seeking fresh air and elegance away from London. (It does not survive but the Paragon at Blackheath, which copied it, does.) Briefly, the area might have become genteel. The Welsh Rolls family, who owned many of the fields along the street and later invested in motor cars alongside the Royces, built Surrey Square to that purpose but it was never completed.

Industrialisation happened suddenly and fast in this bit of south-east London. The Kent Road was linked to the Surrey Canal in 1811 and to the new Bricklayers Arms railway station in 1845. Tanneries, costermongers, bricklayers, gasworks and soap processing all flourished as the 'Great Wen' of London swelled biliously in all directions, and the fields and lanes around the Kent Road were rapidly converted into streets, lanes, houses, flats and workshops. Legally being in Surrey, London's building quality stipulations did not apply.

The Bricklayers Arms station was an exception to the success and squalor. Despite being elegantly designed by Lewis Cubitt, who was the genius responsible for King's Cross a few years later, it was too remote from the city centre and ceased to function as a passenger terminus after only seven years. Passengers travelled to London Bridge instead and all that remains of the station is a bit of the stables, a quietly elegant row of blind brick arches in London stock brick, hidden in a back street – the clear antecedent of King's Cross, if anyone cares to look.

Houses were over-occupied, water was dirty and lives were short. Within forty years, the neighbourhood evolved from toll gates and inns to having one of Europe's highest population densities. It soon became seen as the epitome of working-class, cockney London. The Victorian music hall star, Albert Chevalier, even set one of his most popular songs about a sudden influx of wealth to a poor cockney family in the alleys and lanes surrounding the Old Kent Road.

'Wot cher!' all the neighbours cried,
'Who yer gonna meet, Bill?
Have yer bought the street, Bill?'
Laugh! I thought I should 've died,
Knock'd 'em in the Old Kent Road!

As the Old Kent Road changed in character from rural road to archetypal, working-class high street swarming with market stalls and costermongers, one thing remained profoundly the same. It was still the main road heading south-east. David Copperfield walked to Rochester along the Kent Road, capturing perfectly the brief period of its change from fields to working-class suburb. On the way, he was able to sell his waistcoat for ninepence at a rag shop, but then sleep in a haystack near Blackheath.

By the time George Orwell tramped south in the 1930s, researching the lives of the destitute, it was thoroughly urban:

> We went southward by the Old Kent Road, making for Cromley . . . It was a sixteen-mile walk over asphalt, blistering to the heels, and we were acutely hungry. Paddy browsed the pavement, laying up a store of cigarette ends against his time in the spike [workhouse]. In the end his perseverance was rewarded, for he picked up a penny. We bought a large piece of stale bread and devoured it as we walked.

It was a memory Orwell drew on in his novel *A Clergyman's Daughter*, where the protagonist symbolically finds herself on the Old Kent Road after an attack of amnesia. Unlike George Orwell, Victor Watson and Marjory Phillips almost certainly never saw the road, let alone its cigarette butts and stale bread. You can hardly blame them. The reputation for poverty, bawdy drinking and music hall humour was not designed to appeal to the genteel on day trips to London.

They would have been even less inclined to visit after the Second World War, when change was even faster. Over a third of the road was destroyed or damaged by wartime bombing. The first bomb fell on the Old Kent Road on the very first night of the Blitz at 12:32 in the morning of 7 September 1940. One room was damaged and no one was hurt. The last explosion was not so benign. Four years, four months and one week later at 09:55 on 14 February 1945, a V-2 rocket exploded 200 yards from the Old Kent Road on the junction of Waite Street and Trafalgar Avenue. Thirteen people were killed immediately, subsequently rising to eighteen; a further seventy-eight were injured and ten were saved from collapsed homes by rescue dogs.

CONCLUSION

The police managed the incident badly, permitting too many spectators and a traffic jam, which impeded ambulances. The explosion formed a crater 40 feet wide and 10 feet deep. It destroyed twelve pretty 1850s 'neo Greek' houses and led to the demolition, probably unnecessarily, of twenty-five more; to this day the site remains empty, a crossroads without buildings. The gatepost of one of the demolished homes still stands forlornly on the edge of the site, overgrown with bushes and shielded by green wheelie bins.

What bombs did not achieve, post-war planners, highway engineers, de-industrialisation, crime and corruption completed. The Victorian Old Kent Road was polluted and poor, but it was busy and vibrant, a place of street stalls and gin palaces, activity, work and drinking. Town planners and highway engineers ended that. They asserted an impoverished perception of the street's role as a place merely to *get through*, not a place to *stop in* – and this time at 30 miles per hour. The consequences were disastrous.

In 1968, the authorities opened a flyover, very close to where the medieval lepers' hospital had stood, to increase the traffic's speed and flow. A central barrier was erected, turning the road into a poor man's dual carriageway squeezed into a historic street. As the cars got faster and more frequent, the surviving Victorian buildings were pulled down in the 1960s and 1970s to be replaced with nightmarish, brutalist estates – most prominently the Heygate and the Aylesbury.

Despite desperate and unevidenced attempts to revive their reputation by architectural activists, these estates comprehensively failed as places to live; cruel jokes played upon the working classes by middle-class planners who chose to live elsewhere. Despite the wretched condition of historic streets, one young mother moved to the Aylesbury Estate commented, 'There's nowhere for the kids to play . . . it's like a prison, isn't it, all concrete.' Sir Michael Caine, who grew up nearby and filmed the vigilante film *Harry Brown* in the Heygate Estate, called the development a 'rotten place', which 'should never have been built'.

The planners' intentions were noble. Post-war London was in a miserable and slummy state after war, coal and rent controls. As late as 1961, over half the single-family homes in Southwark, through which the Old Kent Road ran, had no bath. One government minister painted a vivid picture of the sordid conditions in old streets and homes:

> Basement areas used as common rubbish dumps, roofs used for garbage disposal, entrance halls bearing the marks . . . of a common pissoir, with contraceptives strewn in the rickety Dickensian staircases, often with the plaster peeled off and the bare lattice boards exposed; broken windowpanes, exposed and dangerous electrical fittings, and common lavatories and bathrooms of almost indescribable sordidness.

Of course, much of the time a simpler, faster and cheaper alternative would have been to restore the existing buildings (adding bathrooms in the process), or to rebuild using the same street pattern. This was too rarely considered; Islington Council had the best programme of street repair not street destruction. Meanwhile the Old Kent Road's industry shut, pushed out of town by changing land-use policy and rising costs.

By the 1970s and 1980s, the whole area had become a byword for urban decay. Crime escalated, local schools failed, and the few shops provided for in the new estates closed. Post-war planning was well intentioned, but it had not succeeded because it ignored the eternal patterns of human life. By 1999, there were 408 criminal offences per 1,000 of the population; at one point only 17 per cent of local children were achieving five good GCSEs. In 1997, Tony Blair made his first speech as prime minister on the Aylesbury Estate to highlight the challenges of broken Britain.

Have matters improved since? Some have, some haven't. In the 1960s, the Richardson gang (notorious for torturing with pliers, nail guns, bolt cutters and an old army field generator known as the 'Black Box') used to go drinking on the Old Kent Road. Today, even that would be hard. For over forty years the pubs and businesses of the area have been closing; once there were thirty-nine pubs, now there are only a handful.

The reason is that local government, for a second time, has permitted and indeed encouraged the entire district's ruination. Not content with depopulating the neighbourhood in the 1970s, in a series of diabolical planning decisions over the last twenty-five years, Southwark Council has treated the whole area as an out-of-town shopping precinct, even though it is little more than a mile from the City of London.

The result is a dystopia of large, grey shopping boxes – the existential endpoint of traffic modernism in the sterile 'honesty' of their architecture and in their surrounding acres of car parking. It is no place for people to stop and linger, or love to live. Not surprisingly, attempts at local business along the Old Kent Road continue to struggle, stranded between fast cars, large car parks, and depopulated, unpopular estates awaiting their turn at a second round of 'regeneration', even though they are less than a lifetime old.

For, in the perpetual cycle of urban decay and rebirth, the neighbourhood around the Old Kent Road will soon be spanking new again. The Old Kent Road 'Opportunity Area' is being planned and marshalled with a new Tube line and new towers in re-fashionable London stock brick. The age of concrete is over – for now. The Heygate Estate has already been demolished; it lasted less than forty years. The Aylesbury Estate is also being demolished. It will last less than fifty. Both are savage failures of 'sustainable development', while the surrounding streets, and indeed the Old Kent Road itself, march on into the twenty-first century.

Two millennia old and still counting. Simply because it has the good sense to go from A to B.

In the long history of London, human lives are vanishingly brief, buildings' lives often little longer. But streets are the city's most ancient and most persistent infrastructure. Where Celts and Romans journeyed, where we drive, so people of the future and the far future will also travel. Hundreds or thousands of years from now, we have no idea what technology humans will use to propel themselves, what tasks they will do when they arrive, or how they will undertake them. But we do know the routes that they will take.

London's streets, ultimately, are no game. They are the stuff and sinews of London. They are times past and times future. They *are* London.

ACKNOWLEDGEMENTS

Any wide-ranging history stands on others' shoulders. This book would have been inconceivable without the giant-like labours of the editors and authors of the *Survey of London*. It would have been less lively without the sparkling social histories of Liza Picard. And its key theses would have been unwritable without the important studies of London's growth and regulation by Norman Brett-James and Sir Simon Jenkins, whose counsel has been clear and wise. *No Free Parking* would not exist without the generous match-making of Clive Aslet, the intellectual clarity of my agent, Adrian Sington, the elegant typesetting of Graeme Andrew at Envy Design, the superb cover of Emily Rough and the superhumanly patient advice of James Hodgkinson, my editor at Bonnier Books.

This is a history book, and I am by temperament a historian, nevertheless my primary debt is to the non-historians who have encouraged, supported or advised Create Streets. Without a confident, empirical and neighbourhood-led perspective into the types of places in which people flourish and prosper, I would not have dared to embark. In approximate chronological order I owe thanks to Ben Page, Simon Houfe, Alan Powers, Ben Bolgar, the late Hank Dittmar, Yolande Barnes, Alain de Botton, Alexander Stevenson, Tim Stoner, Neil O'Brien, Alex Morton, Rachel Fisher, Dominic Richards, Paul Murrain, David Taylor, Francis Terry, Nigel Franklin,

John Spence, Chris Rainsford, Adam Knight, Pete Gladwell, Robert Adam, Sian Hansen, Isabelle Irani, Aster Crawshaw, Chris Brown, John Moss, Ike Ijeh, Flora Neville, James Wildblood, Harry Phibbs, Jonathan Schifferes, Ben Rogers, Euan Mills, Kieran Toms, Edward Denison, Ruaidhri Tulloch, Elliot Lipton, James Anderson, the late Tony Pidgley, Richard Upton, Martyn Evans, Lord Salisbury, Jonathan Rosenberg, John Myers, Alessandro Venerandi, Maddalena Iovene, Chanuki Seresinhe, Hugh Seaborn, Lord Cadogan, Ann Sussman, John Massengale, Charles Marohn, Charles Montgomery, Ed West, the late Sir Roger Scruton, Sophie Scruton, the late James Brokenshire, Mary Parsons, Adrian Penfold, Steve Quartermain, the Building Better Building Beautiful advisors and officials, Sergio Porta, Samuel Hughes, Ben Southwood, John Simpson, Joanna Wachovia, Robert Jenrick, Zewditu Gebreyohanes, Hugh Petter, George Samaurez Smith, Simon Kidney, Christopher Boyle QC, Michael Gove, Sir Laurie Magnus, Vidhya Alakeson, Matt Leach, Catherine Harrington, Matthew Carmona, Alastair Parvin, Nicole Gray Conchar, Stephen Brien, Baroness Stroud, Lord Glasman, Will Tanner, Katie Fairclough, Nada Elfeituri, Hugo Owen, Lydia Ogden, Lauren Lawson, Robin Edwards, Richard Briance, all of the patient officials at the Office for Place and those of my generous board not already named: Andrew Cameron, Ben Gummer, Sir John Hayes, Victoria Hills, Esther Kurland, Mustafa Latif-Aramesh, Paul Monaghan, Anna Rose and Stephen Stone. To those omitted, apologies

At Create Streets and the Create Streets Foundation daily marvels are made possible by David Milner, Robert Kwolek, Eleanor Broad, George Payiatis, Tom Noble, Lauren Botterill, Edward Leahy, Toby Lloyd, Rose Grayson, Mark Shepherd, Harry Briggs, Lucille Briance, Clare Mirfin, Fabian Richter and Haribo who manages well-being. Constance is the peerless bedrock of my life and work and Alexander and Edward donate infinite hope, purpose and love whose only price is time.

SELECT BIBLIOGRAPHY

Here are the sources I found most useful or enjoyable:

PRIMARY SOURCES, OFFICIAL HISTORIES AND REPORTS

D. Defoe (1724), *A narrative of all the robberies, escapes etc of John Sheppard*

J. Gwynn (1766), *London and Westminster Improved*

M.V Hughes (1934), *A London child of the 1870s*

H. Mayhew (2008 edition), *London Labour and the London Poor*

N. Pevsner (1957), *London volume one*

J. Stow (1908 edition), *Survey of London*

Survey of London

B. Weinreb, C. Hibbert (1983), The London Encyclopaedia

ARTICLES

R. Coates, (1998), 'A new explanation of the name of London', *Transactions of the Philological Society 96,* pp. 203-229.

R. Cowie, R. Whytehead, (1989), 'Ludenwic: the archaeological evidence for middle Saxon London.' *Anglo-Saxon archaeology,* vol. 63, 241, pp.706-718.

UCL Fleet Restoration Team, (2009), *The history of the River Fleet*

BOOKS

P. Ackroyd (2007), *Thames – sacred river*

P. Ackroyd (2011), *London under*

W. Addison, (1980), *The old roads of England*

A. Adolph (2014), *The King's Henchman*

C. Aslet, (2014), *Strands of History*

P. Barber, (2012), *London – a history in maps*

N. Barton (1992), *The lost rivers of London.*

N. Brett-James (1935), *The Growth of Stuart London*

C. Brown, (2009), *Whitehall*

J. Burnett (2004), *England Eats Out: a social history of eating out in England from 1830*

A. Clayton (2000), *Subterranean City*

D. Cruickshank (1990), *Life in the Georgian City*

P. Darley (2018), *The King's Cross Story*

J. Flanders (2003), *The Victorian House*

J. Flanders (2014), *The Making of Home*

B. Freese (2003), *Coal, a human history*

C. Gatty (1945), *Mary Davies and the Manor of Ebury*

M. Girouard (1975), *Victorian Pubs*

R. Goodman (1972), *After the Planners*

S. Halliday (1999), *The Great Stink of London*

S. Halliday (2006), *Newgate*

C. Hibbert (1957), *The Road to Tyburn*

T. Harding (2019), *Legacy*

H. Hobhouse (1971), *Lost London*

J. Holder, E. McKellar (2016), *Neo-Georgian Architecture 1880-1970*

L. Hollis (2021), *Inheritance*

T. Hunt (2004), *Building Jerusalem*

S. Jenkins (1975), *Landlords to London*

S. Jenkins (2019), *A Short History of London*

R. Leslie-Melville (1934), *The Life and Work of Sir John Fielding*

SELECT BIBLIOGRAPHY

T. Longstagge-Gowan (2012), *The London Square*

R. Mace (1976), *Trafalgar Square*

L. Moore (1997), *The Thieves' Opera.*

R. Naismith (2019), *Citadel of the Saxons*

G. O'Neil (1999), *My East End*

B. Paul Hindle (1982), *Medieval Roads*

L. Picard (1997), *Restoration London*

L. Picard (2000), *Dr Johnson's London*

L. Picard (2003), *Elizabeth's London*

L. Picard (2005), *Victorian London*

B. Pimlot, N. Rao (2002), *Governing London*

A. Roberts (2015), *The Celts.*

A. Saint, G. Darley (1994), The Chronicles of London

J. Summerson (1945), Georgian London

C. Thomas (2003), London's archaeological secrets

S. Thurley (1999), Whitehall Palace

T. Travers (2015), London's boroughs at 50

G. Tyack (2022), The Making of our Urban History

M. Waller (2000), Scenes from London Life

V. Watson (2008), The Waddington Story

K. Wedd (2012), Victorian Housebuilding

G. Williams (1990), Augusts Pugin versus Decimus Burton

J. White (2001), London in the Twentieth Century

J. White (2007), London in the Nineteenth Century

C. Wolmar (2020), Cathedrals of Steam

ENDNOTES

1   The phrase 'nation of shopkeepers' is normally attributed to Napoleon. His physician on St Helena cites him as saying it – perhaps originally in Italian. In fact, it was first used by Adam Smith in *The Wealth of Nations*.

2   The phrase is Samuel Johnson's signifying *Magna Carta*'s antecedents and its simultaneously conservative and radical nature.

3   Though see endnote no. 29 in Oxford Street on the dilution of wines in eighteenth-century taverns.

4   © 2020, Rutgers, The State University of New Jersey.

5   Baynard's Castle was rebuilt to the east along the Thames, where it survived until the Great Fire in 1666. Its name lives on, just, in a melancholy and little-used street that threads its sombre way beneath office blocks of 1970s concrete and 1980s glass. It also gave its name to Baynard's Inn, one of the Inns of Chancery linked to Gray's Inn. By the early nineteenth century it was no more than a set of residential chambers. Pip in Charles Dickens's 1860 novel *Great Expectations* lodged here. The building survives and is now used by Gresham College.

6   It is no coincidence that the city's four main prisons were all beside the Fleet: Newgate, Ludgate, the Fleet and Bridewell.
See *Go to Jail*.

7   There had also been brothels off Fleet Street for hundreds of years.

ENDNOTES

In 1389, Gilbert le Strengmaker was accused of keeping a 'disorderly house harbouring prostitutes and sodomites'.

8   See Bow Street and Oxford Street.

9   An advertisement on the front wall of Temple Exchange Coffee House read: 'You see before you the last house of the city in flames, the first in the city to be restored; may this be the favourable and fortunate for both the city and the house.'

10 It was Hugh Audley who bought, at a knock-down price, the Manors of Ebury and Hyde and the grounds of Neate House, which eventually descended to Alexander Davies, Mary Davies and thence to the Grosvenor Estate. See Mayfair.

11 It is possible she was thirty-one or thirty-two. Some historians believe the evidence supports a birthdate of 1501. Most experts think 1507 is more likely.

12 In fact, the French architect, Isaac de Caus, also drew up plans ten years earlier than Inigo Jones. They never made it off the drawing board.

13 The practicalities and symbolism of the location of Charles I's execution were important. His warrant specifically demanded that it should take place 'in the open street before Whitehall'.

14 Despite later images showing him exiting by a window, in fact the windows seem to have been bricked up in 1649.

15 In fact, the scope of Bazalgette's ambition to both sanitise and dignify followed previous schemes – most notably Sir Frederick Trench's 1824 proposals to embank the Thames and create an 'intercepting sewer'. Few ideas are truly new.

16 A culverin was a type of early musket.

17 As early as 1662, officialdom gave up. A Parliamentary Act of that year refers to 'one other street in St James Fields commonly called the Pall 'mall'. In the same year, Samuel Pepys referred to it as the 'old Pall Mall'. Charles II's wife, Catherine of Braganza, who was Portuguese,

also lost Piccadilly to popular preference. It was officially called Portugal Street and the name survived, just, into the nineteenth century. Bow Street is another *Monopoly* street probably named in obedience to common parlance, rather than landowner's decree. Streets are of and for the people.

18   In the eighteenth century, George II's queen Caroline asked what it would cost to reverse Charles II's decision and ban the public from St James's Park. She was told by Robert Walpole, 'Three crowns – those of England, Ireland and Scotland.'

19   Whores 'of the bulk' would use any convenient place (or bulk) to ply their trade. Whores 'of the alcove' preferred somewhere more discreet.

20   For example, one landowner's 1670 agreement with a builder required that every house 'shall build in such manner and forme and with such proportions and scantlings as those houses are built in the Pall Mal.' At the same time, in fact just before, Thomas Wriothesley, the Earl of Southampton, was evolving a similar model at Bloomsbury Square. Earlier developments by the 4th Earl of Bedford and William Newton at Covent Garden and Lincoln's Inn Fields used a different approach, more strictly reliant on royal favour, before changes in the approach to the regulation of new buildings after 1666. See Mayfair.

21   The last reference I can find to 'Leicester Fields' is on 25 October 1830, when George Pattisson gave his address as St Martin's Court, Leicester Fields, in evidence at a trial in the Old Bailey. The earliest written reference I can find to 'Leicester Square' is from 1734. For nearly 100 years both names seem to have been used interchangeably until the banished rurality of the spot ensured the eventual victory of the more urban 'square'. John Gwynn's 1766 book, *London and Westminster Improved*, used both names within the space of two paragraphs. Evidently the distinction was unimportant.

22   The description is of the market in Paris, but the joy of shopping is surely comparable and perennial.

23   As goldsmiths clustered on Cheapside, for instance, so jewellery shops now cluster on Bond Street.

24 Pretty Doll's history, as far as we know it, had a happy ending. She made a good match to a Colonel Poynton. On 6 February 1669, Pepys met her not in the New Exchange, but with her new husband in the King's Playhouse on Drury Lane.

25 She worked under the professional name of 'Lucile' and her London shops were, in point of fact, near but not on Bond Street: on old Burlington Street and then Hanover Square.

26 Engels was probably influenced by a similar turn of phrase in the official 1842 Royal Commission of Inquiry into Children's Employment. Jack Sheppard had also recently been the posthumous hero of what we would now call a 'true crime' novel by the forgotten hack novelist William Harrison Ainsworth. *Jack Sheppard: A Romance* was serially published between 1839 and 1840 in *Bentley's Miscellany*, in parallel with a novel that is better remembered, Charles Dickens's *Oliver Twist*. Illustrations were by George Cruickshank. When Dickens himself visited Newgate in 1835 he almost immediately recalled the 'redoubtable Jack Sheppard'. A few years later, the social commentator and student of London poverty, Henry Mayhew, complained that the novel was 'borrowed from the circulating library, and read aloud in the low lodging-houses in the evenings by those who have a little education, to their companions who have none; and because the thief is there furbished up into the hero . . . of all books, perhaps none has ever had so baneful an effect upon the young mind, taste and principles as this.'

27 See Strand and Vine Street.

28 See Bow Street. Among his many errors, Jack Sheppard failed to 'pay off' the main crime lord of the 1720s, Jonathan Wild.

29 Wine was weak in part because it was doctored and watered down. The Swiss travel writer, César de Saussure, observed that 'though no wine is made in England, yet I am persuaded that three times more is drunk than is imported into the country.'

30 Many witnesses agreed. One visiting Scots Minister concluded, 'My conviction is that, in a moral view, a great number were made worse, instead of better, by the awful spectacle.'

31 The condemned men were not fictional, but were James Pratt and John Smith, the last two men to be executed for sodomy in England on 27 November 1835. The case was unusual in that those convicted under the Offences Against the Person Act 1828 were normally reprieved. The magistrate who had committed them to trial appealed for clemency, but to no avail.

32 Though demolished in the 1890s, part of one of its surrounding ditches survives, some of the cellars can be seen in a nearby pub's basement, and the form of the prison is still reflected in the Millbank Estate's street pattern.

33 Though the Tower of London was briefly reused in times of war. Eleven spies were shot by firing squad in the outer ward during the First World War and prisoners of war were also kept in the Tower during the Second World War.

34 The last living vestiges of London's street merchants were the milkmen and the 'rag-and-bone' men who survived (just) into the 1980s. Their livelihoods were destroyed by deregulation and improved council rubbish collection.

35 The *Survey of London* dates the creation to 1671, however Pepys appears to have visited it, perhaps under a different name, in February 1664.

36 More normally, he who had given offence would be obliged to buy the offended a cup of coffee.

37 The Swiss travel writer, César de Saussure, observed that coffee houses which were also 'temples of Venus' normally had as a sign a woman's arm or hand holding the coffee pot. Most of those near Will's were of this nature: 'You are waited on by beautiful, neat, well-dressed, and amiable, but very dangerous nymphs.'

38 As evidence of the decline of Will's, Fielding preferred to take his coffee at the Bedford Head coffee house round the corner in Covent Garden.

39 Thus began an association between the street and the law that was to last until 2006 and which is still recorded in the street's orange colour on the *Monopoly* board. The other orange streets (Vine Street and the incorrectly named Marlborough Street) were home to police stations and magistrates' courts respectively. Arguably the association between Bow Street and the police still continues, as there is a police museum in the hotel that now occupies the building where the Bow Street Magistrates' Court once operated.

40 In fact, wall width and storey heights were not set for fourth grade houses.

41 Of course, compliance was not universal. There are instances, for example, of box sashes built after 1774.

42 Bedford Square in the 1770s was the first London square to achieve the uniform effect planned for Grosvenor Square.

43 In fact the system of couverture whereby property rights transitioned from the wife to the husband only dated back to 1534.

44 Best known but by no means the only tale of vice is that of the Duchess of Argyll and the salacious photos that led to her second divorce.

45 This story is particularly satisfying, as the St George's Hospital site is precisely located on the point where the two halves of Mary Davies's estates (what we might now call the Mayfair and the Belgravia sides) physically met. It is the geographic hinge of the whole estate.

46 Great Marlborough Street is not the only *Monopoly* street with an eponymous cigarettes brand. Pall Mall was introduced by Black Butler Company in 1899 as a luxury cigarette and is now owned by British American Tobacco. From 1960 to 1966, Pall Mall was America's number-one selling cigarette. It is now a discount or mid-market brand in most markets, but retains a faux aristocratic coat of arms and a spurious Latin motto.

47 The original design was by Robert Lutyens and was skilfully extended in the 1960s, when the building was doubled in breadth.

48   Charles Dingley subsequently promoted the New Road, which extended the New Road directly to the City.

49   The 50 feet rule was reaffirmed by the 1826 Metropolis Turnpike Road Act and used by the Metropolitan Board of Works to reject forecourt shops as late as 1857, but seems to have been de facto abandoned during the 1860s.

50   A word is necessary on the number of 'n's in Betjeman. The firm's Dutch founder had one 'n' in his name, but added a second 'n' to Germanise it due to anti-Dutch sentiment following the Anglo-Dutch War. This German spelling became unfortunate in 1914 when the First World War broke out, so the family returned to the original Dutch spelling, which is the one now known globally.

51   Some shards of G. Betjemann & Sons remain: a curved driveway with iron gates, which the firm created in 1927, still stand together with the workshops at the back of the original houses.

52   From the Latin *fumo* 'smoke' and *fugo* 'to chase away'. John Evelyn was not the only early-modern coal critic. Timothy Nourse published a similar essay in 1700 and the anonymous *Ballad of Gresham College* did likewise.

53   Poor Lord Dundonald was not very good at profiting from his inventive genius. He was unable to sell his coal tar method to the Royal Navy, who waited until the patent expired before using it. He died in poverty in Paris.

54   By a curious coincidence, William Murdoch knew James Boswell and may even have got his first job, with James Watt, in part through the connection.

55   In fact, given his name and his Shropshire birth, Gwynn must have been of Welsh descent, but is usually described as English.

56   Some larger properties were not complete until 1824, but the Crown was receiving considerable rents from 1819 and the street was all but physically complete by 1820.

57   Nash was dismissed from his job and criticised by a parliamentary committee, rather unfairly, for 'inexcusable irregularity and great negligence'.

58   The Café Royale is often said to have opened in 1864. In fact, a precursor existed from as early as 1821.

59   This has been a standard criticism of Nash's work for over a hundred years. However, I am not convinced there is any real evidence that his buildings were any worse built than those of many contemporaries. To those who seek to demolish, all precursors are beyond hope.

60   James Pennethorne was a relative of John Nash's second wife and treated by Nash almost as an adopted son. It is conceivable that he was the natural son of the Prince Regent.

61   In September 1791, the Czech composer and musician, Frantisek Kotzwara, died on Vine Street at the lodgings of the prostitute Susannah Hill, due to an erotic asphyxiation accident involving sexual intercourse, a ligature and a doorknob. She was acquitted of his murder.

62   Arguably the Piccadilly road widening was later. However, although it started later (in 1902), the Piccadilly widening finished much sooner.

63   The reservoir still survives. It was converted into an ornamental basin with a fountain in 1835 and stands just south of Grosvenor Gate.

64   In fact, the high social status of Park Lane in Thackeray's novel, published in 1847–8 is an anachronism. The novel is set in the period of the 1815 Battle of Waterloo, nearly a decade before Burton and McAdam's improvements began the social ascent of Park Lane.

65   When Al Murray's 'Pub Landlord' persona says on prime-time Friday night television, 'We're friends with the French because we had to rescue them,' the raucous applause is, I think, more 'laughing with' than 'laughing at'.

66   Nearby Gracechurch Street was home to a hay market.

67   So uncertain was the London & Blackwall's predecessor line, the London & Greenwich, that they had laid a 'pedestrian boulevard' beside the line for foot traffic. It was rapidly replaced with extra track.

68   The word commuter is an anachronism, not used until the twentieth century.

69   Some were able to move out. Many could not, due to poverty or the nature of their casual work. Until 1874, there was no obligation on the railway companies to rehouse the homeless.

70   As with Pall Mall, there were royal attempts to rename Piccadilly after Charles II's Portuguese wife. It was officially renamed Portugal Street, but the name was almost entirely ignored, with the last reference in a map I can find being in the early nineteenth century. It seems never to have been in widespread spoken use.

71   The description is that of Hugh Massingberd and David Watkin in their history of the building.

72   The very first steel-framed building in London was probably the National Liberal Club on another Monopoly street, Northumberland Avenue.

73   The houses that Stow describes between the City and the Whitechapel church are now Whitechapel High Street. Those beyond are on the west of Whitechapel Road. This was probably true of all early descriptions of Whitechapel. However, as it is not a distinction of which Victor Watson and Marjory Phillips were aware, it is not one over which I propose to obsess.

74   At the time it was 123 Whitechapel Road. The term 'penny gaff' derived from the price of admission (usually one penny) and the old slang for a cock-fighting pit, in turn derived from the metal spurs, or gaffs, historically taped on to cocks' legs.

75   Even the London borough's name has changed. But what's in a name? As Tony Travers has pointed out, the name Tower Hamlets sounds new, but is in fact very old. Revived by the creation of the extended London borough in 1965, the Hamlets refers to the hamlets

of Ratcliff, Limehouse, Poplar and Mile End in the historic parish of Stepney, which once owed feudal service to the Tower.

76   He was not popular with many of his fellow officers or commanding officers and in 1916 was arrested in a Cairo brothel, where he explained he was looking for a diseased prostitute who was infecting his men.

77   Daniel Defoe stood in the pillory from 29 to 31 July 1703, but was garlanded with flowers while his 'Hymn to the Pillory' sold in large numbers to the crowd.

78   Most existing buildings had leases with only short periods to run, so could be purchased for a few hundred pounds. However, the Duke of Bedford and William Howard, the proprietor of the Golden Cross Hotel, received £30,000 for their properties and the Marquis of Exeter received almost £50,000.

79   For many years the height was quoted as 185 feet, until repairs in 2006 revealed the height had been exaggerated by 16 feet.

80   General Napier was reportedly the author of surely the greatest modern Latin pun. Having greatly exceeded his orders by conquering the entire Indian Province of Sindh, his one-word message to his superiors was '*Peccavi*', I have sinned. Napier's statue is bearing a scroll representing the government of Sindh. Other sources attribute the pun to the magazine *Punch*.

81   A five-metre-high fibreglass statue of Keith Park did stand on the plinth for six months in 2009, but he was not promoted to permanent status. A fine bronze statue now stands down the road in Waterloo Place, round the corner from New Zealand House.

82   In African French, they are known as *les wax*.

PHOTO CREDITS